Reviewers Praise *Late Edition*. . . .

"Insatiable joy . . . [Greene's] love song to journalism, a lamentation for the lost world of raffish newspapering . . . populated by crusty but good-hearted editors, sporty photogs, and a cast of characters—'rumpled mutts'—not quite ready for Hildy Johnson's *Front Page*, but nonetheless sweetly lovable. . . . Affecting . . . His heart, as ever, is in the right place."
—*The Wall Street Journal*

"Wonderful."   —*The Advocate* (Baton Rouge, Louisiana)

"Refreshing, respectful, and comical . . . a glowing tribute to the glory days of America's newspapers and the simpler society they so aptly reflected. . . . Noisy reporters, prying editors, artful pressmen, and artisans in the composing room . . . Meant to be read slowly and savored as the current chaotic computerized information business replaces newsprint, banner headlines, and night owl editions."   —*Publishers Weekly*

"A Camelot tale in which, for a brief moment, reporters, editors, and photographers cranked out snapshots of their city for a little pay and a whole lot of fun. . . . A sweet tale with the bitter mixed in . . . The overarching tale of the quirky, scrappy newspaper—a dying breed of journalism—is what makes *Late Edition* hum."   —*The Columbus Dispatch*

"He is the writer of my lifetime. . . . Everything he does is better than the one before."   —Jake Hartford, WCPT Radio, Chicago

"Bob Greene remembers with love and longing those grimy early days when typewriters and Linotype machines were magical instruments. . . . The clatter filled the newsroom. But the sound that Greene remembers most from those days is the laughter."   —*North Platte Telegraph* (Nebraska)

"A valedictory hymn to the daily newspaper . . . the emotional coming-of-age story of a misfit who found a roomful of other misfits . . . He recalls the ecstasy . . . Greene most eloquently describes the atmosphere at the *Citizen-Journal*—the sounds of clacking typewriters and clattering Linotype machines, the clutter and the coffee, and the colorful personalities of his colleagues."   —*Kirkus Reviews*

. . . And Readers Love It.

"Well, you've done it again. It wasn't bad enough that you got me insanely jealous about your guitar playing in *When We Get to Surf City*, but, as you've done so many times, you have brought a simultaneous smile to my face and tear to my eye with *Late Edition*. Thanks for jostling some wonderful memories, and, yes, for a great 'love story.' "

—Mark T. Gould, North Haven, Connecticut

"I have read many of your books and have loved every one. You make readers feel what you were feeling at the time. I think I had a smile on my face the entire time I was reading *Late Edition*. I loved it. Thank you so very much for the pleasure your books have brought me. I can't wait for the next one." —Nancy Gerber, Morton Grove, Illinois

"You nailed it with *Late Edition*. I've been a fan of your writing for years, but you've never done a better job." —Doug Carroll, Chandler, Arizona

"I really, really loved this book. As with all your other books, it made me cry—in a good way. Please, please keep writing books. At least one a year is all I ask. I treasure each and every one. Your style of writing is magical. Thank you for sharing it with the world."

—Susan Ballard, San Francisco, California

"I have long admired your clear and elegant prose, but *Late Edition* is simply the most engaging memoir I have ever read. Ever."

—Walt Sharp, Dallas, Texas

"Before I knew it, I was staring off into space, thinking of all kinds of memories. Maybe that's why I enjoy your writing so much. It allows me the freedom to replay parts of my own life that I can't share with anyone else."

—Jan Cunningham, Largo, Florida

"Every time I read your latest book, I say to myself, 'That's the best book he will ever write.' It happened after reading *Duty*, and then again after *And You Know You Should Be Glad*. But, I just finished *Late Edition*. You did it again." —Roy Lynn, Ashland, Virginia

"Your writing is always a joy to me, a pure delight to read. I could have gone on making little notes on nearly every page of *Late Edition*, of what touched me, informed me, tickled me, delighted me. But I think you get the idea: I loved your book."   —Cynthia Henry, Manteca, California

"Finished *Late Edition* last evening. I was stunned; it was like looking in the mirror or taking a trip in the Way Back Machine. In one of his verses, the poet Rod McKuen wrote about a guy looking for a date on a Saturday night and, failing to find one, going home with thirty-five cents worth of love: the Sunday paper. The price has changed, but the sentiment hasn't. Thank you."   —Carl Golden, Burlington Township, New Jersey

"Yours is the best book by far I have ever read about the newspaper business."
                          —William Conner, Columbus, Ohio

"You have done it again. You've managed to tell a story in a way that no one else could have. No one can capture a period of time, and the feelings associated with it, like you can, and make readers feel as though they were actually there living the experience."   —Jennifer Lewis-Heys, Hunter, Ohio

"Your books make me feel like the final scene in *American Graffiti*, when the Richard Dreyfuss character is getting on a plane to leave his friends behind, while the end credits roll to 'All Summer Long.' As your books end, I feel exhilarated, entertained, yet feeling a great sense of loss all at the same time. That is your gift, I believe: to make your readers feel genuine and complex emotions."   —Jimmy Hester, Clovis, New Mexico

"The feeling of reading *Late Edition* was just as vivid as if I were actually there. I felt the pull of your heartstrings. I couldn't put it down."
                          —Maryanne Burke Battistini, Highland, Indiana

"I started *Late Edition* and loved it by, oh, I don't know—page one or page two, somewhere in there. You are writing better than ever, and that constant, off-the-charts level is because you write with your heart. I see that and feel that in every page. I'm so glad to be where I am, reading your books."   —Brian Rickerd, Lexington, Kentucky

"I am almost finished reading *Late Edition*. I am reading it slowly. Because I don't want it to end." —Michael H. Cunningham, Norwood, Massachusetts

LATE EDITION

BOOKS BY BOB GREENE

Late Edition

*When We Get to Surf City: A Journey Through America
in Pursuit of Rock and Roll, Friendship, and Dreams*

*And You Know You Should Be Glad:
A True Story of Lifelong Friendship*

Fraternity: A Journey in Search of Five Presidents

Once Upon a Town: The Miracle of the North Platte Canteen

Duty: A Father, His Son, and the Man Who Won the War

Chevrolet Summers, Dairy Queen Nights

The 50-Year Dash

Rebound: The Odyssey of Michael Jordan

All Summer Long

Hang Time

He Was a Midwestern Boy on His Own

Homecoming: When the Soldiers Returned from Vietnam

Be True to Your School

Cheeseburgers

Good Morning, Merry Sunshine

American Beat

Bagtime (with Paul Galloway)

Johnny Deadline, Reporter

Billion Dollar Baby

Running: A Nixon-McGovern Campaign Journal

*We Didn't Have None of Them Fat Funky Angels on the Wall of
Heartbreak Hotel, and Other Reports from America*

BOOKS BY BOB GREENE AND D. G. FULFORD

To Our Children's Children: Journal of Family Memories

*Notes on the Kitchen Table: Families Offer Messages
of Hope for Generations to Come*

*To Our Children's Children: Preserving Family
Histories for Generations to Come*

LATE EDITION

A LOVE STORY

BOB GREENE

St. Martin's Griffin
New York

www.stmartins.com

Book design by Phil Mazzone

Library of Congress Cataloging-in-Publication Data available upon request

ISBN 978-0-312-37690-1

First St. Martin's Griffin Edition: June 2010

10 9 8 7 6 5 4 3 2 1

This is for those who, despite everything, are walking through the front doors of a newspaper building today and, with hope in their hearts, applying for their first job

"This next slide shows something even more alarming, which is the decline in readership. This is from a general social survey, and the question is, 'How often do you read a newspaper?' As to the percent who read every day, that's been declining an average of about one percentage point a year, and shows no sign of stopping. You extend that line with a straightedge, you find that the last daily newspaper reader disappears around 2040. In April."

—Philip Meyer, Knight Chair in Journalism, University of North Carolina at Chapel Hill, speaking at the Media Center at the American Press Institute, March 9, 2005

———————

"You and me, Tito, we've seen it all . . ."

"Lots of changes, old Max, lots of changes."

"It's not the changes so much this time, Tito, it's that it all seems to be ending . . . It feels like it's all slipping away."

—resort owner Max Kellerman and resort bandleader Tito Suarez, at the end of the 1963 summer vacation season in the movie *Dirty Dancing*

1

I hadn't been expecting to see the place.

We were rolling through the country in a vehicle that was something out of an old-time science-fiction writer's most vivid futuristic dreams.

This was during the autumn in which Barack Obama was campaigning for president—the campaign which would culminate, that November, with his history-changing victory.

"We'll be at the hotel in a few minutes," Dale Fountain called back to me.

He was the driver of this vehicle—it was called the CNN Election Express, and from the outside it looked like a massive bus. Inside, though, it was a live television studio on wheels—control consoles, editing suite, satellite-uplink hardware, ten high-definition monitors. From the bus, even as it was speeding down a highway, we could transmit pictures and sound that would instantly be seen on television screens around the world. I was writing columns about the presidential campaign every day for CNN's political site on the Internet; we could stop in a town, report on a speech or a rally, interview some potential voters, snap their photographs . . .

And then, even as the bus was on its way, I could write the column, send it and the pictures skyward, and within minutes, before we had reached the next stop, it would be available for reading by an audience in every corner of the globe.

We had been in many places during the course of the long campaign—in the days just before arriving in this town, we had reported from Washington, D.C., from Maryland, from Pennsylvania, from West Virginia, from Mississippi, from Arkansas, from Kentucky. In a new-media age, the bus was an electronic marvel—it provided an almost incomprehensibly advanced digital delivery system for every kind of storytelling imaginable.

So I was writing away in the middle section of the bus—I was a sixty-one-year-old man enthralled by all the ways this three-million-dollar vehicle suddenly enabled a person to communicate his reporting to viewers and readers in the blink of an eye—and I looked up to see that the town into which we were heading was the capital city of Ohio. Columbus.

I stopped typing, and looked out the window.

On a downtown street—the address was 34 South Third Street—there was an old, stone-fronted building.

I had been there before, many times.

There once had been a certain room on the mezzanine.

Inside the bus, transmission-equipment lights blinked silently on and off.

I looked toward the building and tried to recall a sound from long ago.

2

The sound—the sound I can hear even now—was the sound of laughter.

Who would have thought that? The main sound in the room—a sound delicious enough that it was tasted as much as it was heard—was the sound of typewriters banging. A whole floorful of them, all being hit at once, a sound like a low-rent and off-tune concert, fingers pounding keys, keys striking rough sheets of paper curled around hard cylindrical rollers, palms swatting metal return levers, unseen mechanisms low inside the machines clicking like the teeth of steel combs as those worn rollers were hand-forced left to right so the men and women hunched over the typewriters could begin the next lines of their modest deadline compositions. . . .

That was the sound, you would think, that would remain most prominent—that was the sound that constantly filled the room. The symphony of those typewriters—long-gone instruments played upon by long-gone journeymen and journeywomen in the long-gone city room of a long-dead newspaper—was the sound you would think would endure.

And it does. I can close my eyes and listen to it.

But the laughter—the laughter coming every day and every night from the men and women in that room—the laughter is what overrides even all that other joyous noise.

Maybe it's because everything now seems so suddenly grim. Maybe it's because now, with all the dire predictions of a slow death spiral not just for any one newspaper, but for printed newspapers themselves, with all the dark worries and self-doubting and inner-directed recriminations in a trade once so happily cocky and seemingly free from care, a trade that welcomed misfits the way a family would welcome wayward brothers and sisters because most American city rooms were, in large and proud degree, indeed and in fact a brotherhood and sisterhood of misfits. . . .

Maybe, with everything on the business side of the newspaper world today turning gray and measured and fearful, it is the memory of the laughter in that room that stands out, precisely because the absence of laughter—the hollow sound when laughter is gone—can seem so hauntingly loud.

The laughter, at least to the young ears of an absolute beginner in the business, was what made it seem that it must be different from other businesses. You would hear it in that room every afternoon and every evening, as imperfect people put together an imperfect product chronicling the vagaries of an imperfect world, to be delivered by hand before dawn the next morning to doorsteps in one medium-sized and usually overlooked city in the landlocked and half-forgotten middle of the country. At which point the whole unlikely process would begin all over again.

The laughter may have been the laughter that comes with unconscious gratitude—with knowing reflexively, somewhere inside, how lucky you are to be allowed to work in a place like this. And with being blissfully unaware that, somewhere not so far down the line, it would all begin to fade into history.

The room in that city produced a newspaper you undoubtedly never read, and that you in all likelihood never heard of. But in your city, wherever you grew up, there almost certainly was a room just like it. Before the echoes of all that laughter drift away forever—before, one by one, in one big room after another across America, someone thins out the staff and then, eventually, switches off the lights for good—it may be worth the while to listen one last time.

3

Not to make too much of the paper hats, but they did have a way of setting the tone for everything.

How many businesses are there that offer, every day as you arrive at work, and every night as you leave, the sight of fellow workers wearing paper hats?

All right—maybe at certain fast-food restaurants, you see it. But those hats are mass-produced, part of a uniform. And you get the impression that, given the choice, the employees taking orders at the fast-food counters would just as soon not be wearing them.

The paper hats atop the heads of the men who worked around the giant Goss presses on the bottom level of the newspaper plant were made by hand each new day by the men who wore them. I still don't know how they did it—the hats, made from the previous day's editions, were neatly squared off, a wonder of on-the-fly engineering. When you stood and talked with the pressmen, you could read the headlines and stories on their hats. The paper hats were so much a part of their daily routine that the men didn't even seem to know they were there.

The hats served a function—the cavernous rooms that housed the presses were ink-laden, greasy places, and the hats did the job (sort of) of keeping the pressmen's hair relatively clean. But they also served as the signature of the spirit of the place. How could you not struggle to suppress a smile in an office building populated, in part, by men in hats made out of newspapers? By men who *made* their paper hats?

They still do it, I think, at newspapers around the country. The reason I say *I think* is that, more and more, the buildings where newspapers are printed are not the same buildings where reporters and editors and photographers put the newspapers together. The printing plants now tend to be in outlying areas, connected to the newsrooms by satellite links and fiber-optic lines. In many large cities, the people in the newsrooms never set eyes upon the people who operate the presses.

So the paper hats may still be there—but they are seen only by other people wearing paper hats.

A shame, really—a small shame, in the scheme of things, but a shame nonetheless. Coming to work every day, being greeted by the men in the paper hats—what a start to the shift. Made you feel glad to be getting up in the morning.

The story in these pages takes place over a circumscribed span of five years in the middle of the twentieth century, and the setting, in large part, is the mezzanine level of that building located at 34 South Third Street. Though the building is still there, the enterprise that occupied the men and women on the mezzanine is not.

That enterprise was known as the *Columbus Citizen-Journal*, and in the long run it never had a chance; by the end of 1985, it would be gone. The owner, proprietor, landlord, and main tenant of that building on Third Street, the occupant of much more expansive news offices on the upper floors, was and is the *Columbus Dispatch*, the dominant newspaper in town, a considerably more prosperous and influential publication. On top of the building, in soaring, bright, electrified orangish-red Old English letters, was the name of the *Dispatch*, along with its slogan: "Ohio's Greatest Home Newspaper."

And then there was us, down on the mezzanine.

Yet we felt like we were in heaven. We got to put out our paper every day.

Maybe it was just because I was little more than a kid. I was still in high school when in the summer of 1964 I walked in the doorway of the *Citizen-Journal* for my first day on the job; when I walked out four years later to leave for a bigger town, I still had yet to complete college. Maybe, because I was seeing everything through eyes that young, it seemed more heavenly than it really was.

But I don't think that was it. The other eyes in that room may have been older, but it was behind those eyes that I first saw all that laughter.

Numbers are dry. But there is a statistical figure that, as much as any combination of words, explains the way that newspapers—newspapers printed on paper, newspapers that rolled off presses—mattered so much to Americans at one time.

That figure is 123 percent.

Other figures also tell the story of just how rapidly the importance of newspapers in American life has declined. Here's one: the peak year for newspapers sold in the United States was 1984, when 63.3 million copies per day were purchased. By 2007, even though the population of the U.S. had grown, that number was down to 50.7 million copies per day.

And: in 1964, 80.8 percent of adults read a newspaper every day. By 2007, only 48.4 percent read a newspaper every day. Of those newspaper readers in 2007, the most devoted were the ones with the shortest future potential as long-term customers: 63.7 percent of people 55 years old and older were daily newspaper readers, while only 33.7 percent of people between the ages of 25 and 34 were daily readers.

As sobering as those numbers are, though, it is the 123 percent figure that illustrates most nakedly how the country's newspaper habits have changed.

In 1950, the penetration of U.S. households by daily newspapers was 123 percent. By 2004 that number was 49 percent and falling.

"Penetration" refers to the percentage of households in which a daily newspaper is read.

How could a penetration rate be 123 percent—how could it be more than 100 percent?

It could be 123 percent because many American homes chose to subscribe to more than one daily paper. Such a choice was quite common—for American families, having a newspaper in the house was like having electricity or running water in the house: of course they were going to have a newspaper, often more than one. One paper to read at the breakfast table, one to read before sitting down to dinner. . . .

So as dizzyingly quickly as raw circulation has plummeted, that doesn't tell half the story. Newspaper circulation is dropping even as the population of the country is increasing—the numbers are even worse than they seem, because the potential audience for daily newspapers is getting bigger as the nation grows: more citizens are available to buy papers, yet even with that, fewer do.

The social era in the United States when the penetration of households by newspapers was 123 percent—when the average household, as a matter of course and a matter of choice, purchased at least one and often more than one paper a day—made the texture of American life feel a certain way, and made certain things possible in the newspaper business.

One of those things was the existence of a paper like the *Citizen-Journal*—a second paper in a medium-sized town, a paper that families welcomed into their homes even though they already subscribed to another paper, a paper that gave people like those of us who toiled on the mezzanine a chance to do something with our lives.

The assumption throughout the country had always been that newspapers—frequently several in a single town—were necessary because Americans not only wanted them, which was important enough, but also needed them. Part of the assumption was that as people died off, they would be replaced by new newspaper readers—young people who would be just as eager to have papers in their homes as their parents had been, and their grandparents before them.

8

In Iowa, for example, as late as 1957 the *Des Moines Register* and *Tribune*, through an apparent arrangement with Charles M. Schulz, creator of the *Peanuts* comic strip, produced a comic book intended specifically to introduce boys and girls to the idea that the *Register* and the *Tribune* (separate papers produced in the same downtown Des Moines building) were going to be a part of their lives. In the comic book, Charlie Brown and Lucy (evidently drawn by a *Register* staff artist, with Schulz's permission) are given a tour of the newspaper office (while—in one frame of the comic—perched on the tour guide's shoulders). The comic treated the idea of becoming a newspaper subscriber as an inevitable rite of passage, like getting a driver's license: Boys and girls in Iowa were going to be subscribing to the *Register* and the *Tribune* someday, that was a given, so the comic book would get them ready.

Thus, on the way to the newsroom, the tour guide (in the comic book he is a man in a blue business suit and a red bow tie) shows the *Peanuts* characters "enlargements of nearly a century of the *Register* and *Tribune*'s front pages!" ("World-shaking events," Charlie Brown says as he looks at the front pages.) The guide takes Charlie and Lucy to every part of the building: "Here you are, kids," he says, "the big press room—filling the vast basement of the *Register* and *Tribune* building. When the presses are going full blast you can feel the vibration clear to the attic!" A cartoon version of a press operator, wearing a cartoon version of a paper hat, watches Charlie and Lucy watch the presses roll.

The message was clear: If you wanted to know what was going on in the world, this was the way you found out—on folded bundles of paper speeded to your home. The tour guide shows Charlie and Lucy the "fresh-off-the-press newspapers, down the chute from the mail room and into trucks waiting here in the loading dock . . . trucks that fan out from Des Moines in all directions. . . ." The children are informed: "Unrolled, the newsprint used by our papers in one year would cover a patch five feet wide and 290,000 miles long. The papers use $100,000 worth of ink a year."

As the comic book comes to an end, the tour guide asks a newspaper delivery boy—one of "our more than seven thousand carrier salesmen throughout Iowa"—to take Charlie and Lucy home: "Hey, Joe, can you drop off a couple of tired kids on your way 'round your route?"

"Sure thing!" says the delivery boy, and in the final frame, Lucy says: "Well, Charlie Brown, what do you think of the newspaper business now that you've been fully exposed to it?"

And Charlie says: "It's here to stay."

I think we all believed that; wherever in the country we may have been working, I don't think we gave any thought at all to the possibility that newspaper offices—and newspapers themselves—might not feel pretty much like this forever.

When I opened the glass door to the city room of the *Citizen-Journal* for my first day of work in the summer of 1964, Walter Winchell was still writing his column in New York. I was seventeen, and the newspaper world still had one foot—sometimes it seemed like both feet—in the 1930s. Winchell's *New York Mirror* had folded the year before, but he had quickly found work elsewhere in town, and the stereotype of newspaper life continued to be the one that he had helped to popularize in the national mind. It was a life that was determinedly staccato, raffish, hurried, loud, short on reflection, long on hustle, lighted fluorescently, punctuated by indoor shouts, cluttered with balled-up wads of paper under the desks and the stubs of fat black pencils with soft black lead in the typewriter wells . . . the Beatles had arrived in the United States earlier that year, television had all but completed its conquest of the land, but newspapers everywhere, including in the middle of Ohio, were still living in the Winchell model. The nation may have been on the verge of breathtaking change, but it was as if newspapers hadn't gotten the memo.

Walking into that city room for the first time was like encountering some intoxicating sensory buffet. There were two levels of noise—all of those typewriters on all of those desks with reporters hammering away at them, but a separate, more muted, metal sound, too, the sound of the wallful of UPI teletype machines bringing the news of the outside world to the mezzanine. United Press International was the second-tier international wire service—the Associated Press was the big one, but the *Dispatch* had the local rights to the AP, we subscribed only to UPI—and inside those tall cast-iron machines, sitting side by side next to windows overlooking an alley, the machines' own sets of typewriter-style keys received signals from afar as they clacked all day and all night.

It looked like a Houdini illusion—those keys writing their stories, in all capital letters, with unseen typists in UPI offices hundreds of miles away making them move. The reason the sound was different from the sound of the staff typewriters in the room was that on each UPI machine the keys, as they struck the frayed purple/black ribbons and the rolls of cheap copy paper, were shielded from the city room by scratched, dirty, hard-plastic covers, intended to muffle the clatter. It worked, to a degree—the gunshot-cracks of those UPI keys were deadened at least a little by the plastic shields, but they were still clearly audible, even all the way across the room, and as they rapped out their stories, one letter of the alphabet at a time, that was the way—just that quickly, just that slowly—that accounts of events taking place around the planet arrived on South Third Street.

Everything was old; everything was new. That was what it felt like to just be getting started in the newspaper business in that short span of years when I was lucky enough to be one of the people on the mezzanine. The newness of the feeling: One evening I was sent out to cover a shooting in which the victim had been transported by ambulance to a hospital near downtown. I'd had no instructions about how to cover such violent occurrences; this was well before our current era in which every hospital has media-relations specialists hired to provide an official corporate layer between what goes on beneath the hospital's roof and what the public is told about those matters. I made my way to the hospital, walked around to the emergency room entrance, asked the nurses where I could find the person who had been shot, was pointed down a corridor, kept walking and looking into curtained-off examination cubicles . . . and eventually pushed open a set of swinging doors and found myself standing next to an operating table, which

11

was surrounded by doctors and nurses in masks and gowns, and upon which lay the man about whom I had come to inquire, as the surgeons endeavored to remove the bullet from him. One of the physicians turned toward me—I couldn't see his mouth behind the mask, but I could see the surprised look in his eyes, and although he had no idea who I was or where I was from, those eyes told me he was not pleased to see me—and from behind the cloth he said: "Get out of here!" A nurse took my arm to lead me out of the room, and as we walked she said, "What are you *doing* in here?" I introduced myself, and—out of pure ignorance mixed with a certain innocence, because I truly had not known that this was not the way you were supposed to cover shootings— I said to her: "I'm on deadline." To which she replied: "*You're* on deadline?"

There were things to see and hear even when, ostensibly, there was nothing to see or hear. On evenings when I hadn't been assigned anything to do, I would slip out of the city room and walk up an interior stairwell to the composing room, just to watch the men make up the pages for the next morning's paper. They were metalworkers and artisans at the same time, although they probably wouldn't have described themselves as either; the way the Linotype operators and their machines did their work is still one of the most mystifyingly intricate and impressive series of herky-jerky kinetics I have ever observed, with the forming of the hot-leaden-type letters and words being accompanied by a hypnotic high-pitched clicking sound that I'm tempted to compare to a forest rich with crickets on a windless night, but that probably was closer to a gymnasium floor full of stainless-steel dominoes stood on end in a snaking line, at the moment when someone tips the first steel domino and they all begin toppling to the hardwood floor. Not far from the Linotype machines were the men composing the front and inside pages of the *C-J*, laying the metal stories upside down and backward into the page forms, standing over them, pounding them level with wooden mallets, chefs in inky aprons getting something ready for breakfast tables all over town.

Sometimes on a story close to deadline, when I had been sent somewhere to find out what was happening and there was just no time to get back to the city room, I had been instructed in advance to hurry back to the press car I'd taken from the paper's parking lot, the Ford with the skinny wire antenna jutting from its roof. I'd slide across the bench front seat and unhook the big microphone from its moorings and, sitting there, I'd radio back to the city desk the basics of what I had found. It sounds like nothing, now, in the era of universal cellphones—but then, when there were no such things, when calling someone from a car felt like a scene from an outer-space movie, there was a sense of moment and of weight to the act of doing it, every single time: sitting on the edge of the car seat, front door open, feet on the ground outside, broadcasting back to the newsroom, taking it on faith that your voice would travel through the night and be turned into words—words for the next edition—by the person sitting at a typewriter on the other end.

And knowing that as soon as the rewriteman typed the story up, even as you were putting the key into the ignition for the drive back to the office, his sheets of paper would be tossed one at a time into a wire basket atop the night city editor's desk, from where that editor would grab them, quickly read the story, send it sheet by sheet over to the copy desk, where a copyeditor would by hand write a headline, scratching short vertical pencil lines above and below each letter in the headline to make sure it fit the count. I can still do it now, even though there's no need, even though computers measure the fit to complete accuracy. The little lines you'd scrawl above the letters each signified a full count, the lines you'd scrawl beneath the letters signified a half count. Each capital letter was worth a count and a half, except for M and W, which each took two counts, and I, which took one; each lowercase letter was worth a single count, except l and i, which were worth a half. Write the headline, hastily scratch the lines above and below, add up the count, see if it exceeded the maximum total number allowed for the width and font of the headline the copy chief had ordered . . . it was like having to be a writer and a bookkeeping clerk, all at the same time, it was as if someone had told each copyeditor that he had to be Charles Dickens—write the headline—and then turn into Bob Cratchit—add it up and don't be wrong, and if the number doesn't

13

work, turn into Charles Dickens again and take another whack at writing it.

In the morning boys on bikes would ride down every street in town, reaching into their canvas bags, tossing rolled-up C-Js onto front stoop after front stoop. The most efficient way to get the news to the people who were waiting for it—a boy on a bicycle. In all the houses, the alarm clocks would be ringing, the clock radios would be snapping to life, and for those of us with the great good fortune to have worked the night before to put together the rolled-up paper that waited outside all the front doors, there was that feeling—at least there was when all of this was new to us—of opening our eyes and then realizing: "I get to go down to the paper again today." Like when you fall in love for the first time, and you blink to wakefulness in the throes of that new love and, even in your grogginess, you know without knowing why that this is going to be another good day. "I get to go down to the paper again today."

Not a cloud on the horizon. The paper came out every day. Like Charlie Brown said: "It's here to stay."

We were not in the "information business."

That is the phrase that newspaper executives often use today, to explain what they do. It is intended to be heard as a descriptive, even boastful, phrase, but it can sound vaguely desperate. With the newspaper business in trouble, some publishers seem ever eager to proclaim to the public that they're not really in the newspaper business at all. They're in the information business. Web sites, cable television channels, drive-time radio partnerships, e-mail editions, Internet entertainment offshoots . . . a newspaper, the implication appears to say, is only a part of it. It's as if the publishers want the readers to translate that as: only a *small* part of it.

And it's difficult to blame the executives for taking that approach. By every statistical measurement, newspapers—newspapers printed on newsprint, newspapers delivered to front doors—are a dwindling enterprise.

We weren't in the information business. We didn't have thirty different ways to try to reach out to the community. We had one reason for coming to work, and that was to put out the morning paper. It cost seven cents.

If, in winter, that paperboy on his bike misaimed his toss, and the rolled-up *C-J* landed in the snow, the first few pages would be wet and soggy by the time the people in the house retrieved it and brought it inside. The damp stories could be difficult, sometimes impossible, to read. All that work in the city room the day and night before—and you can't read it because the snow has turned it into a soggy mess. You could try to dry the paper in the oven, if you cared that much, but other than that there wasn't much of an alternative.

The father of a boy with whom I grew up—the father's name was Harold Schottenstein—occasionally, in the middle of an evening, would get into his car in his suburban home and drive the ten or fifteen minutes to the intersection of Broad and High in downtown Columbus. This was the city's hub, the center of everything.

There he would purchase something called the Night Green. It was a very early edition of the next morning's newspaper—I think this may have been before the 1959 combination of the old *Columbus Citizen* and the old *Ohio State Journal*, I think the Night Green preceded the *Citizen-Journal* and was in fact an edition of the *Ohio State Journal*. In any event, the Night Green was sold by news hawkers who stood next to lanes of traffic on that busy downtown corner—its name derived either from green paper on which its front page was printed, or green lettering somewhere on the page—and it was intended as a provider of the city's news for people who couldn't wait until morning to be updated.

There were no twenty-four-hour news cycles; there were no news channels telecasting all day and all night. You could purchase a copy of the Night Green only downtown, and downtown, during those years, was bustling enough after dark, with people going to the movies and restaurants and nightclubs and stage plays, that it must have made economic sense for the newspaper company to publish that Night Green, and pay the street-corner hawkers to sell it, for men and women who didn't want to wait until breakfast to find out what in the world was going on.

Harold Schottenstein would hop into his car, the same way that his grandchildren today might log on to their computers in the middle of the evening. "Going downtown to pick up a Night Green," he would say. It made perfect sense.

This isn't some vacation, some temporary hiatus. As the old world of ink-on-paper newspapers begins to drift away, there is a sense among many analysts of the industry that it's never coming back.

"I've been involved with newspapers, in some form or another, for a quarter century," wrote journalist Michael S. Malone, in an essay posted on the Web site of ABC News. "If I don't see a compelling reason to read them, why should anyone else?"

He wrote that he reads news on Internet sites—much of that news cobbled together by search engines, which grab the stories from the electronic versions of newspapers. But in not picking up printed newspapers themselves, Malone wrote, "I'm not alone. In talking with some of my colleagues, men and women who had spent as many years, if not more, than me in newspapers, most of them have also admitted to rarely opening a paper anymore. . . .

"That's why I wasn't surprised when one major newspaper after another in the last year has had to revise downward their inflated circulation. I knew they were lying, not just to their advertisers, but to themselves. I'd been through the whole dance of allowing a subscription to expire . . . only to have the paper call and beg me to come back; or, as a last resort, simply drop the paper for free on my driveway in order to keep the empty subscription numbers propped up."

He predicted that eventually there will be fewer than ten true newspapers, printed on paper, national in scope, remaining in the United States. Computer screens will take over everything else. "As for the local papers: they will be shut down, their presses depreciated and scrapped, their offices leased out. . . ."

As dire and distressing as those words are, and as alarming the language, other media experts, writing in more subdued tones, nevertheless deliver essentially the same message. Merrill Brown, in a report for the Carnegie Corporation of New York, distilled the findings of a survey of young Americans' attitudes toward news: "Newspapers have no clear strengths and are the least preferred choice for local, national and international news." Business columnist Floyd Norris in the *New York Times*: "The consensus Wall Street view of newspapers now is that they are a dying breed, destined to wither" under competition from Internet companies. The *Wall Street Journal*, reporting about its own industry, characterized traditional newspapers as being among American businesses that may be pushed "into the dustbin of history."

There was a series of television documentaries about baseball, consisting of old eight-millimeter and sixteen-millimeter home movies shot at ballparks by players and by fans, mostly before the television era. The documentaries were called *When It Was a Game*.

What was striking about the old home-movie film, much of it in color, was the human scale with which it depicted big-league baseball. Gone was the stentorian mythology of Baseball as Grand Narrative Drama; in the soundless home movies there was a sense of playfulness, of boyishness, of laughter and shyness and fun. These were guys in the summer sun, in the summer of their lives, doing something they loved.

If, in fact, newspapers the way they used to be cease to endure as a ubiquitous part of American life, there will be a multitude of entirely logical, even irrefutable, reasons for it. The story in these pages is not about that.

Instead, it is about that one newspaper in its mezzanine newsroom in that building on South Third Street during the handful of years when, little more than a boy, I was allowed to be a part of it. I tell the story not because there was no other place like that newspaper office—but because there were so many places that were like it.

In some American cities, famous journalists writing for mighty and world-renowned papers changed the course of history with their reporting, and won national awards and high honors for their work. In most cities—including on the mezzanine on Third Street—we didn't. Hardly anyone outside town even knew we were there.

But there was noise and laughter in the night. When it was a game, that laughter—all that happy noise in that room—sounded like a promise. Sometimes, when I listen hard enough, I can still hear it.

4

"This is your country music station. . . ."

It made no sense. Why, during the middle of sixth period, would the public-address loudspeaker on the wall of Mrs. Sara Amos's eleventh-grade English class crackle to life? The PA system was controlled down in the principal's office—no one had the authority to operate it other than C. W. Jones himself. And there was no way in the world that C. W. Jones was going to pipe music—much less country music—into all the classrooms in the building on a Friday afternoon in November.

But there it was: the sound of a radio, through the PA speaker. Within a second, it was gone; we could hear someone twisting the radio dial, in search of something. One station after another came through the speaker, just for a second or two at a time, and there was giggling in the classroom; this sounded like a prank.

And then the words, in the too-sober voice of a radio newscaster:

". . . has been taken to Parkland Hospital. . . ."

A few minutes later we were told that the president of the United States was dead.

Some students put their heads down on their desks. Some just looked around, as if waiting for instructions. Some stared at each other. A few cried, embarrassed, or so it seemed, to be seen that way.

What I did was something I still can't explain, and it changed the course of my life.

There was a typewriter in a little glassed-in workspace at the back of the room. Without asking permission, I went back there, picked up a piece of paper, rolled it into the carriage, and—while looking out at the classroom through the glass—began to type.

The class sits in stunned silence. . . .

I had no idea why I was doing it. None.

. . . not quite able to realize the full impact of the situation. A girl is quietly weeping at her seat. . . .

I wrote about five hundred words. And when the bell rang to end the period, and I walked down the hallway to Mr. Millard's seventh-period history class, I went not to my seat but to his desk. I said:

"I have to go down to the *Citizen-Journal.*"

It was such an odd thing to say, on such a disorienting day, that all Mr. Millard could do was nod yes.

I motioned across the classroom to Jimmy Schottenstein—son of Harold Schottenstein, he of the nocturnal drives downtown to pick up the Night Green—and Jimmy followed me out of the room and I said I needed a ride to the *Citizen-Journal* and he, like Mr. Millard, went along with it without question. It was that kind of day: the president had been murdered, and compared to that, nothing that could happen would seem outside the realm of possibility.

So we climbed into Jimmy's white Chevy, and he drove west on Broad Street until we got downtown and to Third Street, and he waited in the car in front of the building while I went in.

If there was a guard in the lobby, I don't remember it. I know that the reception desk had a stack of free *Dispatch* desk blotters available for members of the public to pick up as promotional giveaways—I know that because soon enough, when this lobby would become a part of my daily life, I would see that there was never a day or a night when the stack of blotters, newly refreshed, was not there. People needed to blot the ink from their fountain pens, after all, so the *Dispatch* provided the blotters as a goodwill gesture to its readers.

I took the elevator to the mezzanine, walked through the glass doors, took a look around me—you can imagine; the president had just been assassinated—and saw, across this room where I had never been before, across this room that I had somehow sought out, a man who appeared to be in charge.

Salt-and-pepper crewcut, white short-sleeved business shirt on the cusp of winter, worried face, cigarette. I walked over to him.

He looked up.

The presence of some kid in the city room on this afternoon—some kid who was a total stranger—did not appear to startle him. Nothing could, today.

"I go to Bexley High School," I said.

"And?" said Bill Moore.

He was the city editor of the *Citizen-Journal*. Soon enough I would work for him.

"I wrote a story," I said, handing him the sheets of paper I had carried downtown.

"We're a little busy today," he said. "The president has been shot."

"I know," I said. "That's what the story is about."

He stared at me, briefly. He laid the story on his desk.

"Thanks," he said. "You've got to let us get the paper out." He went back to the work he was doing.

I turned and left. Jimmy Schottenstein, in his car, said: "What happened?"

"I turned in the story," I said.

"Are they going to use it?" he said.

"They didn't say," I said.

The next morning—a Saturday—I woke up early to retrieve the paper from the front stoop. I went through it three times. Nothing by me.

I had not told my parents about going down to the *Citizen-Journal*; for the same reason I hadn't been quite sure why I had gone to that typewriter in the back of the classroom to write the story, I wasn't sure that I could explain why I had gone downtown on the busiest news day since the end of World War II and had walked, uninvited and unannounced, into the *Citizen-Journal's* newsroom. So I said nothing to my mother and father.

I did call the *Citizen-Journal* that morning, intending to ask why my story had not run. But there was no answer in the city room—no Sunday paper, and thus no Saturday staff. Even on a weekend like this.

So I waited another day, and on Sunday I called the *Citizen-Journal* and Bill Moore said he had read my story and had thought it was fine, but he couldn't talk to me just then. Lee Harvey Oswald had been killed in Dallas.

I could wait. I woke up Monday, went through every page of the morning paper, did not see my story. I called Bill Moore again.

"I was just wondering if you were planning on running my story," I said.

"I don't think so," he said. "It's outdated by now. Your story is about the classroom on the day President Kennedy got shot. That was Friday. Today he's being buried."

"That's why I was thinking it should have run on Saturday," I said. I was sixteen.

"We were a little pressed for space on Saturday," he said.

I hung up the phone. I thought about that room, as it had been at the moment I had walked into it with my story in my hand. All that sound, all that excitement, the motion, the raised voices, the clatter, the sense of something being put together on the fly.

I had never seen anything like it.

I was in love.

I had to be there.

5

I was going to miss playing second base.

I knew it even during that last game—even before my final time at bat.

Our team—Epsilons, it was called—was undefeated in its first two games, and against all odds I was mistake-free, so far, in the field. Every ball that had been hit anywhere near me in those first games I had turned into an out; the year before, in 1963, I hadn't been all that confident, a little unsure of myself both at the plate and in the field, but now our team was one more summer down the line, we were all, at seventeen, a summer older, and the diamond felt more familiar to me, almost like home. I liked the feeling of my shoes scraping over the cracked and dusty surface of the infield, I liked the now-it-begins sensation of being the leadoff hitter, I liked the languorous, sweltering afternoons with the rest of my friends on the team.

Maybe this Beatles/Rolling Stones/Dave Clark Five summer was the American summer when boys would stop dreaming exclusively about becoming big-league baseball players, and instead start dreaming of becoming members of touring rock bands. And maybe this league we were in wasn't much of a league. But we were as good as any team in it, and as the summer had begun I was looking forward to all those lazy Sundays with my friends on the parched-dirt diamonds near Alum Creek.

Before we took the field this Sunday, though, I had told the rest of them that this would be it: I had to quit.

Sundays were days when the most junior copyboy at the *Citizen-Journal* was scheduled to work.

And that, all of a sudden, was me.

"Durante always said goodnight to that Mrs. Calabash, but he never said who she was."

There were only two people in the elevator: one was the woman who, inexplicably, was talking about Jimmy Durante; the other was me. So she had to be speaking to me—either that, or to herself.

This was my first day of work. The woman and I had boarded the elevator car in the lobby of the *Dispatch* building.

I looked over at her. She was talking to me, all right. She was looking right at me. And speaking of Jimmy Durante.

My nose had always been on the prominent side, a fact that, as a kid, had not exactly thrilled me. Could this be what the woman was talking about? Jimmy Durante was the famously big-nosed comedian who invariably ended his television appearances by walking off a darkened stage, through a series of pools of spotlights on the floor, saying, "Goodnight, Mrs. Calabash, wherever you are."

Was that what this woman was doing, on a kid's first day on the job—making fun of his nose? I didn't know what else it could be. Was the world of grown-up work really that casually cruel-spirited? By first impressions, this was not promising.

It was a short ride to the mezzanine. I got off, she stayed on. The elevator door closed, and she presumably ascended toward the higher reaches of the *Dispatch* empire.

I pushed open the same doors through which I'd taken my class-sits-in-stunned-silence story on the afternoon the president had been killed. From the looks of the place, not a single thing had changed in the seven ensuing months:

The same men and women, faces staring toward their typewriter keyboards, fingers smacking away, writing the stories that until this very moment did not exist, but that by this time tomorrow would be delivered to, read by (or at least skimmed by), and most likely discarded by more than one hundred thousand people in Columbus. The same wash of low-level clatter from the UPI machines against the far windows. The same occasional shouts by editors and reporters, summoning a copyboy to scurry over and carry out some demand or other.

When I had walked in with my John F. Kennedy story, it was the onset of winter, gray and bitter outside the windows of this city room; now it was full summer, brilliant and glorious out those windows. It appeared, on first glance, as if the people in the room had not necessarily noticed the changing of the seasons. Eyes aiming down, they banged on. Someone could have stopped a movie projector the moment I walked out of there in November, and started it up again right now. The movie starring the people in the room continued.

Bill Moore looked up from the city desk.

"You're here," he said. "Go see Miss Allison."

I just stood there. He might as well have been speaking in code language.

He went back to editing a piece of copy. When he looked up a few seconds later, to find me still in front of him, he said: "Are you going to see Miss Allison?"

"I don't know who Miss Allison is," I said.

He motioned over toward a regal-looking, white-haired woman who—if I had met her three decades later—I might have mistaken for Barbara Bush. She was the secretary to the editor of the *Citizen-Journal*, Don E. Weaver.

"She'll show you how to fill out your time sheet," Bill Moore said.

So I walked over to Jean Allison, and I introduced myself to her, and she had me fill out the minimal paperwork that in those days had to be completed before a person became officially employed by an American company. Today such a procedure would require visits to a series of various substations of the human resources department, drug testing by an outside contractor, security checks through local law enforcement databases, perhaps a discreet digital pass through Department of Homeland Security computers. At Miss Allison's desk that summer afternoon, the whole process took thirty seconds, maybe forty-five.

She said, in the loveliest, most cultured and welcoming voice: "You and I will be talking to each other. I want you to meet the boss. He's in a meeting now, but I'll introduce you to him when he has a minute."

She sent me back to Bill Moore's desk, but before I even got there I felt a hand on my shoulder.

I looked around. It was Miss Allison. She had followed me the few steps.

"Come here," she said. Her voice was almost conspiratorial.

We returned to her desk.

"I'm worried about your shoes," she said.

I peered down at them. They were Weejuns—brown loafers.

"Look at the backs of them," she said. "That's really bad for your feet."

The backs of the shoes were worn down—the backs had the consistency of old pudding. I liked them that way.

"You can do yourself some long-term damage by walking around like that," Miss Allison said. "Trust me—you want better support from your shoes."

She didn't seem to be kidding. She seemed genuinely to be concerned.

"I don't want to worry about you all summer," she said. "You're young. Don't ruin your feet." She smiled. "Someday you'll thank me."

Wherever Mrs. Calabash may have been—and wherever the Jimmy Durante woman in the elevator may have alighted—this, now, was where I was.

"How many weeks do you still have to work the factory job, too?" she asked, and I said:

"Two."

I'd been hired on a fluke.

For months after seeing the city room on that afternoon of President Kennedy's death I could think of little else but wanting to work there. I was too embarrassed to call Bill Moore again; I might have been ambitious, if quietly so, but I had sense enough to know that the man I'd kept bugging about running my story on the Kennedy assassination had heard just about enough of my voice for one lifetime. *Hello, Mr. Moore? Remember me—the kid who drove you crazy when you were on deadline with the biggest story in the world? Well, I know you didn't want to put my article in the paper—but how about hiring me?* That was a telephone call I wasn't about to make.

So I tried to get in through a side door. I was a big fan of Tom Keys, the sports editor and sports columnist of the *Citizen-Journal*. Not that I knew him, or that he had ever set eyes on me. But I wrote him a letter over the winter, asking if he knew of any copyboy jobs at the paper; he actually allowed me to come down and drop off an application, but he told me there was virtually no chance. I was way too young. The only part-time copyboys the *C-J* ever hired, he said, were Ohio State students who were well along in their college journalism classes. I still had more than a year of high school to go. I never heard back from anyone at the paper.

That summer I worked in the shipping and receiving room of the metal-plating factory my father helped to run. It was grunge work, starting early each morning: unpack the incoming boxes, label the items that were to be refinished, sort them so that they would be dunked into the proper plating tanks. The plant was on a nondescript stretch of East Broad Street, just outside downtown proper. It was a dreary city block that felt as if nothing of consequence could ever happen there.

(Although it's never wise to jump to such conclusions. There was a former Buick dealership next to the plating plant, and one day a guy moved in to start a hamburger restaurant in the showroom where the cars had been. His plan, or so he said, was to sell hamburgers that tasted so good that he would work hard and expand from this block of Broad Street and take his burgers national. McDonald's already ruled the fast-food world, and whatever part of that world McDonald's didn't own, Burger King filled quite nicely. How was this local guy with his one restaurant in the old Buick showroom going to break into that league? He didn't seem to be worried, no matter who doubted him—he knew his burgers were worthy. His name was Dave Thomas, and he named the new hamburger restaurant in honor of his daughter, Wendy.)

The beginning weeks of my summer consisted of opening the packages in a dingy back room of the plating factory, and playing second base in the sunshine on Sundays. And then one day I rode the bus home from work, and there was a message: a man named Bill Moore, I was told, had phoned. He wanted me to call him right away.

Was he finally going to run my Kennedy story, half a year later? Not likely—even I realized that. But why else would he be calling? When I reached him he said Tom Keys had told him about my job application. The Columbus newspapers had been on strike; during the strike the college school year had ended, and the copyboys and copygirls he had hired from Ohio State for the summer had gone home to their families, because the jobs he had promised them had evaporated when the strike had begun. Now, though, the strike had been settled; the papers were going to print again. And the *Citizen-Journal* needed a copyboy.

I was on the next bus back downtown. The meeting was short. If I wanted the job, it was mine, provided I was willing to start immediately. Sixty-five dollars a week, and I'd be required to work nights and Sundays. Come in the next day to fill out the paperwork.

My dad said he'd let me do it, but only if I'd give the proper two weeks' notice at the factory, and work both jobs until those two weeks were up. No one in the metal-plating receiving room had ever commented about my footwear, but now, on South Third Street, Miss Allison was fretting aloud about what the backs of my shoes were doing to my feet. Quite a week: It had begun with playing baseball, and with ripping open packages in that shadowy room on the street where only Dave Thomas would ever visualize potential grandeur. It ended with my life being changed forever. "So do you want the job?" Bill Moore asked. Yes, I said. I wanted the job.

"Let me ask you something," said Ronnie Rummel, in the singsong rural Ohio twang to which I had become more than accustomed.

I knew this would be good; it always was. He was a guy in his early

28

thirties who worked in the shipping and receiving department at the metal-plating factory; he and I had been laboring side by side near the loading dock every day that summer.

"If you had a choice," Ronnie Rummel said, "would you live in an average apartment, or in a really great car?"

"I don't know, Ronnie," I said. "Which one would you choose?"

"I think the apartment, but maybe the car," he said. "Like if it was a Cadillac."

"Where would you go to the bathroom if you lived in a Cadillac?" I said.

"Filling station," he said.

We were still having these conversations each morning. Standing next to Ronnie, I would unload the cartons that had arrived from all over the country, take out the items for plating, fill out and attach the required identification labels. Then, right before noon, I would excuse myself from my colloquy with Ronnie, step behind a tall row of shelves, strip off my filthy T-shirt, put on a white shirt and tie, and emerge looking like a different person. Sort of like those scenes in the *Superman* TV show—except I wasn't Clark Kent turning into Superman, I was some kid turning into Clark Kent. I was ready to go to my other world—my new newspaper world.

Thus each day after my factory shift I would step out of the grim dourness of that plant, walk due west on Broad Street, make my way to the *Dispatch* building on Third Street, hurry up to the *Citizen-Journal* newsroom . . . and it felt like going from gloom to happiness, like magically traveling from shadows to light. Fifteen minutes earlier I had been handling tarnished teapots and worn-out knife-and-fork sets, sending them on their way to be dipped into electrolytic solution so they could emerge appearing a little less dull; now I was in this brightly lighted room where news was being born.

Not that, in those first weeks, I had any direct connection with the birth of that news, at least not any connection with shaping the words that would make it into the paper. "Get the pastepots," Bob Moeckel, the senior editorial clerk (he must have been twenty-two), would command me, and I learned quickly what that meant. I would go from desk to desk and pick up the ancient white coffee mugs that, the day before, had been filled to the brim with absurdly thick white paste; each coffee mug had a bargain-basement brush with hard black bristles jammed into the white gunk. That's how the reporters would organize their stories after they had typed a first draft and wanted to revise the order of the narrative—by cutting paragraphs out and pasting them together.

I'd carry the coffee mugs—the pastepots—into the men's restroom back by the mailboxes, and I'd stand at the sink running hot water into each mug and over the bristles of each brush. This would loosen up yesterday's paste. I'd then grab low-grade paper towels from the metal dispenser on the wall and scrub the inside of each mug until it was close to pristine, ready to have a new day's load of fresh paste poured into it. The old congealed paste would slowly slither down the drain of the sink—I hesitate to think what all that paste, year after year, had to have done to the plumbing at 34 South Third. I would do all of this while, directly next to me, men would urinate. Sometimes now, when I read about the public's supposed feeling that the news media are elitist and highfalutin, I wish they could have seen this: a guy scrubbing pastepots while, a foot away, reporters pissed.

"Get these for me, Bob," some of those reporters would call to me when I returned to the city room—I felt triumphant that they actually knew my name. They wouldn't be looking at me—they'd be staring at the stories they were writing while, one arm extended, they thrust pencils in my direction. There was one pencil sharpener in the office—a stand-up type bolted to the surface of a table, with a lever to be rotated by hand. The trick was to make the pencils sharp but not too sharp— too fine a point and the lead would break off as the reporters hurriedly edited their own copy.

Everything was a remnant of the industrial age—straightedges to trim the copy paper, carbon sheets to provide backup, dangerous-looking metal spikes sticking straight up from green iron bases, upon which the editors and reporters were expected to jam the carbon copies of their stories in case the originals somehow got lost. The spikes were razor-sharp at their tips—today I doubt that newspaper companies' corporate law departments would allow them in the building, those spikes were workers' comp cases just waiting to be filed, yet the men and women in the C-J city room would barely glance at them as they plunged their copy down over the spikes, seeming to take pride in instinctively knowing how to do it so the paper, and not their palms, would be impaled.

"Tube!" someone on the copy desk would yell toward me, and I would hustle over, accept the piece of copy they would hand off to me, roll it up, and then grab a scuffed-up cylindrical tube made out of yellowing hard clear plastic. Each tube had a fraying leather fastener at its top, with a short strap that snapped closed. It was my task to stick the rolled-up news story into the tube, fasten the leather strap, then insert the tube—bottom up, always—into the opening of an iron pipe that descended from the ceiling. The pipe was the business end of a long and hollow pneumatic device that snaked with many twists and turns from the city room to the composing room. I learned to pull down a hinged metal cover that was attached to the mouth of the pipe: immediately an insistent rush of compressed air would be heard, to be silenced only after I stuck the tube into the hole. Then—*thwuck*—the tube bearing the story would be sucked forcefully into the pipe, the metal cover would clang closed, and for a few seconds you could hear the tube banging its way through the pipeway, somewhere above the ceiling tiles, en route to the Linotype operators waiting on another floor to transform the copy inside into metal words.

If it felt like working in a submarine—sometimes you could hear that the tube was stuck in there, and you'd have to send an empty tube after it to knock it free and on its way—this was all in the context of a wider 1964 world that, like the world inside the city room, was teetering on a ledge that separated all that had come before from all that would soon follow. The young British Invasion bands from England may have been changing the sound of the music that filled that summer's air, but Alan Ladd (who had died in January) was still a leading man in downtown movie theaters, starring in his last film (*The Carpetbaggers*); Garry Moore and Red Skelton and Jack Benny and Jackie Gleason still were the headliners on network television; Rudy Vallee was still a part of the national cultural fabric, hosting a weekly TV series called *On Broadway*

Tonight. Things were changing—but not all that fast. The old ways continued to dominate.

So when, two days into the job, someone would call "Bells!" in my direction, I already had figured out how to translate that. Rush over to the UPI machines, read the stories that were emerging from the tops of each of them, discern as quickly as possible which of the machines had sounded two bells, or sometimes three, to signify that the story coming through was one of particular urgency. How else would the people in this room know that some piece of important news was breaking somewhere in America, or beyond America's shores? Bells were the way—like firebells in the night. "Bells!" someone would shout, and I was the courier entrusted to find out for the shouter just what those bells might be heralding.

In the morning, in those first weeks, I'd be back in the catacombs of the metal-plating-factory receiving room, standing with Ronnie Rummel, sorting scratched serving platters and discussing the pros and cons of making one's home in a luxury automobile. But soon enough each day, I'd be chasing bells—if the queen of England were to stumble and fall on the palace stairs, if the governor of Mississippi were to threaten to shut down the public school system, I was the guy on the mezzanine who was expected to find out first. "Bells!" someone would call, or "Tube!" I came running, gleefully.

There were just two of us—a young woman named Doris, and me.

I was the copyboy; she was the copygirl. She was probably twenty or twenty-one, no longer really a girl, but that was the title, that's what she was called. "You must be the new copykid," she said to me the first day, smiling and extending her hand like a businesswoman.

There was something slightly chilly in the smile, something stiffly formal in the handshake, and it took me a while to figure it out. Doris had a little bit of a Natalie Wood look, had Natalie Wood come from a family where the father and the brothers made their livings in the searing indoor heat of the pig-iron foundries down in Jackson County, Ohio. She was here because this was her chance to get a foothold in a world where men wore ties to work, and women wore dresses or skirts, and where, when the shift was over for the day, you didn't have to go home streaked with sweat and covered with grime. Our days at the *Citizen-Journal* overlapped only by an hour or two; she began early in the morning, and by the time I arrived to work the afternoon-and-night shift she was in the homestretch, almost ready to depart.

She had a ponytail, and wore a nice dress to work virtually every day—I got the sense that, copygirl classification or not, she was determined to make this entrance to the world of white-collar commerce something that would stick, something she could stay with and build upon. There were times, in those first days, when she could be sort of condescending and a little didactic—"This is something that the senior copykid hands down to the junior," she said more than once, passing some menial task to me, apparently feeling she needed to spell out that I was now the low man in the office—but that was all right, she seemed nice enough. It wasn't until she took me up to the composing room floor that I saw what she had to deal with every day.

Going there—fetching proofs, passing messages from the news editor on our floor to the makeup foreman up there, ferrying revisions in layout sheets—was a constant part of the routine. And the first time I accompanied Doris on her rounds, I was startled by what I heard the moment she stepped onto the floor.

They started barking—the men in the composing room, the Linotype operators, the men making up the pages, the maintenance guys whose job it was to keep the mechanics of the operation running— just about all of them, or so it seemed, let out a loud, collective, howl the second they set eyes on her. It couldn't really have been every one of them; certainly some must have refrained. But the sound was so overwhelming—so loud, so jarring—that it seemed to be coming from every throat. Dog sounds, rude hoots, yelps—I could hear her name being shouted, this was something obscene, like the sound you might encounter in a burlesque house, or so I imagined, never having been to one. The wailing persisted the entire time Doris was on the floor—and she kept her head up, she looked straight forward, she did not visibly react to it in any way.

"They do that to all the women," she explained to me one day when I got up the nerve to ask her about it. She was matter-of-fact in explaining to me: On that floor, where the men working with the hot type produced the paper, this was the welcome that women could expect. Any woman who went to that floor, she said, got the yowling, keening greeting, at least any relatively attractive woman under the age of fifty. It was like a mass wolf whistle, or that was the intention, she said. "They don't mean anything by it," she said. "I just try to ignore it."

Never having worked in a newspaper building before—never having worked anywhere, except at the metal-plating factory—I had nothing with which to compare this. On the mezzanine, among the reporters and editors, Doris was not treated like this; it was only on the composing floor (and, I would later see, in the big room that housed the printing presses) that she faced the hoots. It was how the men there reacted to women—apparently it was a tradition. I would hear in later years, from women who worked at newspapers around the country, that they had endured it, too. It's somewhat astonishing, to recall it now: a time when a young woman coming to work each day at a newspaper knew that, on certain floors, this was what would await her.

The odd thing was that on the composing-room floor, when Doris would be talking face-to-face with whomever she had been sent there to see, the man would invariably be courteous and respectful. Even as the howling sounded all around them, Doris and the man or men with whom she was specifically speaking would be all business: direct and professional. Yet no one ever told the men doing the shouting to stop. And, I noticed, the men barking and braying never made eye contact with Doris as they were doing it. It was almost as if they were afraid to look at her.

Maybe that was it—the ugliness was unmistakable, but maybe there was an aspect of fear present, and not necessarily fear on Doris's part. The men who bleated and yipped at the mere sight of a woman visiting their floor: maybe they were afraid of certain things that they couldn't even begin to articulate. One era of American life was coming to a close; another was about to begin. "Now let's go drop these off in the engraving room," she would say to me, with the howls from the men still filling the air and the men who were doing the howling looking every way but at Doris. She seemed not to take it personally, as if it had nothing to do with her, and in the most elemental and troubling of ways, it probably didn't.

The city room windows faced out over Third Street and Broad Street, and because we were only one floor up from the lobby you could stand at those windows and look at downtown—look at it, if not at eye level, then at just above eye level—and it was sort of a lifeguard tower's view of the center of the city's life. If you were to spot anything out of the ordinary going on down there, anything to catch your attention, you could scramble down off the tower to check it out.

Not that I would be the one to scramble; that job would fall to the reporters and photographers. But being downtown in those days, when downtown was still the place where anything considered of true note-worthiness in an American city transpired, and when an event's being recorded in the pages of a city's daily paper was the one way the fact of that noteworthiness was certified—if it didn't make the paper, then how could it have mattered?—being downtown in those days felt to me like being at the core of something.

I could see the Statehouse from the city room windows—the governor of Ohio was working in there, the state's laws were being written by the legislature—and if I went to one set of windows I could see the Lincoln-LeVeque tower, the town's one and only skyscraper, and all of this felt right, the idea that you could see downtown from that lifeguard's-perch vantage point made it feel that of course this newspaper and the people who worked here knew exactly how to cover the city, all of this was set up like a game board, everything was in its place and ready each day for the next roll of the dice.

I was trying to memorize the names of the members of the staff and connect the names to faces, although some names I already knew—the quiet older guy in suspenders over there, sad look always in his eyes, Nixon-style five o'clock shadow on his face, hands typing away duti-fully, was Wink Hess, a byline I'd been seeing since I was old enough to read, the jaunty, insouciant feel of that byline not matching the worn-out and somehow deflated look in Wink Hess's tired eyes; the young man just out of college, eager and nervous in his crisply starched shirt as he peered around the room, hoping that someone would throw him an assignment, was Jim Sykes, a recent graduate of Ohio University down in Athens, his hair already thinning, his desire to do well and make Page One and keep this job as visible as a flashing neon sign. . . .

Dick Garrett and Hank Reichard would dash in and out of the city room's side door—no time to wait for the elevator in their world, they'd take the staircase—and the phrase "ace photographer" seemed to have been invented for each of them, from fifty feet away they might have been middle-aged twins: dark hair, sharp facial features, cameras slung around their necks on heavy straps, all but sprinting toward their cars on the street below. They knew the angles, I could see—they *were* the angles, all jagged edges and elbows, like something from a great comic book. I'd been seeing their credit lines on front-page photographs for just as long as I'd been seeing Wink Hess's name atop banner-headline stories, and how I wanted to go out there with them, how I wanted to hit the streets with them and see the things that they saw.

But it felt good enough just to be here, in this room, and in those first weeks I would sleepwalk each day through the receiving-room job at the plating factory, then hasten on foot to this better world, one day arriving soaked to the bone from a driving rainstorm, and on a certain afternoon, with all the phone lines ringing at once, Bill Moore, busier even than usual, called over to me with some impatience: "Bob! Get it!"

He gestured with his head toward a ringing phone. I picked it up and, for the first time in my life, answered a telephone by saying the words:

"City desk."

I half expected the person on the other end to laugh—"City desk?" It was just me, seventeen years old—but I heard not laughter on the other end, but in the person's voice something close to nervousness, a sense of tentative intimidation—whoever was calling was talking to the city desk of the *Columbus Citizen-Journal*, after all, and making such a phone call was not something that people undertook lightly.

On the first Friday I was there Jean Allison carried a long sheet of paper to the cork bulletin board on the wall near the glass doors, and as soon as she tacked it up I could see everyone in the room beginning to wander over. I joined them.

Across the top of the sheet were typed the days of the week to come, each day lined off with a descending vertical rule, and on the left side of the sheet were the names of every member of the newspaper's staff. For each staff member, Miss Allison had typed in the hours of which days they were assigned to work.

There was some grumbling from those gathered at the bulletin board about Sunday shifts or late-night shifts, but not much—most of the staff got their same days and their same hours every week—and I stood with them and looked at the names. Moore, and Hess, and Sykes, and Garrett, and Reichard, and all the others, all the names I knew from all the years of reading the morning paper.

And then—I guess I should have expected it, the only surprising thing was that I was surprised—I saw it.

My name, right there with the others. The staff of the *Citizen-Journal*, and all of a sudden I was on it.

I tried not to stare. I tried not to grin. My summer had started off in the Epsilons lineup at second base, and now I was on this lineup sheet, and I suppose I stood there looking at it longer than I should have, as if looking at it long enough would make me believe for certain that it was real.

6

It was a good era in American journalism to be a kid who was a little shy, because the coffee runs were guaranteed to knock any bashfulness out of you, and, in the process, to almost instantly expand your circle of acquaintances.

"The coffee runs are the junior copykid's responsibility," Doris said to me right away—it was starting to seem that just about everything was the junior copykid's responsibility—and, thinking back now on what that particular task was like, I understand why nothing exactly like it typically goes on in newspaper offices today. Too seemingly demeaning, in our egalitarian-on-the-surface contemporary times; not that newspaper reporters wouldn't welcome such a regular service by a junior-level staff member, but they might be embarrassed to take part in it.

This is the way it worked:

Three or four times a day someone—me, during the time I was there—would go around to every person in the office—every reporter, every editor, every photographer, every artist, every clerk—and ask them what they wanted to eat.

"Coffee, two sugars."

"Cheeseburger with onion, pickles and mayonnaise."

"Hot tea, no sugar."

"Fried egg sandwich, on toast."

"Coke, no ice, and a hamburger with nothing on it."

"Grilled ham and cheese, rye bread."

Dozens of orders, writing them all down, accepting the money from the people, promising to bring them change.

And then I'd leave the building, and walk south on Third Street to Paoletti's, an old-style family Italian restaurant just down the block. I'd go to the service counter in the back and start reading off the orders, which I'd already consolidated to make this go more speedily:

"Eight coffees, two black, three cream and sugar, one black with two sugars, two cream no sugar. Seven hamburgers, one with tomato and pickle, two plain, one with onion and lettuce. . . ."

There was a poor old guy who was coughing his life away as he helped to take the orders—I think he may have been a patriarch of the Paoletti family, but I never found out for sure—and the health aspects of this made me a little queasy (there was never a time when he wasn't hacking loudly as he wrapped up the food and put it into big cardboard boxes for me to haul back), but mostly I was scared that I would forget an order, or get one wrong.

There were Western sandwiches, which featured some sort of omelet between the pieces of bread; there were bacon-and-egg sandwiches; the men and women of the *Citizen-Journal* ate as if there was an office pool that would pay the jackpot to the person who keeled over first. Hot brown trickles of coffee would leak out the tiny slits in the plastic tops snapped onto the paper cups; the ice in the soft-drink cups would slosh back and forth against the sides. The sound of the old man behind the counter hacking and heaving may have been revolting, but the smell of that food as I walked back to the office—all of those fragrances mixing together, wafting up from the big box—overrode the old man's sound; as soon as I was out the front door of Paoletti's I was able to push him out of my mind until the next coffee run (which would be only an hour or two away).

What this did for me was to immediately introduce me to every member of the newspaper staff—something I never could have brought myself to do under other circumstances. Without the coffee runs, I would have looked at them typing frenziedly, or cropping pictures, or marking up copy, and I would have feared that I'd be bothering them by saying hello and presenting myself. What was I going to do—pretend that this was some version of a Rotary Club meeting? Extend my right hand, plaster a big smile on my face, stride up to them and call out: "Hi, I'm the new guy, and I just wanted to say hello . . ."?

The coffee runs made it easy, because the people in the city room were happy to see me approaching. It had nothing to do with me, of course—it had to do with their grumbling stomachs, their thirsty palates. I wasn't disturbing them—even if they didn't want anything this time around, they'd tell me, "Make sure you come back on your next round, and don't miss me." By the time I was two or three days into this, I knew them, knew the sounds of their voices, knew which ones liked to tell jokes, knew which ones were looking for excuses to stop working for a moment and gab, and which ones were the most jittery on deadline, which ones seemed kind and which ones were constitutionally distant and which ones seemed to see, somewhere inside the new copyboy, reminders of who they had been themselves, not so very long ago.

And—even more than seeing my name on Miss Allison's schedule sheet—this made me feel that I was a part of the staff. It had happened just that quickly. I'd go to Paoletti's for the third or fourth time of the day, and that sorrowful old man would still be coughing, as if he hadn't stopped since I'd walked out two hours before, which he probably hadn't . . .

And I was the kid from the *Citizen-Journal*. Whoever I might have been at the beginning of the summer—my parents' son, my buddies' friend, my brother and sister's brother . . .

Whoever I had been up to this point in my life, I was something else, and someone else, now. I was the kid from the *C-J*, walking into Paoletti's like I knew the lay of the land—and then walking back into the newsroom full of reporters eagerly waiting for me, or, more accurately, for the sandwiches and the drinks I was lugging. Fine by me. I was one of them now, against all odds I was a part of this staff, which was all I had wanted in the first place.

"E-*nun*-ciate!"

That's the kind of thing that passed for career advice as I circulated taking the coffee orders, and the bestower of that advice—Ron Pataky, the *Citizen-Journal*'s officially designated theater-and-film critic—was undoubtedly correct.

"Bob, you're never going to make an impression on anyone if you mumble and slur your words," he said to me one day. "Don't walk up like you're afraid to talk. Say the words! Enunciate!"

"I was just wondering if you wanted a sandwich now," I mumbled. "I can come back later."

Because he covered the theater—although the theater scene in Columbus, in those years, consisted mainly of an occasional touring Broadway show at the ancient Hartman Theater a few blocks from the *Dispatch* building, some traveling warm-weather productions brought in by the Kenley Players to the Veterans Memorial Auditorium, and the Playhouse on the Green summer-stock tent on a patch of grass north of the city—Pataky was considered quite theatrical himself. He didn't have much competition, in the setting of that city room, where I found that I was just one of many non-enunciators. Broad-browed in a Joe Namath way (although the face of Joe Namath himself had not yet come onto the national scene), dark-haired, booming of voice and flashing of eye, he would end up, during his tenure at the *C-J*, surprising people all over town because of two personal accomplishments quite removed from his assigned and predictable routine of reviewing every new movie that opened in Columbus:

He wrote songs that Jerry Vale recorded. And—no one could figure out how this happened—he dated, at least briefly, the actress Anna Maria Alberghetti. Dating a Hollywood actress, for a guy in that central Ohio newsroom . . . well, the only reason people believed it was true was that there was a picture taken at Port Columbus as he greeted her upon her arrival one day, and one of the papers—I think it was the

Dispatch, I think they thought they were sticking it to the *Citizen-Journal* by showing a *C-J* newspaper guy going high-hat by dating a famous actress—printed the picture, which was examined in town as closely as if it were some fake document designed to trick the citizens into believing the Loch Ness monster was on the loose.

"*E-nun*-ciate!" he directed, and I told him I would really try, and took his coffee order.

I don't think many of the people in that room ever attended a school of journalism—certainly not the older reporters and editors. Most of them seemed more blue-collar, which was at the center of their appeal to me: the room itself was a school of journalism; if you paid attention to how these men and women carried out their trade, you could learn to do it too. They were the opposite of haughty—they were just writing stories about the news of their city, and doing their best not to make mistakes and get bawled out by their bosses.

So I studied them as I brought them food. Al Getchell had the title of editorial cartoonist, but in practice he seldom was permitted to express his opinions on the editorial page; he was a short, rumpled, unhappy-looking man who was missing part of a finger, and who spent most of his days retouching photos on the orders of the managing editor, Jack Keller. On his easel he would lay the photograph that Keller had tossed at him, and he would paint beneath a newsmaker's eyes, to make those eyes appear more conspicuous; or darken the area next to the main subject of the photo, thus removing whoever else might have been standing there, and making it seem as if the man at the center of the story had been posing alone; or whiting out whatever buildings or wall decorations were behind a person in a photo, so that the person's face would appear as if he or she had sat for a studio portrait for the *C-J*, and not been grabbed candidly.

None of this would be permissible today: to alter photos in that way would be cause for hand-wringing and immediate dismissal in the standard twenty-first-century newsroom. But Getchell wasn't doing anything that wasn't going on in most newsrooms in America in those years—it didn't occur to him, or to his editors, that there was anything wrong with cleaning up a photo. That was the phrase: "Clean this up, will you, Al?" He would get out his brush and his paint, and, on command, try to make a picture look better before it got into the paper. If he was professionally frustrated that, at the very most, he was assigned to do little line sketches to illustrate feature stories, or caricatures of local celebrities in the news, and was seldom allowed to create a real editorial cartoon, like the Bill Mauldins and Herblocks of the newspaper world—well, on the mezzanine on Third Street a man did what he was asked to do.

I watched it all, every day. There were the locally well-known writers who got their headshots in the paper with their stories: Ben Hayes, the been-there-forever man-about-town columnist, who wore a straw hat and wrote eccentrically paced, amiably toned stories full of whimsical items about Columbus, whose smile sometimes curled upward on only one side of his face, the way Dick Cheney's would years later, but seemingly much more softly than Cheney's—Ben Hayes was a newspaper columnist with no perceptible ego or lust for power and influence, he was just spinning his daily yarns; Jo Bradley Reed, the birdlike television critic, always jetting off on network-underwritten junkets to meet the stars so they could plug their shows in the pages of the C-J (like Getchell fixing up the photos, Jo Bradley Reed wasn't doing anything that hundreds of other television writers on hundreds of other newspapers weren't doing in those days; the networks sent the plane tickets and paid for the hotel rooms because . . . well, because that's how it was done, no one had yet pointed out there was anything wrong with it, press junkets paid for by the big, rich television networks were part of the business, and papers like the *Citizen-Journal* certainly didn't have the budgets or the inclination to on their own tab be sending Jo Bradley Reed to soundstages in California just to interview the cast of *Bonanza* or *The Beverly Hillbillies*). . . .

The newsroom stars were the exception, though. Most of the people I would stop and talk with on my coffee runs were journeymen and journeywomen like Dave Scheen, an excruciatingly withdrawn young reporter who wrote fluidly and seemingly effortlessly, but whose shy eyes were always averted, as if too timid to look at other people; and Gail Lucas, a women's-page reporter whose countenance was as opened up as Dave Scheen's was closed down, who brimmed over with brassy self-confidence and good humor, and who seemed always to bristle just beneath the surface at being assigned not to cover politics or murders, but, more often, ladies' club meetings and society dances; and Ed Colston, the paper's sole African-American reporter, who invariably would be sent out whenever there was said to be trouble in Columbus's "Negro community," and who, in his spare time (I would eventually learn), was an oil-painting-and-pastels artist of such breathtaking skill and heartbreaking sensitivity that the mundane crime-reporting tasks to which he was so often assigned by the C-J city desk seemed like, if not an insult (for he was working here by choice, and underwriting his artistry with his newspaper paycheck), then at least a waste of what he appeared to have been put on this earth to do.

I would talk with them all, every day, taking their food orders but listening for more. They were not like anyone I had ever known. They had all found their way here, to this place, to this kind of work, to this room.

And, every morning when I would wake up at home after my copyboy shift the night before, they would have made it to my family's doorstep. That was one of the things I loved most that summer—finding the names of those men and women waiting on the pages of the *Citizen-Journal* when my father, my mother, my sister, my brother and I would get up for breakfast.

The newspaper itself—the tall sheaf of newsprint pages that bore the bylines of Wink Hess and Dave Scheen and Gail Lucas and Ed Colston and Ben Hayes and all the other people I'd talked with and carried food to during the twenty-four hours since my family had sat down for their last breakfast—felt to me, by morning, like both a part of what I'd been involved in the day before, yet something completely separate. The newspaper on our front stoop was a finished product—each morning it felt, on the one hand, like an artifact devoid of any remnants of the noise and the joking and the roomful of frowns and smiles I'd immersed myself in the previous day, an artifact removed, both by the intervening hours and by the distance from the *Dispatch* building to our front door, from the sights that had surrounded me: the bearers of those bylines leaning back in their chairs, arms clasped behind their necks as they stared at the ceiling and considered whether it was time to begin writing their stories, the vision of them reaching into pockets as they fished for a dollar or two to give me for their portion of the city-room order I would be taking over to Paoletti's. . . .

The newspaper waiting for my family and me in the morning seemed at once a cooled-off and bloodless thing compared with my memories of what I had seen and heard during the effectuation of that paper, yet also a recondite reminder, on every page, of those private memories. Under a headline on some inside page in the paper at home I would read a lead paragraph of a story, and I'd recall seeing the reporter who wrote it as he had tried out one opening sentence for the article, then rejected it in frustration, tearing the copy paper from the typewriter carriage, balling it up and heaving it toward the tall trash can across the aisle, impatiently rolling in a new sheet and giving the lead a fresh attempt; I'd see in our paper at home the layout of a page, and know immediately where I'd seen it before—in the composing room, inverted, upside down, the metal of each letter jutting ceilingward as the men in printers' aprons had assembled that page, carefully placing the stories one by one, as if fashioning a fragile jigsaw puzzle that only they had the answer to, while I had stood next to them with some instructions from the newsroom in my hand, waiting for them to look up from their work so I could give it to them, as I'd been directed. . . .

The paper would arrive at our front door before breakfast, and I would see both things: the product, prim and standard, an American newspaper just like American newspapers on doorsteps in every city in the nation on that morning—and at the same time I would see my collection of vivid and happy memories of what I had observed, what I had heard, as that product had been invented from scratch, story by story, photo by photo, page by page, the afternoon and night before.

I suppose the pages of the *C-J* were not especially elegantly designed or meticulously thought out, measured against how newspapers now are put together. They were a hodgepodge—local stories, statewide stories, national stories, features, profiles, all thrown in together, one-paragraph newsbriefs dropped in next to longer articles as if they were positioned where they were just because there happened to be a hole available (which, oftentimes, is in fact how those tiny stories ended up where they did). Today American newspapers are intricately organized—"navigation" is the operational word in newsrooms, great emphasis is placed on making it easy for the reader to plot his or her journey through the pages of a local paper; there is a place for every-thing and everything is expected to be where it is for a reason. Readers are in a hurry; that is the presumption, and with it comes the assumed necessity of helping the reader locate what he or she may be looking for as swiftly and seamlessly as possible.

From what I could tell that first copyboy summer, the men and women who put the *Citizen-Journal* together didn't assume the reader was looking for anything in particular, and certainly not that the reader was in a big hurry. The jumble of stories and photos that filled the pages of the *C-J* was a pleasing jumble—it looked like what a scrap-book of the town would look like, all kinds of things thrown in to-gether, with nothing in common save the fact that the people on the mezzanine on Third Street who had assembled the daily scrapbook had figured that readers at their breakfast tables the next morning might, for a few minutes, deem it all, or at least some of it, interesting. If there was any grand concept behind the page design of the *Citizen-Journal* on a given morning—and I don't know that there was—then it was just that the pleasing jumble was being presented as something for the read-ers to look around in, to wander about inside of, to discover things on their own.

The readers were reading the *C-J* because they wanted to, right? Where else were they going to find out about their town this morning? That seemed to be the unspoken premise in putting the pages together—that the people of the city picked up the *Citizen-Journal* each new dawn because they liked doing it, and because there was no alternative, that morning, to the scrapbook that had been cobbled to-gether for them after the sun had gone down the day before.

"Bob, I've got something for you to do," Bill Moore would call out from the city desk as I arrived on Third Street for a new shift, and already the edition of the paper that my parents had read at breakfast was obsolete, already the men and women on the mezzanine were working on a new one. On the wall across from Bill Moore's desk were two big maps, one of the city of Columbus, one of Franklin County, each map with a specially marked long, narrow band of cloth tacked to it, the band of cloth calibrated to tell a staff member how many miles it was from one point to another. This was the area of the world the men and women in the room were expected to cover; these were the parameters that contained the raw material for the daily scrapbook delivered to all those doorsteps. "Run this up to the engraving room for me," Bill Moore would say, and the next day's scrapbook was already beginning to take shape, even now, one random idea, one sweated-over paragraph, one wet-from-developing-fluid photograph, at a time.

"The boss would like to see you," Jean Allison said one afternoon, and that was the day I found out what a "D.W. Page One Must" was—and its significance to the newspaper-as-city-scrapbook theory that was forming in my head.

Don E. Weaver, who looked almost exactly like Popeye, but older and even knobbier—you somehow got the impression that he had looked like that even as a baby—was a holdover from the *Columbus Citizen* who had been retained to serve as editor of the *Citizen-Journal*. The *C-J* as a distinct and separate enterprise was only five years old the summer I joined the staff—it was a hybrid that had been born in 1959 when the owners of the evening *Citizen*, published by the Scripps-Howard chain, and the morning *Ohio State Journal*, published by the proprietors of the *Dispatch*, had worked out a joint operating agreement with the federal government. The new *Citizen-Journal* would continue to be owned by Scripps-Howard, but would be printed in the *Dispatch's* headquarters, on the *Dispatch's* presses, with all advertising, circulation and other business functions overseen and carried out by the *Dispatch's* managers. Families who had subscribed to the *Citizen* and to the *Journal* were told that the papers they had welcomed into their homes for generations were going to be consolidated into one even better paper, one they would like even more. We were one of those families; I actually believed it when I first read about how much better we were going to like the new paper, and it took me a few weeks before I began to realize, even as a kid, that when two newspapers combine into one, it's never a better deal for the readers. It's a better deal for the owners.

The *Citizen-Journal* was the underdog from the start; down on the *Dispatch* building's mezzanine it maintained its own news and editorial staff, but that's all it controlled. The joint operating agreement virtually guaranteed that the C-J would never be the city's dominant newspaper, no matter how hard its reporters and editors tried. Scripps-Howard did get to name the editor, and it named Don E. Weaver, who, according to Miss Allison on this summer day, wished to see me.

"So you want to be a newspaperman," Mr. Weaver, pipe in hand, said to me from behind his desk. Perhaps at bigger papers, to call on the editor-in-chief you would have to go to a different wing of the news floor, or even a different part of the building, to reach his office. Here, he was just twelve or thirteen steps from Bill Moore's city desk, through an ever-open door. I would never see him without the pipe, either in his mouth or in his hand; the Popeye resemblance included his face, the pipe, and, beneath rolled-up white shirtsleeves, a thick set of forearms that would have looked just as at home on a southern Ohio farm. He seemed swell.

He said he was glad the paper had been able to give me this job for the summer, and that he hoped I'd do well, and he said he had his first assignment for me, which was to take a piece of paper that was atop his desk to Jack Keller, the managing editor, who sat even closer to Mr. Weaver's office—I'd say eight steps—than did Bill Moore.

And I could see that, handwritten in big letters on the piece of paper, was: "D.W. Page One Must."

As I recall, the sheet of paper was a press release saying one of the local banks was building an ambitious new branch office—but I may be mistaken on the specifics, it might have been a local department store that was erecting a new branch. What I'm certain of was that it was a bit of commerce that had the potential to boost the Columbus economy, and that Don Weaver—D.W.—with his notation was telling the managing editor that not only should a story be written about the announcement, but that that story had to be featured on the front page.

Now . . . there's not much of the romance of fearless stop-the-presses journalism in that—and if an editor today were to send to his subordinates such an explicit message concerning placement of a story about a leading local business, that editor's staff members would be leaking the memo to Internet media critics within minutes, and within an hour online voices from around the country would be mocking the editor who did it, and in the most derisive terms, calling him a sellout to advertising interests. You can make a case that the critics would be right.

But on that day, in that era, it didn't feel as if Mr. Weaver was doing anything especially controversial. The bank (or the department store) was a leading player in the life of the community; the readers of the C-J would likely be interested in the availability of the new branch; Don Weaver was responsible for what the readers of the paper saw; and he thought they should see this, first thing in the morning. Not exactly an investigative piece—the *Citizen-Journal* didn't have any reporters who were assigned to an investigative unit. But the construction of the new branch was part of the scrapbook of the town, and Mr. Weaver had determined that, tomorrow morning, news of it was going to be on the front of the scrapbook.

"Mr. Weaver wanted me to give this to you," I said to Jack Keller, who glanced at it, showed no reaction one way or another, and flipped it to Bill Moore to be assigned to a reporter. The next day, over breakfast, my parents read, on Page One, that the new branch would be going up.

If they were bothered that the story seemed a little like an advertising promotion for the bank or the department store—if they would have preferred a hard-hitting piece questioning the dealings of the town's power elite—I don't recall them expressing that thought. What I do remember was them noting, with appreciative surprise, that the town was going to be changing again, was going to have a new commercial landmark that hadn't been there before. The two of them talked about it with approval as they read the paper.

Me? At that point in my life, I just thought it was amazing that I had known it was going to be on Page One before anyone else knew—even before Jack Keller or Bill Moore. Popeye himself may have been powerful—he may have been able to rip the lids off spinach cans. But he wasn't any more powerful than Don Weaver. Popeye couldn't put his pipe down and decree that something appear on the front page. Mr. Weaver could. And did. I'd seen it with my own eyes.

"You sure you don't want one?"

Bob Moeckel, his arm extended, held an open pack of Lucky Strikes in front of my face. We were sitting in the dark on the roof of the *Dispatch* building.

"No, thanks," I said.

"Suit yourself," he said. He did this little thing with his thumb—he knew how to take a matchbook and, using one hand only, somehow remove a match, scratch it against the sandpaper part of the matchbook, make it flame, and light his cigarette. Astonishing—one hand.

The match flared in the night, he lit his Lucky, and we kept talking.

This is where he would take his breaks in the evening hours—on the roof. He looked like something out of *Rebel Without a Cause*—he may have been a C-J editorial clerk, one step elevated from copyboy, but I don't think he had any journalism aspirations above his current job, or any desire for schoolroom training in the field. His short-sleeved shirt rolled up high on his biceps, hair greased back, he was a guy who might have found himself working in a gas station, but who had landed in the city room of a daily newspaper instead. Nothing so unusual about that, in that era.

Sometimes he'd invite his non-newspaper-world buddies—guys from his neighborhood—to join him at night on the roof of the *Dispatch* headquarters to sit there and shoot the breeze and try to catch looks into the windows of the YWCA. It was a straight visual shot into the side of the YWCA building, where, on nights when Moeckel and his pals hit the jackpot, a young woman might decide to get undressed and neglect to pull down the shades.

Occasionally he'd ask me if I wanted to join him on his break. It was quiet up there—it was a view of Columbus at night I'd never had before. Moeckel's day—the most important part of it—would have peaked after the New York stock markets had closed. He was the last link between the high-powered financial traders on Wall Street and the readers of the *Citizen-Journal*.

He would use this handheld chrome-and-steel device—it looked like a big, boxy scissors—and as the ticker-tape strip from the stockmarket wire in the city room would come streaming out late each afternoon, he would hold his machine over long mock-up pages that had been imprinted in advance with the symbol of every company that was listed on the New York Stock Exchange. His job was to paste the final numbers for each company next to the corresponding symbol on the page; when he was finished, it was sent to the Linotype operators to be set in metal. Today all of this is done in an eye's blink, via digital computer transmission. In 1964, setting the stock-market results was still one of the most painstaking and labor-intensive parts of the daily production of a newspaper. All that tiny type—the day's opening numbers, and highs, and lows, and percentage of change—thousands of numbers to be set in type, each of them having to be accurate, and before that could happen, Bob Moeckel, the newsroom James Dean, had to paste it all up. It was no coincidence he could do the lighting-a-match-with-one-hand trick; that was nothing, compared to the dexterity required to work the handheld stock-ticker-pasting machine.

(One day that summer, he blew it. On the long sheet with the preprinted company symbols, he somehow was off by one line—every line. He pasted the strips of stock numbers just like he always did—the way the machine in his hand worked, he would paste down one set of numbers next to a company symbol, push a lever, the machine would snip the strip as he pasted it and thus free him to position the next numbers as they came out. On that particular day, he pasted everything just one line too low. In the morning, business-page readers all over town spat their coffee out as they checked the stocks they owned and felt their hearts freeze as they saw weird, way-off prices that made it seem their fiscal worlds had suddenly veered out of control.)

"So I can make you that press card," he said on the roof, drawing deeply on his cigarette.

"Really?" I said.

"Sure," he said. "I figured out a way. You bring the picture?"

I had—I'd brought a black-and-white school photo of myself.

"Come on," he said.

We walked through the door that led us off the roof, and took the stairs back to the city room. He led me to a desk in the back, where he kept some supplies.

He cut a little rectangle from the side panel of a manila filing-cabinet folder. He rolled it into a typewriter, and typed, in capital letters: OFFICIAL PRESS. He typed in my name, the words "Columbus Citizen-Journal," and then typed a dotted line across the bottom of the card.

He removed the stiff little rectangle from the typewriter carriage, and, using a brush from a pastepot, adhered my school picture to it. For good measure, he also cut the Scripps-Howard lighthouse logo ("Give Light and the People Will Find Their Own Way" was the newspaper chain's slogan) from a piece of C-J stationery, and pasted that onto the card, too. Then, across the dotted line he'd typed, he scrawled a signature that was intentionally indecipherable. As the final step, he took me back to the morgue—the newspaper's library—where there was a laminating machine utilized to preserve the wire-service pictures that intermittently and slowly emerged, on flimsy paper, out of the newsroom's UPI photo receiver. Tonight Moeckel used the laminator to encase in plastic the newly crafted press card. "Here you go," he said, handing it to me. "Flash it at a cop, and you can go anywhere."

"Like fires?" I said.

"Fires, crime scenes, movies . . . anywhere," Moeckel said.

I slipped the card into my wallet. When I inspected it later, I knew I'd be nuts to ever try to use it. It looked like exactly what it was—a forgery, and not even an artful one. It wouldn't have fooled a four-year-old.

But I really liked having it. Moeckel had said, one previous night up on the roof, that he'd get me a press card like the ones the real reporters carried. And tonight he'd come through—sort of, in his own manner. How many ways had he risked getting fired on this night? Sneaking onto the roof of the *Dispatch* building, peering into the windows of the YWCA, counterfeiting an official press card, using *Citizen-Journal* office supplies to manufacture it, forging an authorizing signature (although not a signature that anyone could read) . . .

How many ways had he risked getting fired?

Probably none. Not back then. This was just what young guys who worked at newspapers did at night. Fooled around. Looked for a little fun, as the rest of the city slept.

Water, heat, suction:

One afternoon I knocked over the postage-stamp wetter that the women at the public-service desk by the C-J's front door used. It was a little contraption that moistened the backs of stamps for them, so they didn't have to lick them every time they mailed a brochure or a C-J football schedule to a reader who had requested one. I inadvertently hit it with my hand as I was walking past, and all the water from the stamp wetter poured onto the desk's surface. I felt like it was the biggest mistake in the history of newspapering—I thought the women were going to yell at me, maybe banish me from the building. They just smiled sweetly and wiped it up with paper towels.

One evening a ribbon frayed, and then snapped, on one of the UPI machines. "Hey, quick, get over there and change it," Bill Keesee, the assistant city editor, shouted toward me. I fumbled as I tried to put in a new ribbon—it was different than a typewriter ribbon, switching it was a more complicated task, and there was heat inside the wire-service machine, that's what caught me off guard; there was heat coming up from beneath the hard plastic cover, and every second I wasted before getting the ribbon successfully changed meant that the national and international stories that were coming across weren't reaching us. They didn't get put on hold—we just missed those stories during the time I had the keys turned off, and we'd have to ask to have them retransmitted later. I felt like James Bond, trying to defuse a bomb before it ticked down to zero—I felt that kind of pressure, with the heat from inside the UPI machine on my hands.

The suction in the pneumatic tube next to the copy desk as I would send stories to the composing room on deadline—the feeling of the pressurized air yanking the cylinders out of my hands, the cylinders that, very late at night, carried the last-minute stories and headlines for the C-J's front page, the late-closing material for what would be the next morning's most urgent and prominently displayed news articles . . . as the air in the tube tugged the cylinders from my hand, transporting the stories toward their next step to being read in houses and offices all over the city the next dawn, it felt to me like the most important thing I had ever been entrusted to do.

Most nights I took the bus home, but on some nights my parents would drive downtown to give me a ride. I'd come out of the front door and onto all-but-deserted Third Street, and I'd hand my dad a copy of the early edition, and he'd say, joking but not joking, "How was work, Scoop?"

It took a few weeks for the lag in the office paperwork to kick in, and for me to receive my first paycheck. Miss Allison had to remind me that it was payday. I hadn't even thought about it, since the day I was hired. Payday? A check, for doing this? I would have paid them. Gladly.

It was $58.50 after taxes, and on my first day off afterward, when I had time to take it to the squat, gray Ohio National Bank branch near my parents' house, to deposit it in my passbook savings account, I hoped against hope that the teller would give the check more than a cursory glance before processing it. The press card that Bob Moeckel had made for me might have been a phony, but this wasn't, and I wanted the bank teller to see it—I wanted the teller to know. The person standing on the other side of the counter worked for the *Columbus Citizen-Journal*. Truly. It said so, right on the paycheck.

7

One person in that city room who didn't much care what anyone would think of him when he cashed his *C-J* paycheck was Bill Moore.

The reason I'm sure of this is that he would have me cash it for him.

He'd ask me to do that, and to buy him his cigarettes. The cigarettes were Larks—he'd hand me a quarter and a dime and tell me to run over to the gift shop of the Sheraton-Columbus and fetch him a fresh pack. The first time, I was worried that the clerk wouldn't sell them to me—I was too young to legally purchase a pack of cigarettes. But the woman behind the counter just took the thirty-five cents and put the Larks into my hand, and within minutes I was putting them into Bill Moore's hand. This would go on all summer.

The paycheck, I was a little surprised about. I grew up in a house where how much money my father made was never discussed—to this day, years after his death, I still don't know what his salary was. So when Bill Moore gave me his paycheck and asked me to go to the bank to cash it for him, I wasn't quite sure how to handle the logistics. Should I look to see what he earned? I couldn't very well avoid it—he wanted me to bring all the cash back to him.

He endorsed the back of the check before sending me, and the first week I went, the teller didn't want to give me the money. She had an assistant manager make a phone call to Bill on the city desk, to make certain this was all legitimate—that I wasn't some kid who had found someone's lost check, and who was trying to improperly withdraw the money.

His take-home pay was, I believe, one hundred fifty-three dollars a week. He was responsible for the entirety of the newspaper's local report. That wasn't a lot of money for a man to make, even in 1964 dollars, and I was someone who worked for him, and you might think he wouldn't want one of his employees to know his salary. But apparently that mattered to him not at all.

Beneath his crewcut, I would sometimes see a current of tension in his eyes, but his voice was ever steady, and he never raised it to me in anger. He was in charge of making sure the city was covered, that no story was missed, and he was up against a much larger and better financed operation upstairs, at the *Dispatch*, where there were more layers of editors to provide backup for each other. On our city desk, on the five days of the week when he worked, it was just Bill.

I didn't know anything about him, other than what a good guy I thought he was, and how much I admired his self-evident professionalism. Almost forty years later, when he died in a small town in North Carolina, I received in the mail a package from a member of his family. Bill had written a personal history for the family, and they said that he had told them that he and I once knew and liked each other, and because of that, they wanted me to have a copy. He had been a bomber pilot in World War II and the Korean War, it turned out; that's what he had done as a young man before entering civilian life and deciding that, after years of combat aviation, being a newspaperman sounded like something he'd like to try.

I think the reason he always sent me for his cigarettes, and to cash his paychecks, was that he didn't want to be away from the city desk. Being at that desk was his responsibility. I'd run out to the Sheraton for his Larks, I'd run out to the bank for his cash, and the one thing that made me curious, something I never asked him about, was that his hands always seemed to shake a little. Whatever pressure he may have been feeling, that's where I would see it: in his hands. But I didn't say anything.

One day he said to me:

"You ought to start doing the emergency runs."

I had been hoping to hear something like that. I'd been talking with some of the reporters about it; when I would go out to dinner by myself, and I would run into some of them at various bargain restaurants around downtown—the Woolworth's soda-fountain counter, Mills Cafeteria—I would tell them, if the course of our conversation permitted it, that I was hoping I could write something that would get into the paper.

Downtown after six o'clock at night, when the businesses and government offices had emptied out and the employees had gone home to their families, felt suddenly desolate—just a few hours before, the sidewalks would have been packed, the noise level on the streets would have been high. But after six, when I would head off alone to take my dinner break, the population around Broad and High would be quite sparse. So as I'd have a cheeseburger at the Woolworth's counter, or a Salisbury steak from the Mills buffet, I would notice other *C-J* staff members at other stools or tables, usually, like me, eating solo. They, too, were a part of the decimated downtown tableau after the daytime workers had returned to the suburbs.

They'd invite me to join them: Gail Lucas, eating from a dish of Jell-O at Mills, Jim Sykes, dining on a hot dog at Woolworth's, and as we'd talk I'd look around the restaurant, at the few other customers who were present, and I'd think to myself: Gail and Jim get their bylines in the paper almost every day, their words are some of the most widely read work in town, yet no one here on High Street tonight knows who they are. Tomorrow morning, some of the men and women who are here now— that fellow over in the corner, slurping up his soup, the woman in the Mills uniform adjusting desserts atop the clean glass counter, trying to make the display of puddings and pies look more appealing—tomorrow morning, they may be reading the stories Gail and Jim will write after we all go back to the city room when dinner is finished. But they have no idea.

So it felt sort of like being in a private guild, sitting with them at dinner, sort of like knowing their secret: they wrote the news that the other people in the restaurant would read at breakfast. And they'd ask me about my own ambitions—"What do you want to do with your life?" Gail asked me one night—and I said that what I wanted to do was be like them, I wanted to do what they did, and I said it would be great if, in addition to my copyboy duties, I could write some words that would be part of the newspaper.

I don't know if they told Bill Moore what I had confided to them— he must have known it anyway, I was, after all, the kid who had arrived unannounced in front of his desk on the afternoon the president had been killed, beseeching him to print my story—but, whether or not they had let him know, one day he informed me that I should do the emergency runs, and I knew that, by getting the assignment, I would be given entrée, however modestly, into the pages of the C-J.

"*Citizen-Journal* calling, anything new?"

So the colloquies would begin. I would call every city, suburban and small-township police and fire department in our circulation area, every day, right before deadline. "*Citizen-Journal* calling, anything new?" I was nervous the first few times I did it, I could feel my voice shaking a little, but the police and fire dispatchers on the other end had heard it all before, from C-J staff members and *Columbus Dispatch* staff members who had come along years before me, and they'd be hearing it from new C-J and *Dispatch* staffers years after I'd be gone. It's what the people on the other end of the phone had come to expect: newspaper people in search of bad news.

For that, at essence, was the reason behind our pursuit: if nothing had happened, then there was nothing to put in the emergency runs, but if something had happened—an accident, a heart attack, a fire that destroyed a home—then that something was, by definition, bad. Happy events didn't make the emergency runs.

"Harry Denison, 438 S. Hamilton-rd, found unconscious in garage; treated and released." "1179 W. Seventh-av, electrical fire in kitchen, fire department responded and extinguished."

That's how the emergency runs I wrote would read. Few newspapers today publish emergency runs; some editors believe they violate the privacy of the people named in them, some think they take up too much space. The specificity of them was always their major appeal. In the C-J they would appear in agate type, near the back of the morning paper, and although it was difficult to take any pride of authorship in the emergency runs—it felt a little like writing for the telephone book—the words were mine, I'd selected them, and this felt like something constructive, this was something that, had I not typed it up, would not be appearing in the newspaper in precisely this way. I liked the feeling.

Bill Moore instructed me: the *Citizen-Journal*'s style for "Road" in an address was "-rd" after the name of the road, "Street" was "-st," "Avenue" was "-av." I was not to forget that; it was very important not to break style. And to this day, I still do it when I address an envelope or write down directions; to this day, I'll write "2722 Bryden-rd," or "532 N. Main-st." It's a style I've never seen anywhere else, but Bill Moore's admonition rings in my ears: Do it this way. Our readers deserve consistency.

I would call the police and fire dispatchers night after night, and they would give me the bad news. The worst news they would give me always had the three initials "D.O.A" in it—dead on arrival. The dispatchers said it so often that it lost its punch: "D.O.A." became just another common phrase, no more unexpected than "said" or "the." One night, when talking about an emergency run his department had made, a dispatcher—he knew my voice by now, we had spoken scores of times—gave me the name and spelling of the victim, and then said: "D.F.M."

"'D.F.M.'?" I said into the phone. "What's that mean?"

"Dead as a fuckin' mackerel," the dispatcher said, summing up a life just lost, and this was my new world. I typed it up as dead on arrival, and was just as glad that the family of the deceased would never be aware of what the dispatcher, bored in the midst of one more shift, had said about their beloved.

"You are Miss Citizen Fair."

This is how a fairgoer was required to say it, in order to become the winner. If a person on the midway were to say, "Are you Miss Citizen Fair?", that would not count. If the person were to say, "Are you the girl?", that would not count. It had to be those exact words: "You are Miss Citizen Fair." If the person had approached the right young lady, that person won the money.

It was a promotion that had started at the old *Columbus Citizen*, and evidently the decision had been made not to alter the wording when the *Citizen* became the *Citizen-Journal*. The way it worked was this:

A young woman in her late teens, maybe her very early twenties, was hired to walk the Ohio Fairgrounds every day during the two weeks of the Ohio State Fair, carrying a copy of that day's *Citizen-Journal*. On the first day of the fair, the vaguest of photographic clues—perhaps a picture of one of her hands—would appear in the *C-J*. If a fairgoer spotted a young woman carrying the paper, recognized that her hand matched the hand he had seen in his *C-J* that morning, approached her and said, "You are Miss Citizen Fair," he would win the cash prize. If he said the words any differently, she would ignore him and walk on.

As each day passed without Miss Citizen Fair being identified by a fellow fairgoer, the clues in the paper would become more obvious: maybe a photo of her shoes one day, then, if no one picked her out, her skirt the next day, then, the next day, a photo shot from behind, showing the back of her hair. She could be anywhere—by the dairy barn, in the bleachers at the prize hog competition, standing in line for the Tilt-a-Whirl, looking at the butter cow. Miss Citizen Fair could be any young woman on the fairgrounds.

On one of my days off that summer, my friends and I went to the fair. They asked me if I knew who Miss Citizen Fair was—they wanted to claim the prize. I told them the truth: no, I didn't know. It was closely held information, possessed by only a few executives at the newspaper.

"You are Miss Citizen Fair," one of my friends said to a woman who was walking past us.

But she wasn't. "You're the third person who's asked me that to-day," she said.

One person we did see from the *Citizen-Journal* was Al Getchell, under an umbrella.

The editorial cartoonist had been sent out to the fairgrounds, as he was every summer, to sit at his drawing board beneath a big parasol that protected him from the sun, and draw free caricatures of fairgoers. The idea was to generate good will for the paper.

"Hey, Al!" I called to him. He looked toward my voice, not show-ing much interest—a lot of people were yelling "Hey, Al!" at him, the sign next to his table and umbrella announced to all in the vicinity that he was Al Getchell of the *C-J*—but when he saw that it was me he grinned and waved me over, which made me feel good: it proved to my friends that the people at the newspaper really did know me.

"What are you doing here?" he said to me, as if my natural habitat, like his, had now become not the outside world, but the city room. He looked happier than I'd ever seen him at the paper—there, under the fluorescent lights, Jack Keller was always tossing photos at him to re-touch, there he always seemed to be contemplating the fact that his pro-fessional life had come to this: not to making art, not to expressing visual editorial-page ideas about stories in the news, but to whiting out unwanted areas of pictures before they appeared in the paper, touching up the wrinkles on a newsmaker's photographic likeness. At work, there seemed always to be a sombrous cloud hovering over Al's head, even as he hovered over his drawing board.

At the fair the sun was high in the sky, and dozens of people crowded around him, hoping that he would select one of them as the subject of his sketch. "Mr. Getchell! Mr. Getchell!" they called out, and he beamed in their direction. I looked at him there, I saw his hand with the missing finger, I saw the people whom he'd already chosen, walking away with their prized, signed Al Getchell sketches. "Mr. Getchell!" they called, and he smiled toward me and shrugged, as if to indicate: *What can I do? I'm in demand.* He looked as if he never wanted to leave the fair.

"Let's see if we can find Miss Citizen Fair and win the money," one of my friends said, but we didn't try very hard. It was hopeless: how, out of all the young women at the fair, were we going to find the right one?

And of course, the bittersweet part, looking back on it from the perspective of today's world, is this:

It was a time when newspapers were still such a fundamental part of everyday American life that there really were too many young women on the fairgrounds who fit the Miss Citizen Fair profile, too many young women for us to narrow down the field.

Too many young women walking around the Ohio State Fair carrying copies of that morning's local newspaper. It was utterly common: a person at the fair, young or old, carrying the latest edition. It's what people did: purchase a paper every day, and carry it around with them.

Even at the fair.

I noticed that when there was a mistake of any kind in the paper, the editors had a way to make note of it.

In green grease pencil, each day, one or more of the bosses—usually Jack Keller, sometimes the news editor, an ever-embittered but paradoxically friendly enough fellow named Ted English—would mark up that morning's edition to show what they thought was wrong.

There would be slash marks on the front page to indicate their displeasure with the design of a layout; there would be big circles around words or names that were misspelled; there would be peeved comments written over headlines that the editors felt were pedestrian, or photos they thought were poorly shot. On every page of every edition, within hours of when that edition had hit the street, the thick, angry lines of the green grease pencil would show just how much of that day's paper the editors didn't like.

And yet, the *Citizen-Journal*, like most newspapers of the era, had no formalized corrections column in the paper, where the readers could see it; very seldom did the *C-J* tell its subscribers that the paper had made an error. If you were a reader of the *C-J*, you may have assumed that your morning paper was all but infallible—there was almost never a word admitting that a mistake of any kind had made it into print.

This was just how things were done, then, at newspapers all across the country. Today, newspapers not only routinely run daily corrections and clarifications, but they often engage in self-flagellation meant to demonstrate the new and highly prized quality called "transparency." It's becoming harder for even the most dissatisfied readers to want to beat their papers up; the papers seem to enjoy doing it to themselves with such vigor, some readers may almost feel like a compassionate boxing referee who wants to step in to stop the fight—in this case, to ask their daily paper to stop hitting itself.

But that's now. Then, as I saw each day in the city room of the *Citizen-Journal*, any criticism of the product was kept in-house. Even the edition with the green grease pencil all over it wasn't circulated to the staff. It just lay for most of the day on one of the desks. I wasn't certain for whose eyes it was intended. We weren't instructed to study it, to learn from the mistakes—we weren't told not to look at it, either. It was just there, like an echo from a private tantrum. Like something the editors had gotten out of their system, before moving on to the new day's work. To try again.

"Shee-*it,* Henry!"

I could scarcely believe the photographers would allow me to sit with them, back in their office/darkroom, and let me listen to them complain about the bosses. But they did, just about every day.

"Shee-*it*, Henry!" Dick Garrett, as cop-shop natty as Dick Tracy, would say to Hank Reichard, as glum as Sad Sack. You could just about set your watch by it. It didn't matter what new grievance Hank had come up with on a given day—he had been sent all the way across town to shoot a picture he knew would never get in the paper; or Jack Keller had looked at all the exposures he brought back from an assignment and then had selected the one frame among them that Reichard knew was lousy, and had put that one abysmal shot on Page One; or he had retrieved a scrawled note from his darkroom mailbox informing him that he had to start at five A.M. the next day for some break-of-dawn story—and, in his constantly mournful hangdog voice, Hank would elucidate the depth of the incompetence, the sheerness of the idiocy, that he discerned in the men who ran the *Citizen-Journal*. Two beats later, three beats at the most, Dick Garrett would sum it all up: "Shee-*it!*"

Meaning: What else can you expect? Meaning: Our bosses are dimwits.

And the photographers let me be there to hear this. I shouldn't have been surprised, I suppose—newspaper people complaining about their bosses is hardly a shocking concept, but I had never witnessed it before. It made the whole place even more appealing to me: not only were these photographers the same men whose work I had been seeing in the newspaper since I was old enough to look at a newspaper, but now I was among them, and apparently they trusted me enough to insult our mutual bosses in front of me.

There were stacks and stacks of yellow Kodak film boxes back in their offices—more film than I had ever seen in my life, even in a drugstore display. "Yeah, the company gives us our cameras, and all the film we want," Garrett had explained to me one day when I had remarked upon it. It was a different world back there—the pungent smell of the developing fluid, the curtained-off area where they would hand-print their photographs, the little heating machine that would get prints dried and ready on deadline—it was like a boys' clubhouse, a members-only place removed by more than geography from the main newsroom. Garrett and Reichard would hang out there between assignments, joined by the other photographers—Lloyd Flowers, Herb Workman, names as famous to me as those of United States senators—and, gesturing for emphasis, they would explain to me the latest indignities visited upon them by their superiors, and if this guys-in-a-treehouse atmosphere was separate from the larger social order of the city room, then all of it was so much more separate from the world to which I traveled back and forth in my off hours.

On a day off I would be mowing my parents' lawn, listening to a brand-new hit—"House of the Rising Sun" by the Animals, "Tobacco Road" by the Nashville Teens—through the earplug of my plastic transistor radio; I would be sneaking beers with my friends during evenings when I wasn't on the *C-J* schedule; I would be driving around town with my buddies as, out of the car radio, a WCOL disc jockey shouted the rules for a new contest ("Two gift certificates for dinner at the Big Bev drive-in for the listener who sends in a postcard with the best answer to this question! You walk into a party, and everyone is watching the door as you arrive—and you slip and fall flat on your behind! The question is this! What do you say as you're lying on the floor?").

I actually sent in an answer to that one on a postcard: "For my next trick, I will try the amazing . . ." It didn't win, but that was the world I was living in away from the *Citizen-Journal*. A world like the one in which any other kid resided that summer.

And then would come the next work shift, and I would be back in the newspaper business, standing with Garrett or Reichard in the darkroom, watching as one of them gently moved a piece of photographic paper through the chemicals, making a rocking motion with the paper as if it were a baby at bedtime. I would see the image begin to form, first a faint hint of gray, then bolder, emerging into recognizable shapes—people, buildings. Then sharper still—eyes, noses, doorways. Magic.

Sometimes they'd ask me to run the newly born photo up to the engraving room. There would be a paper tag on the back, with a one-word slug to help identify where in the paper that picture was supposed to end up. Inside the newspaper building was a quiet little interior bridge that led to the engraving department, a bridge that was the most silent place I'd found in the whole *Dispatch* headquarters, and when I'd cross the bridge and arrive in the shop where the engravers worked I would hand them the photo so they could transform it into dots on a thin metal plate.

It all felt very urgent—the engravers, in their smocks, would be waiting impatiently for me to relay the deadline photo to them. Yet I would always notice, in the corner of their room, hollow wooden carts piled high with engraving plates very much like the one they were about to manufacture from the photo I'd delivered to them. The plates that had been tossed into the cart were from today's paper, which was already history, and yesterday's paper, and the day before's—they were obsolete. The photographic images on those metal plates had, a day or two earlier, seemed as timely as the photo I had just hurried to the engravers. Now those plates were useless—outmoded, the definition of old news. They were part of the scrap heap in the wooden cart—waiting to be melted down. What mattered was tomorrow.

Tomorrow morning, at breakfast, my father would pick up the *Citizen-Journal* and look at a photograph—perhaps this photograph, the one I had seen Dick Garrett or Hank Reichard, just a few minutes before, bring to life in the chemical bath, the one that the engravers had not yet turned into something ready to be pressed onto newsprint. I pretended to be getting used to this, I pretended that it was all very routine to me by now, but inside myself I couldn't get over the exhilaration of being involved in what went on here.

Tomorrow, in the darkroom, Hank Reichard would gloomily say: "You won't believe where they're sending me now." If not those exact words, words very much like them. Words full of dismay and protest—a newspaper photographer complaining that his bosses couldn't be any more dense.

"Shee-*it*, Henry!" Dick Garrett would say tomorrow, expressing his customary solidarity.

Tomorrow I would shake my head in commiseration, wanting them to know that I was on their side.

Maybe that—my knowing that I was on their side, sensing that they seemed to be on mine—gave me the courage one Sunday to try to write more than the agate emergency runs.

Today a kid who wants his words to be read by the outside world can satisfy that desire within a matter of seconds. Sit down at the computer, post an entry on a personal blog or send a message to a public board—done. Minutes after the kid first has the thought, it's out there in the cyberuniverse, available for reading by anyone who stumbles upon it. There used to be a famous and oft-paraphrased dictum that was seldom challenged: "The power of the press belongs to the man who owns one." The person who owned the printing press—and his lieutenants—would decide whose words got disseminated.

That's gone now, and its departure—the loss of absolute control by the men who owned the giant presses in America's cities—is a change so profound that it will take us generations to fully realize its implications. During my first copyboy summer at the *Citizen-Journal*, the only way a person could have his words read by the whole city was if an editor in the newspaper building judged those words meritorious of publication.

In retrospect—our recent democratization of public discourse notwithstanding—this may not have been an altogether bad thing. It made the act of being published feel more precious. It made having one's words presented for strangers to read feel more like an accomplishment. It made getting past the gatekeeper—past the person who determined whose words would be printed—something close to thrilling.

On that summer Sunday afternoon I was calling all the fire departments and police departments, trawling for items for the emergency runs, when a dispatcher told me that a man had been transported to a hospital because a golf ball had blown up. The man—or so the emergency dispatcher informed me—had been fooling around with the ball, and its liquid center had squirted into his eye.

I instantly knew this could be it—I knew this was good enough to provide me a way to get my first real article in a daily newspaper. This was better than a one-line emergency run. This was a story.

But how to proceed? If I just typed it up with the other emergency runs, it would be buried, would disappear into the paper as one line of tiny type among all the others.

If I told the editors about it, and they liked it, they might assign it to a staff reporter. Which was the last thing I wanted—if a staff reporter wrote the story, that would mean I didn't write it.

So I looked up the phone number of the man the dispatcher said had been victimized by the golf ball. His name was Samuel Self Jr. His wife answered. I identified myself. Mrs. Self told me that Mr. Self was resting after his ordeal.

She explained the sequence of events. Her husband, she said, had long wondered what the center of a liquid-center golf ball looked like. So he had taken such a ball down to the family basement, and had tried to cut it in half.

Bad idea.

I took notes, thanked her, then typed up a three-paragraph story. I must have read it a dozen times to make certain I wasn't leaving out any of the pertinent facts.

Then I walked over to the city desk, where a bespectacled assistant editor named Bill Keesee was filling in for Bill Moore. I had typed my last name up where the slug was, so Mr. Keesee would know that I was the author.

I dropped it into his in-box, the same place where I dropped the real reporters' stories every day and every night. He didn't look up. I stood there.

I told him what I had done, even though he wasn't looking at me.

I was afraid that he might ask me what right I thought I had to assign myself a story. My heart was racing as he picked up the sheet of paper, read it . . . and then smiled. "This is good," he said.

I went back to the desk where I'd been doing the emergency runs. I tried not to stare at him. He had no idea just how important this was to me.

I could see him doing something to my story with his editing pencil (later I would find out that he had condensed my three paragraphs into two). He sent it over to the copy desk; I couldn't help it, there was no way I was going to observe this from afar, I edged behind the copyeditor. His name was Charlie Stine—this little newsbrief meant nothing to him, Charlie Stine processed copy nonstop every work shift of his life—and I looked over his shoulder, hoping he wouldn't notice I was there.

I watched his hand as he wrote the two-bank headline for the one-column story:

> *Golf Ball*
> *Fights Back*

I scooped it up with all the other copy that was waiting to be shot up the pneumatic tube, I sent it on its way to the composing room, and a few hours later I went up there on my dinner hour just to stand and look at my story on a galley sheet that dangled from a metal hook. My words, in newspaper type. Ready to go into the next edition, hanging there on a proof sheet with all the other news stories poised to be delivered to the readers of the *C-J*.

I spent the entire dinner hour in the composing room that night. I just stood next to my story. It hadn't existed, and then I'd talked to that emergency dispatcher, and had worked up the nerve to try it, and here it was—those words, in actual *Citizen-Journal* typeface, set by union Linotype operators. I might as well have been a bodyguard assigned to protect that two-paragraph story, so close to it did I hover during that dinner hour.

The next morning, at six o'clock, I was at my family's front door when the paperboy arrived. I heard the paper hit the front stoop, I opened the door and grabbed it, I rolled the rubber band from it and unfurled it. . . .

I went through the whole paper, page-by-page, and I didn't see it. I was terribly disappointed; each night some stories never made it, they were left as overset on those proof-sheet hooks. Each night, space invariably ran out.

But I went through that morning's *C-J* a second time, and I don't know how I had missed it, but there it was, at the very bottom of the obituary page.

GOLF BALL
FIGHTS BACK

A seemingly harmless golf ball erupted Sunday, sending an unsuspecting victim to the hospital.

Samuel Self Jr., 35, of 4815 Carbondale-dr, was removing the cover of a liquid center golf ball when it suddenly exploded, sending a portion of the goo that fills its inside into his eye. He was released after treatment.

It may have been the most wonderful moment of my life up to that point. I sat there reading it again and again until my parents woke up; when they came downstairs to breakfast I showed it to them. Two-paragraph briefs, of course, did not carry bylines, but it didn't take much to persuade them that I was the author; they could see the excitement in my eyes.

I have no idea whether, today, a kid posting his thoughts on an Internet board—with no one standing sentry between his sentences and their appearance on the Web, with no Bill Keesee or Charlie Stine to evaluate the worthiness of the words before they go up . . .

I have no idea whether a kid today would feel the kind of pride I felt that day.

To have my words printed in the morning paper. To have had my words be granted safe transit past the city-desk gatekeepers.

It was a big deal, being in a newspaper.

Hard as it is to believe, it really was.

(Although undoubtedly, when I told the guys back in the darkroom about my first printed work, and explained to them that Bill Keesee had crunched my three paragraphs into two, they almost certainly shook their heads in disdain, as they always did at what they saw as the constant and nagging need on the part of editors to meddle. And undoubtedly, instead of letting Garrett and Reichard see how honored to the point of giddiness I was to be one of them now, to have had my work appear in the same pages of the *C-J* as their own work, I probably pretended, in front of them, to be annoyed at Bill Keesee's editing, pretended to be offended that my exquisite words had been fiddled with. What else was I going to do, back in the brotherhood of the darkroom? Shee-*it*.)

Immortality—the immortality of words that appear in a newspaper—was conferred and configured differently then.

Today, once a newspaper story is published it becomes part of an electronic database that will be in existence long after the people who assigned, reported and edited the story are dead. The story—any story—will live eternally in digital form. You couldn't get rid of it if you wanted to.

During those *Citizen-Journal* days, however, once a story had appeared in the paper, it was gone by the next sunrise. Stories weren't meant to stick around, and they didn't.

Except in one place.

The newspaper's library—the morgue where the clippings were filed, available for viewing only by members of the staff—was a cramped rectangular space next to the women's department. In the daylight hours, it was presided over by a stern-faced, perpetually silent woman who wielded a pair of stainless-steel scissors, and who, from breakfast time until just before dinner, spent her entire shift snipping up multiple copies of that day's *C-J*, circling names in every story she snipped, placing those clips in worn little manila envelopes. The envelopes—labeled alphabetically—were stuffed into multi-drawer metal filing cabinets that filled every inch of wall space in the morgue.

I found the newspaper morgue to be an endlessly fascinating place. After the *C-J* librarian had gone home for the evening, I would often go back into the morgue just to fish around the metal cabinets and read old stories. I seldom looked for any subject in particular—I would open a file drawer, see what piqued my interest, and pull out an envelope. Some newsmakers had envelopes of their own—the mayor of Columbus, Maynard Sensenbrenner, had many envelopes, as did James Rhodes, the

governor of Ohio. Most of the envelopes, though, simply had a few letters to indicate the scope of their content: BA-BE would contain clipped
stories about everything ranging from bakeries throughout Columbus's
history to an interview with Dr. Joseph Benis, a local dentist; SO-SU
would include stories about the Southern Hotel, one of the city's oldest,
and robberies that might have taken place over the years at central Ohio
Sunoco gas stations. . . .

The randomness of it was what I liked. The clippings files contained
stories not just from the *Citizen-Journal,* but from its two predecessors, the
Citizen and the *Journal.* I'd look at the old bylines, read the old news
stories—some of the more ancient stories would crumble in my hands, so
brittle was the newsprint. I'd notice which of the long-departed reporters
had been fine wordsmiths, I would learn about crimes and controversies
that dominated coverage decades before, crimes and controversies that
had faded from memory, whose heat had long since cooled. The morgue
felt alive to me—sitting there by myself at night, rummaging around the
file drawers, I could imagine the noise and tension in the city room on
the nights those stories had been written.

On the streets of the town each day as I'd arrive for work, everything
was bright and full of summer, and the sounds of a crowded downtown
would cram the air: horns honking, city buses groaning and puffing as
they pulled away from the curb, voices on the corners mingling and
melding. Sometimes I'd see people from the paper approaching the building at the same moment I was: Ben Hayes would tip his straw hat—he
truly did it, he was a man-about-town columnist who tipped his hat in
greeting—and Ron Pataky, in that booming Broadway-in-the-Midwest
basso profondo, would jokingly call out from the sidewalk, "Robert!
You're going to be late for work!" It was lively, out there on the street.

But the life that would carry on far into the future—or so I
thought—was back in that little newspaper morgue. I would go there
by myself in the evenings because, in my mind, this was the proof that
what newspaper people did would last forever, their work preserved in
ragged envelopes. And one night, a week or so after my first story had
seen print, I opened a certain file drawer on purpose, reached for a cer-

tain envelope on purpose, allowed myself to hope that I would find what I was seeking.

The envelope was labeled SA-SE. From it, I pulled out all the clippings, old and newer.

And it was there—the librarian had clipped it and filed it. A two-paragraph story about Samuel Self Jr. A golf ball, it seemed, had exploded and sent him to the hospital. GOLF BALL FIGHTS BACK, the headline said.

Immortality. That's what it felt like. Something I'd written, something that would endure.

8

Because this was, in every way that mattered, first love, there wasn't much about the *Citizen-Journal* that I found fault with. As with all first-time romance, the loyalty toward my beloved was absolute, my fidelity unyielding. When the evening *Dispatch* was delivered to my parents' doorstep, it, under my uncharitable gaze, seemed chilly, distant, an entity that exerted no magnetic pull. Never mind that it covered the same news of the same city that the C-J did (and more thoroughly—it had a bigger budget and a bigger staff and a bigger news hole); never mind that we shared the same building, the same presses, even the same rolls of newsprint. I would look at the *Dispatch* and allow myself to feel nothing. To regard it with affection would have felt like cheating.

Yet, the very typeface of the *Citizen-Journal's* headlines, the font used in its photo captions, the look of its page designs—I felt this overwhelming and outsized swell of allegiance toward it, this protective urge toward every aspect of it. In my eyes, it could do no wrong. I liked its face, even on days when it doubtless wasn't all that pretty.

First love is like that.

Which made my reaction to the Our Readers Write letter—a letter I found in a desk drawer—so jarring.

Our Readers Write was the name of a column in the *C-J* that published requests for help from readers. When the letters would arrive in the day's mail, they would be put into an "ORW" manila file folder in one of the desks; as I recall, the feature didn't run on any set schedule, but would go into the paper when there was enough space for it.

One afternoon, looking for supplies, I came across the ORW folder. There were several letters inside, and I started to read them.

One—I've never forgotten it—was from a man who said he was severely, even morbidly, obese, was jobless, and lived alone. It was as direct and naked a cry for help as I have ever read. "If I could just have some underwear and socks, so I could feel clean," he wrote. He wrote that, having so little money and no prospects for work, he wore the same underwear and same pair of socks day after day. I can still see his handwriting. The letter went on for several pages; what I recall most vividly is how he gave voice, with his written words, to his desire to feel clean, and how grateful he said he would be if he could have the underclothing that would make that possible. It must have taken such resoluteness, for that man to reveal thoughts as private as those to whoever at the *C-J* would read them.

I watched the paper every day, to see if his letter would appear in Our Readers Write. I didn't know which member of the *Citizen-Journal* staff was responsible for putting the column together, but I was hoping that the column would run soon, and that the man would get the help he needed. It was a sweltering, muggy summer; I couldn't imagine any reader of the paper being unmoved by the eloquence of his anguish.

Then, one day, the column ran. It contained several letters that had been sent to Our Readers Write. Including his.

I was aghast. It had been boiled down to a sentence or two. Something along the lines of: "52-year-old north side man requests underwear and socks."

That was it.

All the life had been taken out of it. Everything that had made it human—everything that would have reached the hearts of the readers of the paper—had been excised. The man's yearning to feel clean? His wrenching portrayal of his obesity, and of what it felt like to be without a proper change of undergarments? Gone. The readers would never know.

It couldn't have been an effort to protect his privacy or his dignity; the Our Readers Write letters were just signed with initials when they were printed, and readers who wanted to assist the writer of a specific letter sent the requested items to the paper in care of those initials; the paper would then send the donation on to the person who had written. So whoever put the Our Readers Write column together that day couldn't have cut the soul out of it for the man's own benefit. Maybe it was because space was short; maybe it was because whoever edited the column had no ear for the poetry of despair and longing.

I found myself wondering what the man would think when he read the paper that day: if he would feel embarrassed for having revealed himself the way he had, only to have the revelation discarded. I found myself wondering if any reader even would think to send underwear and socks. Maybe not; the indifferent way the letter read in the paper, it could have been from any man looking for a handout.

There wasn't much about the *Citizen-Journal* I found fault with that summer. This was, after all, first love.

And as much as I wanted to tell Bill Moore or Jack Keller what I had seen, and what I thought of it, I didn't.

What did I know. I was a copyboy.

"Is that him?"

One of my friends asked the question. It was difficult, at night, to tell; from our vantage point in the seats at Jet Stadium, west of downtown, we could look up toward the wooden press box and see a few shadowy figures—a couple of them hunched over portable typewriters, another talking into a microphone.

The guy at the microphone, we knew, had to be Joe Hill, the Jets' play-by-play radio broadcaster. So that meant that the person for whom we were looking—Tom Keys, sports editor of the *Citizen-Journal*—must, by process of elimination, be one of the other two men. The *Dispatch* sent a writer every evening to cover the Jets, Columbus's minor-league

79

baseball team, and the *C-J* sent Tom Keys. Actually, Tom Keys sent Tom Keys; he was the boss, and he also covered the Jets. The *C-J* sports department wasn't exactly overstaffed.

"I think that's him on the left," I said. I sort of waved—you didn't want to wave too wildly in the midst of the sparse crowd at a minor-league ballgame, you'd look goofy if you did. So I waved a half-wave, and Tom Keys, seeing me, stood up and waved a half-wave back.

"That's so cool," one of my friends said.

And it was. If the Our Readers Write episode had emblemized the unhappier side of life inside a newspaper office, what Tom Keys and the sports guys did represented a part of the newspaper world that seemed, from the outside, like the most enjoyment a grown man could have at work. Go to ballgames as your *job*? Spend your shift doing the thing that the rest of the people in town did in their leisure hours?

Tom, in one of the golf sweaters or garishly colored sport coats that he customarily wore, sat back down in the press box and resumed his tasks. I hadn't had much contact with the sports department—I took their coffee and sandwich orders every day, that was about it—but to readers of the *C-J*, they were the newspapermen with the names that glistened. You read the sportswriters because you wanted to, not because you had to. Jim Sykes or Dave Scheen or Wink Hess covering a city council meeting was one thing—the front-page story that resulted was the adult-world equivalent of required reading in school. But the sports pages were pleasure—pleasure on purpose. And the men fortunate enough to work on the sports pages had, it was widely thought by the outside world, the best jobs on the paper.

One weekend that summer the PGA Championship came to town, to be played at Columbus Country Club. On a day off, two of my friends and I went out to watch. As great as it was to follow Arnold Palmer and Gary Player and Jack Nicklaus around the course, the best moment for me was when Dick Garrett—assigned to photograph the tournament—saw me, and brought Tom Pastorius and George Strode, two of the *Citizen-Journal* sportswriters, over to say hello.

Now . . . I knew Pastorius and Strode, I took their sandwich orders every day. But to have my friends see for themselves that Pastorius and

Strode knew me—knew my name, knew my face—was as warming an instant as I had all summer. There was no ESPN back then; being known by Tom Keys and Tom Pastorius and George Strode, in that town, was like being known by Dick Vitale and Chris Berman and Mike Tirico today. Everyone, even kids, read the sports pages every day. It was the Miss Citizen Fair syndrome: in those years, having a newspaper in your hands, even if they were young hands, was second nature. Newspaper sportswriters, in any medium-sized town, were legitimate stars. Pastorius said something to me about work, and my friends looked at me as if Dwight Eisenhower had wandered over to say hello to me.

And newspaper sportswriters got paid for having fun. That's what it seemed like. But at Jet Stadium, when the ninth inning was over and we headed for the car, I looked up toward the press box one more time. Tom Keys wasn't leaving. He was in his fifties by then, maybe his sixties; a gray fringe of hair framed his bald head, and as the fans went home he began to write one more story on one more night, a story about ballplayers in their late teens and early twenties, ballplayers who were in Columbus this summer only because they wanted to get out. Who were here en route—or so they hoped—to the major leagues.

The kids whose pitches and catches and home runs Tom dutifully recorded for all those morning editions were kids who desired to make this city, and this old ballpark, a distant memory, and as soon as possible. Tom wasn't going anywhere; this summer, as every summer, it was his job to watch the boys in the Jets uniforms play, to ask them soberly presented questions, and to write it all up. Five summers before, none of these young players had been here; five years from now, they all would be gone. But Tom had been here then, and he'd be here in five years, and here he was tonight. Supporting his family by covering the Jets. In the eyes of others, it was a job that seemed like endless delight, a free ride through life. Tom, head down as the ballpark emptied and another midnight deadline loomed, typed.

One day Bill Moore asked me to go out and find Dr. Sam Sheppard.

The Fugitive, based on the Sam Sheppard case, was already a hit on

television, with David Janssen playing Dr. Richard Kimble. On the
TV show, the Janssen/Dr. Kimble character was on the run after being
accused of the murder of his wife—a murder he claimed was really committed by a one-armed man. Dr. Sheppard—an osteopath from Cleveland who had been convicted in the 1954 murder of his pregnant
wife—insisted that it was a bushy-haired stranger who had murdered
her. The Dr. Sam case had been called the Crime of the Century—it
could be fictionalized on television because Dr. Sam was safely locked
up in the Ohio Penitentiary.

But then, one summer day, an up-and-coming attorney named F.
Lee Bailey managed to get Dr. Sam sprung. And for the C-J, it was as
local as a local story could possibly be. The Ohio Pen—the state's
maximum-security prison—was less than five minutes from our office.

Bill Moore immediately sent his reporters and photographers into
action—to the warden's office at the pen, to the governor's office across
the street from us at the Statehouse, to Columbus police headquarters.

And then, after all the reporters and photographers had fanned
out, a phone tip came in: Dr. Sam Sheppard was allegedly drinking at
Benny Klein's.

Benny Klein ran a hole-in-the-wall bar and steakhouse downtown,
near Broad and High; he was a Jack Ruby–type figure in Columbus, a
fellow whom all the cops and criminals were reputed to know, a holdover
from the Guys and Dolls era of American life. If Dr. Sam Sheppard
was going to hang around Columbus after getting out of prison, Benny
Klein's might be the logical place where he would have his first drink.

Bill Moore looked around the office for someone to send. But they
were all out on other aspects of the story. So he motioned me over.

He told me to go to Benny Klein's. And to bring Dr. Sam to the city
room.

"Just walk up to him and talk him into coming back to the paper
with you," Bill said. The idea was that we would take a picture of
Dr. Sam in our photo studio for the morning edition.

By this point in the summer, it didn't even seem especially odd
to me. Go to Benny Klein's. See if the most famous convicted mur-

derer in America is there. If he is, ask him if he would mind inter-
rupting his first hours of freedom to walk over to the *Citizen-Journal*
with me.

"OK," I said to Bill Moore.

What complicated the assignment was that, at seventeen, I feared I
might be too young to legally walk into Benny Klein's bar—and that I
was not at all certain I would recognize Sam Sheppard if I were to see
him. Dr. Sam was reputed to be with a German woman with whom he
had corresponded while in prison—a woman referred to in news stories as a "blonde German glamour girl," a woman who was, according to
at least one news report, "a wealthy divorcee whose half-sister-in-law
was Mrs. Magda Goebbels, wife of Dr. Joseph Goebbels, Hitler's propaganda minister."

So here I was. The summer had begun with me playing second base
for Epsilons; now I was being sent to see if the nation's most notorious
criminal was sitting around a central Ohio bar with the blonde half-
sister-in-law of Hitler's propaganda minister. Not bad, as summers go.

"She looks like a hoor," Al Getchell said to me as I was leaving the
office.

"Pardon me?" I said to him. He was sitting at his drawing board.

"Dr. Sam's girlfriend," he said. "You'll know it's her because she
looks like a hoor."

Hoor, I surmised, was Al's pronunciation of *whore.*

"Thanks," I said, although I had never seen a whore in my life, never
mind a famous murderer.

I walked over to Benny Klein's. I wondered if I should be armed,
going into a situation like that.

I entered the dim little place—no one stopped me—and it was
empty. No Sam Sheppard. No blonde German glamour girl. No one
but the bartender.

By the time I got back to the *C-J,* word had come in that Dr. Sam
was on his way out of town—the Benny Klein's tip had been bad
information.

What a world this was, inside that city room: Go out and find

Dr. Sam Sheppard—and when you're finished, swab out the pastepots, and see if anyone wants a fried egg sandwich from Paoletti's.

The press cars, as I recall, were Fords, light blue in color, and that first newspaper summer I drove them only infrequently—usually on Sundays, when Paoletti's was closed and I would be sent out to a drive-in to bring hamburgers and beverages back to the reporters and editors. There was a certain weekday when, after a man had died under unpleasant circumstances, I was instructed to take a press car and go to his widow's home to pick up a photograph of him. I dreaded the drive, it felt like a trip to make a terrible intrusion, and I was surprised when the woman was not angry at my knock on her door, was not visibly offended. I was just one more lamentable part of her husband's passing— one more dispiriting detail to be dealt with as swiftly and wordlessly as possible.

Some nights, when I got off work, my friends and I would go out on the Three-C Highway to a place called Bounceland—a plot of land consisting of a series of open pits with sheets of rubber stretched tautly over their tops. The industrial-strength rubber slabs formed de facto trampolines—I think the price was fifty cents for thirty minutes of bouncing, and we would spring high into the summer air while the bored proprietor looked at the clock and waited to close up. Driving a *Citizen-Journal* car to retrieve a dead man's photo in the daylight, bouncing skyward next to the Three-C Highway under the Ohio moon—that was the new dichotomy of the life to which I was becoming accustomed.

And always, the people in my new world at work:

"They only care about Ethel Merman because of her bustline," a copyeditor stood and announced to the city room at large one night.

No one paid the comment much attention; the man who said the words was an eccentric and loquacious flannel-shirted gent, he was always making pronouncements that seemed to emanate from the deepest recesses of a convoluted psyche. On this particular night he appeared especially geared up.

"As talented a woman as she is—and men just *use* her because they like her bustline," he said, and the fact that in 1964, in a newsroom in the middle of Ohio, he was talking about seasoned Broadway show-stopper Ethel Merman as if she were still a vital part of the national culture and conversation, as if of course everyone within earshot of him would be interested in his analysis of Ethel Merman and the root of her appeal, was part of that same Bounceland/dead-man's-photo dichotomy. I was living in two separate universes.

It was the first summer of the Beatles; A Hard Day's Night was in the movie houses, and one day at work Bob Moeckel was on the phone and he called me over to demonstrate to me what he had discovered: if you dialed the Esquire Theater, one of the places where A Hard Day's Night was playing, the number was always jammed by young people who were calling to see what time the shows started. The line was so clogged that the Esquire's phone had gone haywire, and you could talk to the other callers over the busy signal—it was an inadvertent party line, you could meet and speak with other Beatles fans just by dialing in. Which, in the C-J city room, we did.

It was the same city room inside whose walls toiled the copyeditor who expounded on Ethel Merman. Two worlds: the Ethel Merman world and the Beatles world, the newsroom world and the Bounceland world. I had no idea at all if Ethel Merman even had an ample bust-line, or, if she did, if it was a factor in how people treated her. It was all just part of the general newsroom wash. On the afternoon before the first night of the Republican National Convention the UPI wire ran the advance text of the keynote address by Oregon Governor Mark Hatfield, and as I scissored the speech from the wire machine Don E. Weaver was walking by. The wire machines had carbons between two rolls of paper—there would be an original and a copy of every story—and I asked Mr. Weaver if I might keep the carbon of the keynote as a souvenir.

He said if it was all right with the wire editor it was all right with him. At dinnertime I asked Bill Moore if I could borrow a press car for thirty or forty minutes, and he tossed me the keys. I drove home, where I knew my parents would be having their evening meal. I pulled the press car into the driveway—the driveway that passed beneath my bedroom window—and it felt like arriving home in a police car, with the antenna sticking out of the roof.

I went in to where my parents and my brother and sister sat at the dinner table and I gave my father and mother the keynote address. I knew they'd be watching the Republican convention in a few hours, so I gave them the advance text of the speech to follow along. I suppose I was showing off; I suppose I wanted to let them know that this was the kind of mystical thing I was encountering at work—they would know Governor Hatfield's words before he said them. With the Beatles coming out of the dashboard radio I drove the press car back toward the *Citizen-Journal*, back toward the Ethel Merman world of the newspaper office.

And a newspaper office is what it was and all it was. I had never heard the word *media*; in Latin class in school we had studied Medea, but *media*, as a descriptive term for the far-flung tentacles of the global news business, had not yet come into usage. The word would have elicited quizzical facial expressions in the city room had anyone ever uttered it, which no one did.

I think the circulation of the *Citizen-Journal* was around 112,000—maybe a little more or a little less. So these men and women I was seeing every day and every night would have their work—the stories that bore their bylines, the photographs they snapped, the headlines they wrote—seen by those 112,000 readers each morning.

That's a lot of people. The America of an all-encompassing media culture may still have been years away—no satellite television transmission yet, no cable, no personal computers, much less a worldwide computer network—but 112,000 readers was and is a lot of people. The men and women who worked in the C-J city room may or may not have had certain boundaries on their dreams (though I never would have presumed to ask them about those dreams), yet 112,000 is more readers than all but the most successful and bestselling authors of books have for their work. And even for the most productive of authors, there is at least a year between the publication of each successive book.

At the C-J, the authors of the newspaper stories got to do it all over again every shift, knowing that their reading audience would be waiting in the morning. Where else were those 112,000 readers going to get their local news? That was a big part of the pull of the work, I sensed, as the staff reassembled each day to produce another *Citizen-Journal*. It was like being on the home team, and knowing that the stands were always going to be filled.

Each night, as the presses powered up and then began to roll, you could feel it in your feet. Under your desk the floor would begin to sort of hum, if not exactly vibrate, and the tingle would shoot up through the bottoms of your shoes, that tingle so insistent that your toes could almost hear the presses, and this was it, this was what you had worked for all day. Ethel Merman may have belted out "There's No Business Like Show Business," but that was her opinion—for the men and women feeling the presses start up each night, there was no business like this one.

It was the newspaper business, not the media business, and I suppose that in many ways the people who were drawn to it could be seen, in the eyes of the more conventional and rigidly starched business community, as a group of society's misfits. And I realized anew as the presses groaned to life each night, announced by the hum beneath my shoes, that the men and women in this room—loose, laughing, unburdened by pretensions or power-lust, praising Ethel Merman, dialing into Beatles busy signals—were, for a bunch of misfits, the most gloriously and grandly easy people to fit in with that I had ever been lucky enough to meet.

Sometimes on Sundays I would be the first person there.

The staff on Sundays was small anyway; most of the reporters and editors got the day off. And if I arrived downtown a few minutes early, and walked up the stairs to the mezzanine and let myself in through the back door of the city room, there were Sundays when the room was dark.

I suppose it was to save electricity; because there was no Sunday

Citizen-Journal, and thus no Saturday staff, the room would have sat unused on Saturdays. Whoever had been the last to leave on Friday night would have turned off the lights, and they would still be off when I got there.

Letting myself into the C-J city room was beginning to feel like letting myself into my home. For a few minutes, before the next person showed up for work on the Sunday shift, I had the newspaper office all to myself. The November before, with the president dead, I had walked into this room for the first time—so noisy a room that day, bright and bustling and full of cacophonous energy—and I had been an outsider. Everything had happened so quickly. Within the year I was letting myself in on a silent Sunday, and turning on the lights. One by one they would flicker on across the city room ceiling, and in the quietude the place felt like it was mine.

The first thing to do on those Sundays was to strip the wire machines; they would have stayed turned on all weekend, to have shut them down would have meant to miss out on all the news of the world that transpired since Friday midnight. So in the darkness the machines would have clacked and clanged for the whole weekend with no one to hear them, and the long rolls of paper filled with words would have curled up in haphazard piles on the floor behind each machine.

I'd pull the paper up from the floor and, with a straightedge, separate the stories, one piece of news at a time. I'd place them on the proper desks: the stories about events in Ohio on one desk, the stories about events around the United States on another, the stories about international events on a third. When the editors would begin to arrive, the world—what had happened in the world since Friday night—would be waiting for them. Arranged by me.

Downtown was empty on Sundays, and the area in the city room around the wire machines would smell like heated-up ink ribbons, and in those minutes before anyone else arrived, the minutes just after I had switched on the lights, I was alone, in a place that somehow had begun to feel like my own.

It seemed like a place where no one could ever grow old. I wouldn't have put it in exactly those words back then—growing old, when you are as young as I was that copyboy summer, isn't a concept that even occurs—but in retrospect I think that was the underlying allure of being in that room. No matter what the age of those men and women—even Don Weaver, in the editor's office, and Wink Hess, with his tired-beyond-tired face and his worn suspenders, even the men and women who were far closer to their final newspaper summers than to their first—they seemed younger than grown-ups were supposed to be. The twinkle, against all odds, had not been beaten out of them.

Part of that could be ascribed to the nature of news—when your job involves observing and chronicling the unexpected each new day, that tends to keep you alert and on your toes. None of the men and women of the *Citizen-Journal*, when they walked through the doorway each shift, could know precisely what awaited them. Whatever the office routines may have been in other businesses downtown, here the nub of the routine was that there was no routine. No one could predict the news; no one could know what might come at us on a given afternoon or evening. We were batters at the plate, waiting for an unseen pitcher to deliver his best stuff.

Yet it went beyond the basic definition of news always being new. The reporters and editors just didn't seem as solemn, as burdened, as their chronological years might dictate. One night the UPI photo machine received a picture of something called the topless bathing suit—a new national fad that summer (although one of those fads that seemed invented only for publicity purposes—women weren't really wearing the things at America's beaches and country club pools). Modeling the suit in the UPI picture was blonde bombshell movie star Mamie Van Doren—in the photo (which we received on the tissue-thin paper that emerged from the machine) she was holding martini glasses in each of her hands, strategically positioned in front of each of her breasts. We were all passing the photo around, looking at it—I felt honored to be included as the picture was relayed from staff member to staff member, it would have been easy for them to leave me out—when Charlie Stine (the copyeditor who was the author of the GOLF

BALL FIGHTS BACK headline) called out from next to the photo machine: "Look, here's another picture on the machine—and the martini glasses broke!"

We all scrambled over, realizing too late that he was joking, but that's how it was, that's what life felt like in that room. Years later I would understand that beneath the surface there must have been more than a little anxiety; when Bill Moore died early in the twenty-first century, and his family sent me that personal history he had been working on, I sensed in his written words that he had not been quite as self-assured a person as he appeared to the new copyboy who worked for him, that maybe, just as I nervously wanted him to approve of the work I was doing, just as Jim Sykes, the first-year reporter who always seemed so intent on searching for, in Bill Moore's eyes, some clue as to how well Sykes had done on the story he had just turned in, the story that Bill was reading and editing as Jim peered across the room at him . . .

I came to believe that Bill, too, was a man who constantly and maybe fretfully hungered for the approval of his own bosses, that even as he assigned stories to the staff every day he was hoping that the editors above him would think he had been creative and thorough enough. Bill didn't have all the answers, although we weren't supposed to know that; Bill's self-confidence, like all of ours, had its limits.

But so much of this was new every day, so much of what would pass through our little world by deadline on a given night was unknown and unknowable when we had arrived at work eight hours earlier, that it seemed there was no time to grow old in such a place, the freshness of each day was an antidote to the gloomy prospect of that. The very sound of the place—the stillness in the air when I would get off the elevator on the mezzanine, the stillness lasting for the two or three seconds it took to walk from the elevator landing to the glass doors of the city room, and then, as soon as I opened those doors, that wondrous hubbub inside, the voices and the laughter and the crazy chorus of the typewriter keys . . .

If you were trying to create an effect for a movie, you couldn't do any better than that: the dull blanket of quiet just outside the city room doors and then the gladdening racket inside, the swift change in the tone and texture of life each day as all of us moved once again into the happy clamor of that room.

The possibilities seemed infinite. Late at night I would ride the bus home, the newly printed edition of the *Citizen-Journal* in my hands, and some nights I would glance at a certain apartment building on the north side of Broad Street, and as the bus rolled by it I would tell myself that life's prospects truly are endless, that even in the landlocked middle of Ohio you never know just how far your ambitions might someday take you. I would look up at the apartment building, not sure which was the right window, but I would know, after midnight, that behind a certain darkened pane in that building slept one of our fellow townspeople, one of our readers, John Glenn, back from space now and living among us. You never had to grow old. That was the illusion, as on the bus I read the morning paper while it still was night.

On my last day of work—school would be starting soon—I went into the little glassed-in area next to Jean Allison's desk. There was a table in there, where the editors would gather to make decisions about what to put on the front page, but my reason that last day for entering the room was to look at the papers on the bamboo binding sticks.

That was how all of the editions for the past three months were preserved: fastened to these long bamboo rods, with the rods themselves stored horizontally on metal racks. For clippings of specific stories, there was the morgue, but if you wanted to read entire newspapers this was the place where they were kept. Seek out a given week, lift the bamboo rod from the rack, carry it over to the table and take a look.

The papers were there so the editors could conveniently refer to past editions—maybe to check on how a continuing news story had developed, maybe to be certain they weren't duplicating the design of a recent front-page layout. For me, though, on that last day, it was like taking one more unhurried trip through my summer.

All those stories—I'd seen them all be born. Starting with the copy of the newspaper from my first day on the job, I leafed through the pages of every edition, letting myself be reminded, story by story, photograph by photograph, of the voices and visions that had filled my days and nights. An article might be about a school board meeting, but I would recall bringing its author a cup of hot tea as she was writing it; a photo might be of Mayor Sensenbrenner cutting a ribbon to open a new shopping center, but I would remember Hank Reichard grousing in the darkroom that the mayor had been late to the event, and had caused Hank to miss his lunch hour.

The papers on the bamboo rods felt, to me, like a scrapbook of what I'd just been a part of. If the newspapers of that era felt like daily scrapbooks of their towns, then this was more private—this was a scrapbook of my summer, of some of the most valued and eye-opening times I'd ever had. Some of the pages on the bamboo rods were more personal to me than others: there was the day when there was a surprise party in the city room for Al Getchell's twenty-fifth anniversary at the *Citizen-Journal* (and the *Citizen* before it); Ed Colston, the African-American reporter with the talent for oil painting, had done, on his own time at home, a portrait of Al, and the entire staff had been asked to sign it, and in the next day's paper there had been a photo of Al holding up the painting. In the room with the bamboo rods I looked at that photo in the already-old paper, and I felt quietly pleased that they had asked me to sign the portrait along with all the real staff members.

I read through every paper from my time at the C-J, and no edition felt like a stranger to me, reading them all felt like a return visit to a treasured path upon which I'd recently walked, or even like opening up a diary. Just before my shift ended that last night I went over to Jack Keller's desk to tell him I'd be taking off; I didn't know what the proper procedure was on one's final evening at the paper, but I thought I should say something, so I told him I was going, and I thanked him for having me there.

I didn't want to bother anyone else; I thought it might be pretty goony, to approach each desk and inform the people I was leaving. What did they care? I had been going up to their desks several times a day all summer to take their food orders, but this was different, I didn't want to interrupt them just to say this was the last night at the C-J for me.

So I opened the side door next to the maps, next to the bulletin board where the schedules were posted (the next week's schedule was already up; my name wasn't on it). Bill Keesee, filling in for Bill Moore just as he had on the day I wrote the golf ball story, saw me departing and called: "You're not going to leave without saying anything, are you?" I walked back to his desk. "I hope I'll be printing bigger stories by you one of these days," he said.

It was a very nice thing for him to do. It made me think that it would be all right if I said goodbye to the others. I went to every desk. I shook every hand. Ron Pataky said I should come down and have a cup of coffee with him some afternoon; this time, he said, he'd go out on the coffee run for me. Tom Pastorius said if I ever wanted to hang out with the sportswriters, they'd be there; they weren't going anywhere. They were beneficent to me that night and they were considerate in what they said and they were on deadline; I knew that as soon as I walked out the door they would go back to writing their stories for the next day's paper, and then tomorrow they would return to this room to do it all over again, and I wouldn't be a part of it.

I left and, as always, it was the reverse of the switch in sounds that occurred as I arrived each day; coming to work at the paper, there was that change from flat silence outside the city room to frenzied, joyful clatter inside its walls. Now, as I walked out the door, the clatter disappeared, and I was already missing it by the time I got to the bus stop.

9

The paper would thump down on our front stoop as it always had, after
which the paperboy would ride his bicycle on up the street, tossing the
C-Js toward just about every door. If there was a family on our block
that didn't subscribe to the *Citizen-Journal,* I wasn't aware of it; not subscribing to the morning paper would have been just about as unthinkable as not owning a television set. There was no law that said you had
to do it, but there might as well have been. How else were your mornings supposed to begin?

Back in high school for my senior year, I would pick up the C-J in
the mornings—sometimes I'd be the one to go get it from outside the
house, sometimes, if my father was up early, he would already have
brought it inside to the breakfast table . . . and something felt different.
Something felt vaguely removed, detached, about the paper, in a way I
couldn't at first quite put my finger on.

The headlines and typefaces hadn't changed; the bylines of the reporters, the names of the photographers in the caption credit lines, were
still the names of the people with whom I'd spent all those days and
nights. Yet there was an unanticipated remoteness.

The feeling was the opposite of being in the room with the bamboo-
rod newspaper binders. There, every story, every photograph, every page

of every edition, had felt familiar. I'd been a part of them—a very small part, yes, but that was all right, being a small part had been enough to addict me. It didn't take long—a few weeks into autumn—before the reverse of that feeling set in. The paper would come to our house every morning, and I would look at it . . . and it had nothing to do with me. Because I'd had nothing to do with it.

I didn't like the feeling. It had the effect of a taunt: the *Citizen-Journal*, each new day, would look up toward my curious eyes, and it was telling me that it didn't need my presence on Third Street. It had managed just fine before I ever walked into that city room, and it would do just fine now that I'd walked out.

The first-love syndrome, yet again. Was I ever there? That's what would occur to me as I looked at those new C-Js, the ones for which I'd had no preview the night before. Did all of that really happen? As the months wore on I would discern an uncustomary byline or two popping up. Some new reporters had been hired; I didn't know them. The first-love syndrome, after your first love seems to have moved on.

If the enlivening thing about newspaper work was knowing that you got to start from scratch again each day and build a new edition from nothing—if that was the lure that made going back every day such a kick—then this realization was the flip side of that. The exhilaration—the invigorating feeling—had a very short half-life. It could go away just as rapidly as it first arrived. There's only one way to maintain the feeling: be there. I would read the *Citizen-Journal* as the air turned cold, I'd go to school in the day and hang out with my friends at night, and downtown on the mezzanine, I knew, they were getting the paper ready. You had to be there. That's what I now understood. The one and only trick was, you had to be there.

On the Saturday afternoon before Christmas, because I was an editor of our school newspaper, I got to go downtown to a Dave Clark Five press conference.

The Beatles never came to Columbus, but the Dave Clark Five were the second most popular British band that year (the Rolling Stones wouldn't really hit their stride until 1965), and the Dave Clark Five had been booked for a December concert at the Ohio Fairgrounds Coliseum. Before the concert they had agreed to hold a White House–style press conference for high school editors at the Deshler Hilton hotel, at Broad and High.

Walking into the hotel, I could turn and look across the Statehouse grounds at the *Dispatch* building. For a moment I had the urge to go up to the C-J and say hello to everyone—hoping they would remember me—but then I remembered: Saturday. No C-J staff at work on Saturday.

The Dave Clark Five were hours late arriving, so all of us waited around a too-crowded sort-of-ballroom in the hotel—boys and girls from schools all over central Ohio. One girl said to me:

"Why do you have it folded up that way?"

I looked down. In preparation for writing notes, I had taken eight or ten pieces of typing paper and folded the sheaf three ways. That's how I had seen the reporters do it all summer—the three-way fold was the way they took their notes, they would grab a handful of copy paper before leaving the office and fashion the paper into the three-way vertical fold. It was easy to hold in your hand as you covered a story, you could jam it into the inside pocket of a sport coat, or into a back pocket of your pants—none of the reporters used store-bought notebooks. The three-way fold, I had observed in the city room, was the way it was done.

I looked around the room in the Deshler Hilton. All the other kids had brought spiral-bound school notebooks.

"This is the way I always do it," I said to the girl, feeling a twinge again for what I'd loved in that city room.

When the Dave Clark Five finally did arrive—Beatle hair, Beatle suits, Beatle boots—they stood at the front of the room and said they only had a few minutes, but they had time to answer several questions.

Most of the students asked about things like what the Dave Clark Five's favorite colors were, or what they thought of American girls. I raised my hand and the concert promoter—a local guy who was running the press conference—pointed toward me.

I stood and said, toward the general direction of Dave Clark himself, the words I had carefully rehearsed in my head:

"Where to from here?"

"We're going to Cleveland tomorrow," Dave Clark said, his speaking voice a little like Paul McCartney's, at least as close as we were ever going to hear in Columbus. "And then I think we go to Detroit."

I wrote it down on my three-way fold of paper.

Off to the side of the room were five young women wearing short red costumes with white fur trim. The promoter had brought the women here; they looked like pretty tough customers: beehive hairdos, bored expressions, chewing gum cracking in their mouths. They wore sashes across the fronts of their costumes that said they were "Miss Christmas and Her Snow Princesses."

A little gift from the promoter to the Dave Clark Five. Al Getchell might have pointed them out as *hoors*. I'd still never seen one, but I was pretty sure. As the press conference ended the Dave Clark Five got onto an elevator to go to their rooms, and Miss Christmas and Her Snow Princesses got on with them.

Because the band had been so tardy in coming to the press conference, it was dark by the time I left the Deshler Hilton. Now, across the way, the OHIO'S GREATEST HOME NEWSPAPER sign was blazing in the black December sky. My three-way fold of notepaper was stuck into my back pocket, just the way I'd learned to do it when the downtown nights were full of summer's warmth. I looked over at the newspaper building. Where to from here, indeed.

The next summer the metal-plating factory was moving—leaving the downtown block where it always had been, setting up operations in a contemporary-looking, single-story new plant out near an interstate cloverleaf, away from the congestion of the center of the city—and my dad informed me that I would be helping with the move.

So that's what I did that summer—loaded equipment into crates, assisted in clearing out every corner of that sooty old brick building on Broad Street, rode in the trucks day after day as everything was transported to the new place on Alum Creek Drive, unpacked the boxes once we arrived there.

Downtown, the factory had been just the short walk from the *Citizen-Journal* newsroom. Out by Alum Creek, the newspaper office, and my memories of it, were something off in the distance. By the end of that summer the factory, in its new quarters, was all set up and running smoothly, as if it had never been a part of downtown at all. I knew the feeling.

I went off to college, to study journalism—after the *C-J*, there was no question in my mind about that—and although the courses were well planned out and efficiently instructive, and although I never doubted my decision, there was something missing: the laughter and the looseness. The college courses were earnest and staid, in a way that life in the *Citizen-Journal* city room never had seemed to be; there were afternoons in winter, during long lectures in overheated classrooms, when I felt myself drifting off to sleep. At the *C-J*, regardless of how late at night, everything always felt wide awake. That city room, I realized even as I was studying at college, was my real school. The mezzanine was my alma mater.

The summer after that first year away at college, I got a job at the *Dispatch*.

The *Citizen-Journal* was full up on copyboys—they had enough full-timers that they didn't need or have the budget for summer extras—and they said that I was too young, under the rules of their parent company, Scripps-Howard, to work as a summer reporter. So I applied at the *Dispatch*, and was told that I'd receive my assignment when I arrived in the city room.

The assignment was the library—the *Dispatch's* morgue.

It was up a little half-flight of stairs at the back of the newsroom—it was hidden away, crammed into what felt like a makeshift floor-between-floors. I was told that I was to work the early shift—I was supposed to arrive before the regular library staff, and start to clip the papers.

The library staff was very nice, and I hated the job. Being stuck in that claustrophobic crow's nest of a room, cutting stories from both the *Dispatch* and the *Citizen-Journal* and stuffing them into files, felt like being filed away myself. When stories broke and the newsroom phoned up requests for clippings on deadline, I could only imagine what the tumult and the bustle were like down there. You couldn't even hear it, from up on that half-floor where the library was.

One morning the big national news was that eight nurses had been murdered in Chicago, and that a man—a "drifter," according to the story—named Richard Speck had been arrested. Chicago—just north of Chicago, Evanston—was where I was enrolled in college, and seeing the story, recognizing the names of the neighborhoods and of the top Chicago police officials, I felt energized and revved up, as if I could somehow lend a hand in some way with the coverage. But in the small library I just clipped out the articles and the photos and filed them away in the proper envelopes.

Years later, when I would interview Speck at Stateville Penitentiary in Illinois, and he would break his long silence and for the first time confess to the murders—and in gruesome detail—I would think back to that day in the *Dispatch*'s alcove of a library. Speck was in handcuffs and leg shackles as I spoke with him inside the prison walls, which was pretty much the way I felt in the *Dispatch* library. I wanted someone in the city room that summer to come up and spring me, to get me out of there and give me an assignment, even if it just was to go to Paoletti's. But I was in solitary confinement, or something like it.

One day on my lunch hour I was walking up Third Street and I saw Ben Hayes pausing as he waited for a stoplight to turn. "Mr. Hayes!" I called, and it took him a second or two to figure out who I was. But when he did he smiled and said hello to me by name, and tipped that straw hat. It was sunny out there, and he was a reminder of life at the C-J, and I went back to the *Dispatch* morgue to snip more newspapers.

It didn't last long. They, and I, both knew that, cut-up newspapers aside, we weren't cut out for each other. I got a job offer to run some municipal tennis courts for the rest of the summer, and in the *Dispatch* library they let me know that they wouldn't object if I accepted the job, which I did.

Had I been paying a little closer attention to what was right in front of my eyes—or had I been a little smarter—I might have noticed the first traces of the change that was already overtaking the world of newspapers.

Just before dinnertime each night, when my father would arrive home from the office, he would go to his favorite chair and read the *Dispatch*. Same chair as always, the one closest to the front window in our living room; same *Dispatch* as always, bringing the end-of-the-afternoon news to our home the way the *Citizen-Journal* brought the first-thing-in-the-morning news.

Yet, I realize now, he didn't seem to be spending as much time with the paper. He and my mother had developed a nightly routine: no matter what else was going on, they would repair to the television set in the den to watch the *CBS Evening News*, presided over by Walter Cronkite. Occasionally they would stray, and watch Chet Huntley and David Brinkley on NBC—but what didn't vary was their faithfulness to the schedule. They had to watch "the news."

What this cut into was my father's time with the *Dispatch*. It happened in the morning, too, with the *Citizen-Journal*—he would zip right through the C-J as he ate a quick breakfast before backing out of the driveway and going to work—but the morning dash seemed to make more sense, the C-J was a skinny paper and most men didn't tarry on their way out the door. The *Dispatch*, though—fat, dominant in town, an institution in the evening—was made for leisurely reading, was constructed with the thought that people could and would spend a lot of time with it.

But as the network television news became an institution of its own—in our house and almost certainly in just the same way with just the same effect in houses across the country—my father appeared to spend more minutes with it than with the *Dispatch*. The *CBS Evening*

News was a thirty-minute broadcast, and my parents watched every one of those thirty minutes. I don't think he gave thirty full minutes to the *Dispatch*.

Not that this recently incurred and conflicting set of habits was diminishing newspaper sales—not yet. Because reading the paper was second nature, not to be questioned, it never would have occurred to my parents to cancel their subscription to either the morning or the evening paper, even if it had been pointed out to them that they were spending more time with the television set, less time with the newspapers. The newspapers remained welcome members of our household.

In one of the northern suburbs of Chicago, there was a restaurant where, during my college years, I would often go on Saturday evenings—it was called Mr. Ricky's, it had the feel of a Miami Beach ultra-delicatessen, a cold-weather version of Wolfie's or the Rascal House. Piled on the floor next to the cash-register counter on Saturday nights were the massive weekend editions of all four Chicago daily newspapers—the early editions of the *Tribune,* the *Sun-Times* and *Chicago's American*, and the Saturday edition of the *Chicago Daily News*, which was an all-weekend paper. Those papers were stacked up in towers at Mr. Ricky's, and people grabbed two, three, even four of them, on Saturday nights, just to get a jump on their Sunday newspaper reading.

To look at the crowds snapping up those papers, it seemed that the inclination would never die—the American newspaper industry, from the vantage point of the Mr. Ricky's cash-register counter, was like the American steel industry or the American auto industry: indestructible, immortal. People were constantly hungry for the product.

(When I think of the stacks of newspapers at Mr. Ricky's, and of the apparent hunger for them, I have to smile, because the kid behind the cash-register counter selling the papers—the kid who took the customers' money—was the son of the owner. In fact, the restaurant had been named by the father in honor of the son—the kid was the Ricky in Mr. Ricky's. The newspaper devotees in the delicatessen weren't fooling him—the hunger that wasn't going to go away, he understood, was the more traditional kind, the kind that was satisfied by pastrami sandwiches and strawberry cheesecake. When his father turned down his request to be partners in Mr. Ricky's—the father didn't think Ricky was ready yet—the kid quit to start a restaurant, and then many restaurants, on his own. Ricky's name was Richard Melman, and what he founded was the Lettuce Entertain You restaurant conglomerate, one of the most successful and admired in the United States. He might have sold hundreds, maybe thousands, of those early Sunday papers at Mr. Ricky's every Saturday night—but, as he stood at the cash register, something must have told him that the path to his own future riches was not necessarily lined with newsprint.)

Every city had at least one big out-of-town newsstand, where readers went to learn what was going on in other places. You could pick up a *Philadelphia Bulletin*, a *Miami News*, a *Cleveland Press*, a *New York Herald Tribune*, a *St. Louis Globe-Democrat*—all newspapers that, like the *Columbus Citizen-Journal*, would, by the time a new century arrived, be dead. You would go to the out-of-town newsstands to find out the news of those cities, how the sports teams were doing, what the people in those places thought about things. There were invisible walls around America's cities that made them feel self-contained, specific to themselves, and the news—at any rate the workaday, mundane, news of those cities—was kept inside the invisible walls. If you lived in another part of the country, the only way you could avail yourself of a city's local news was to go to your out-of-town newsstand and pick up a copy of a paper that had been brought in by plane or train. The out-of-town papers were invariably two or three or four days late—they were no longer technically news—and they cost a lot more than they did in the cities where they were published, usually three or four times the cover price. But a lot of people thought it was worth it, to read what life was like in another town.

No one could have envisioned the day when virtually every paper in the United States would be available for free on home computers—when a man could sit in his den and read up-to-the-minute editions of newspapers from Missouri, from Florida, from California, from Pennsylvania . . . from everywhere . . . with the tap of a key. Could read those newspapers without having to pay a cent—as, meanwhile, the owners of the newspaper companies in those future years would worry deep into the night about what all of this meant for their businesses, and about what they could do to stem the ever-plummeting circulation numbers of the newspapers, the actual news*papers*, that they printed on their presses.

My father would put down the *Dispatch* each night a minute before Walter Cronkite—before "the news"—arrived in our home. Had I been smarter—had I been paying proper attention—I might have sensed what this signified.

Newspapers may not yet have been dropping out of the sky and onto home computer screens, but the Big Ten Skywriters were dropping out of the Midwestern air and onto football fields, and that sounded decidedly glamorous, emphatically so.

Late in that summer when I hadn't prospered in the *Dispatch* library, I would read the *C-J* at home and see that the Big Ten Skywriters were at it again. It was an enthralling concept—one of those concepts that made newspapers themselves seem enthralling. To be a member of the annual Big Ten Skywriters Tour—that was the official name of the expedition—was a goal that seemed unreachable, so electric was the notion.

Each summer, a sportswriter from every paper in every town that had a university in the Big Ten athletic conference was delegated to go on the Skywriters Tour. The Skywriters would fly to each Big Ten school to interview the head football coach, to observe practice, to size up each team's prospects, and to write a ten-part series of preview stories for the paper back home.

Could anything be more fun? To this day I don't know how the whole operation really worked—did they have their own charter plane? Did they all travel together? Did they eat their meals at one big table? This was never explained.

The implicit mystery of the logistics made it sound all the more enticing. The very phrase: *Big Ten Skywriters*. In your mind you could conjure a picture: the droning of airplane engines off in the distance, the football players on the practice field looking up, shading their eyes against the sun, catching sight of a glistening silver DC-3, the plane gliding onto the nearest airstrip, and then, rushing out of the plane's door, the Big Ten Skywriters, maybe wearing old-time leather flyboy helmets. . . .

Or, an even dizzier fantasy: the plane buzzing the football field, and, up in the sky, the door next to the cockpit opening, and then, parachuting to the gridiron, the Big Ten Skywriters themselves, chutes opening just in time, the Skywriters landing in perfect formation on the forty-yard line. . . .

We, the readers, didn't know—we didn't know how they did their work and reported their stories, and it's just as well: the facts of the journey couldn't have been as spiffy as the concept of the Skywriters. Never mind that their exotic ports of call were places like Iowa City, Iowa, and West Lafayette, Indiana, and East Lansing, Michigan, and Champaign-Urbana, Illinois. It didn't have to be Paris or London—France and England didn't have football teams in the Big Ten.

I would read Kaye Kessler's datelined reports in the *C-J* that summer—each of his stories was accompanied by a special *Kaye Kessler on the Big Ten Skywriters Tour* logo, hand-drawn by Al Getchell—and it didn't matter that the *Dispatch* library hadn't worked out so well, it didn't matter that my father was spending less and less time with his newspaper, more and more time with Walter Cronkite and Eric Sevareid and Charles Collingwood.

Newspapers heading toward trouble? Newspapers facing an uncertain future? Not a chance.

The Big Ten Skywriters were newspapermen, weren't they? If there were storm clouds for the business looming somewhere ahead, how ominous could the clouds be? The clouds had a pigskin lining.

At the public tennis courts where I worked, the job consisted mainly of unlocking the gate in the morning, cleaning up the surface of the two courts, and sticking around all day to make certain that, if people were waiting to play, no one hogged too much time.

I was being paid minimum wage, and to sweeten the deal a little the head of the community's recreation department said that if I wanted to give lessons, I could keep the money I earned from that. I said that sounded fine, although I didn't know why anyone would want to take a lesson from me. I wasn't all that good.

But the recreation-department chief said that some residents of the community probably wanted lessons, and he wasn't about to go out and hire a real tennis pro. Thus, I was it.

I thought that $3.50 for a half hour, $5.00 for an hour, sounded right. Only a few people came around asking for the lessons—several housewives during long summer afternoons, some older people wanting to brush up on their games—but then, early one evening, about an hour before sunset, a boy showed up with his father.

The boy looked like he was ten or eleven. He walked up to me and said he wanted to learn how to play tennis, and asked me how much the lessons were. Then he went back to his father, and returned to me again and asked a few more questions.

I thought this was a little unusual; I didn't know why the father wouldn't be asking me himself. But I looked over and I thought I recognized the father's face, and when I saw the boy using sign language to communicate with him, I knew I was right.

The father worked in the composing room of the *Citizen-Journal*; he was deaf. I'd seen him many times during my copyboy summer—sometimes he'd be wearing one of those paper hats. It was the kind of work that was well suited to a person who could not hear; working with printed words all day, making sure they got into the paper correctly, was his skill.

At the tennis courts, I don't think the man recognized me. I was in a pair of shorts and a T-shirt; it had been two years since I had hung around the composing room.

His boy's hearing was unimpaired. He talked back and forth with his dad, both of them using the sign language, and then the boy came back to me and said they would take the half-hour lesson, the $3.50 one. The whole thing made me feel like crying—the memory of the man working all those eight-hour night shifts down on Third Street, and here he was trying to give his son a gift, trying to help the boy learn how to play a sport, and he was spending his money on me. And I wasn't even a real pro.

I wanted to give the lesson for free, but I thought that would insult the man, would make him feel diminished in front of his son—he didn't know that I knew who he was, he just knew that I knew he was deaf—so what I did instead, as we approached the end of the half hour, was tell the boy that I thought he had a lot of potential talent, and that since the courts were empty except for us, I'd like to extend the lesson to the full hour. He ran over to tell his dad; the dad reached for his wallet, as if to ask if he should pay more, and I shook my head no.

I worked with the boy for a long time, with his dad watching from a wooden bench. I did my best to correct his serve, to show him how to hit a proper backhand, to explain how to play close to the net. At the end of the lesson, with the sun dropping behind the trees, I told him that I thought he could be really good if he worked at it. I told him to tell that to his father.

He went over to the bench and, with his fingers, spoke to his father. The father smiled and waved over to me. They walked off together. I suppose it was the dad's day off; soon enough he'd be helping to put the C-J together again, because he was a newspaperman who worked nights.

The Charity Newsies were so much a part of life in town that children used the phrase when they were playing pickup games of basketball.

The Charity Newsies was an organization of businessmen who, on one Saturday each Christmas season, would go out on the streets around town to sell papers on the corners for as much as they could persuade people to give. The proceeds went to purchase clothes for needy children. The assumption behind it was that of course people were going to buy copies of the newspaper every day—that's what people did.

The Charity Newsies were there to urge them to spend a little more on their paper than they did every other day of the year.

So enmeshed was this with the fabric of what the city felt like—the newspapers themselves, and the Charity Newsies—that it became a part of the civic lexicon, something picked up by children almost as soon as they learned to talk. When a kid was fouled during a playground basketball game he would step to the free-throw line—the charity stripe—and, before shooting, he would yell out: "Charity Newsies!"

The idea of readership slipping away—where was it going to slip away to? It was possible to conceive of readers of the morning *Citizen-Journal* deciding to switch to the evening *Dispatch,* or readers of the *Dispatch* switching to the *Citizen-Journal;* we all knew of families that subscribed only to one paper instead of to both, although that seemed like an idiosyncratic thing to do. But people drifting away from newspapers altogether? That thought just didn't occur.

There were still towns in America with competing evening newspapers—not just competing newspapers, but competing *evening* papers. Evening papers as a commodity, as a part of the national life, were already starting on their path to near extinction, because of the competition from television and the difficulty of trucking the papers through rush-hour traffic in a timely manner to the new suburbs, far from downtown. But meanwhile, in bigger cities, the old-line evening papers, like punch-drunk prizefighters blinded past the point of reason by perspiration and blood streaming into their eyes, battled away at night—I saw it during the school year in Chicago, with the *Daily News* and the *American.* It seems like something out of a rotogravure-and-woodcuts era, which in its lineage, it was.

The vending boxes for the *Citizen-Journal* were dark green, with little cylinders welded to their sides, and slots on top of the cylinders for readers to drop in their seven cents. The part of the boxes that contained the newspapers could be opened whether or not coins had been deposited; readers were counted on to do the right thing and pay the seven cents. It was the honor system. And, one Saturday each year, the readers of the town felt honored to be asked to hand over much more than seven cents for their daily paper. The Charity Newsies were on the streets, selling something the citizens had to have.

I went back to college for my second year, and during the winter I wrote a letter to Don E. Weaver asking if the *Citizen-Journal* might have a place for me when summer came.

Mr. Weaver wrote back saying that they needed a fill-in on the copy desk, and that if I wanted the job, I could have it.

Although it wasn't exactly what I had in mind, I told him that of course I'd be there. The copyeditors, I always thought, seemed locked involuntarily into their chairs, locked onto the copy desk; it was a characteristic of their work. They went over what other people had written, line by line, they looked for errors and wrote headlines and were the last stop the stories made before they went to the composing room. The copyeditors never left the office and thus were constrained from being freewheeling; that wasn't part of their job description.

But I thought it would be a good learning experience for me, and Mr. Weaver sent me a *Citizen-Journal* style book to study at college. Which I did, all during the spring (although I already knew what *C-J* style was; I was, after all, the guy who was writing *Main-st* on envelopes instead of *Main St.*, who was writing *Ardmore-rd* instead of *Ardmore Rd.* I had already made the *Citizen-Journal*'s style my own style, without anyone asking me to do it).

When June came I returned home to Columbus from Chicago, and walked onto the mezzanine—hearing that city-room sound again was like what a parched man must feel as he gulps a glass of cold water after being lost in the desert—and when I reported to the copy desk I received one of the biggest surprises of my life.

Sometimes the world will deal you a spectacular hand.

10

Mr. Weaver, it seemed, had retired.

He had offered me the summer job during the winter; he had retired in the spring.

His replacement as editor of the *Citizen-Journal* was Charles Egger, brought in by Scripps-Howard from out of town.

Mr. Egger—a somewhat formal, almost reticent man with a gentle voice—came over to the copy desk as I stood there. He introduced himself.

"I know that Don Weaver said you could have a job on the copy desk this summer," Mr. Egger said. "But when I arrived here I went over all of our staffing needs, and I just don't think we have a place for you on the desk."

I did my best to hide my dismay. Great, I thought. Back to the municipal tennis courts, if they'll have me.

Mr. Egger appeared to understand my wordless reaction. He looked straight at me.

"Since we don't have anything for you on the copy desk, I don't suppose you'd be interested in working for the sports department?" he said.

It took a second or two for it to sink in.

Christmas morning. That's all it felt like: Christmas morning, in a five-year-old's heart.

"Hello, Brownie!" Clarence Young called out. "I hear you're joining us."

I sighed a little under my breath. Clarence—the oldest man on the sports desk, the layout man—had, for almost the entirety of my copyboy summer, addressed me as "Brownie" every time I came by to get the sports guys' coffee orders. It had taken him many weeks before he realized—or before someone told him—that my name was Greene, not Brown, and only then did he adjust his greeting to "Greenie." Two full summers had passed, though, and here I was again, and—at least temporarily—"Brownie" it was going to be.

Clarence reminded me of Andy Devine, the slightly daffy-and-disconnected sidekick on the *Adventures of Wild Bill Hickock* television series. He had the wavery, high-pitched voice, the thickest of glasses, a constant smile—Clarence moved slowly, as if negotiating his way through a fog not perceptible to anyone else in the vicinity, and was so immediately likeable that "Brownie" was just fine with me: if Clarence thought I was Brownie, there was no way I could possibly hold it against him.

There was no wall around the sports department—it was literally five steps from the desks of the news reporters, in the same big room. It had no door, no sign on the wall setting it apart—it consisted of six office desks jammed together, three on each side, facing each other. Which was a good thing for me, because the *C-J* sports department had only five employees, which meant that I would always have a chair and a desk.

Tom Keys's desk was often vacant after dinnertime—he was out covering the baseball games at Jet Stadium, but most days he would come in earlier in the afternoon to shoot the breeze with the others. As the sports columnist as well as the sports editor (and Jets beat writer), he was the only member of the sports staff to get his picture in the paper—that's why my friends at the ballgame with me that night had been eager to wave to him up in the press box, that's why they had recognized him even in the shadows high above home plate. Tom, beneath that fringe of hair, behind the nineteenth-hole golfers' garb that covered his skinny frame, had the bearing of a retired United States Marine Corps officer—always pleasant and softspoken, never visibly angry, he nonetheless gave off the aura of a man whom it would be unwise to cross.

Kaye Kessler and Tom Pastorius were, to me, like Frank Sinatra and Dean Martin, though Kessler's physical resemblance was closer to Kirk Douglas—the strong features, the unfailingly self-confident, name-above-the-title voice, the wavy hair (like Douglas's, Kessler's was blondish, but unlike Douglas's, Kessler's was going prematurely silver). The Sinatra/Martin parallel was what had occurred to me during the copyboy summer, because although my only contact with the sports staff was during my preparation for the Paoletti's runs, Kessler and Pastorius struck me as the two coolest guys I had ever met. Casual beyond anything I had observed in grown men, constantly laughing, joking with each other even as they wrote their stories, Kess and Pasty, as they (and everyone else) referred to themselves, were the movie stars of the mezzanine. As with Sinatra and Martin, Kessler, without anyone having to announce the fact, was the leader; as with Sinatra and Martin, Pastorius was the low-key, studly-without-seeming-to-try, heartbreaker. Pasty even looked like Dean Martin—dark hair graying at the temples, everybody-loves-somebody whimsy in his speaking voice, something behind his eyes that said he had figured out the world's secrets, and had found them preposterous.

George Strode was the kid of the staff—Archie Andrews face, perpetually amazed expression even at something as unexceptional as a baseball score coming across the wire (if Pittsburgh was playing Philadelphia, one of the two teams had to win, but Strode always reacted as if it was a miracle of the ages when he saw what a final result was); he wore two-toned saddle shoes, which only added to the impression that Betty and Veronica, accompanied by Reggie and Jughead, would be coming around the corner any second now. John Stewart—the sound of West Virginia or Kentucky in his voice, an intimation in his manner that spoke of coal mines and a hard early life, a hint of Joe Palooka somewhere south of his crewcut—was the fifth member of the sports department, a relentlessly sunny man who, it seemed to me, had to silently fight off the impending onset of certain clouds.

"Take that desk in the middle, Brownie," Clarence Young said to me. "The one next to Kessler's."

Christmas morning. That's what that first day in sports was like.

"You want to try the standings tonight?"

Pastorius—in his sleepy Dean Martin voice—was asking me the question. I'd been there less than a week.

He tossed me the frayed statistics-tables book with the ripped pages, the one whose cover had long ago fallen off. He'd taught me how to use it the night before.

"Start with the National League, and then show it to me," he said.

He didn't want to do it. Doing it was drudgery. And in the C-J sports department, where it never felt like anyone was really in charge or really wanted to be in charge (Tom Keys, Marine aura or not, wasn't one for giving imperious orders), this counted as an assignment.

So, using the wire-service results of that evening's major-league ballgames, I started to figure out the standings. The torn-up book was composed entirely of numbers, page after page of them—if a team had won, say, forty-seven games during the current season, and lost thirty-two, you were supposed to locate the proper page of numbers, run your finger across a column, and find out what that team's winning percentage was as of tonight (.595). You'd do that for every team, as the final scores came in. Next you'd figure out how many games behind the first-place team (GB, in the parlance of the standings) the team whose position you were determining was. Then you'd type it up on a piece of copy paper, and it would be sent to the composing room to be set in type for the next morning's paper.

Today it would all be done electronically; today, the moment each successive game ended, the standings would be revised by the wire service and transmitted to sports department computers all around the world. But there were no computers then, of course—either in the wire-service headquarters, or on sports department desks, or in composing rooms. At the C-J—as Pastorius had informed me—they didn't like to wait until too late at night, when UPI would send its updated standings. They preferred to do it themselves, to save a little time.

The standings book in the sports department had been published before 1961—before the major leagues went to 162-game seasons—so it only went up to 154 games; someone at the C-J had added a home-made list for those extra eight games.

"Don't get it wrong," Pastorius warned me. "If you do, we'll be answering the phone all day tomorrow."

It felt so national, and at the same time so local—nothing could be more big-time American in scope than the major-league standings—but here we were, here I was, calculating those standings on my own, using the beaten-up book with all the numbers in it.

Games behind? Subtract a team's number of wins from the number of wins the first-place team has; then subtract the first-place team's number of losses from the number of losses of the trailing team; then add those numbers together, and divide by two. . . .

"Sports!" Clarence Young would call out, as if greeting Wild Bill on horseback, picking up a ringing phone.

"The Indians?" he would say. He would shuffle through the scattered pieces of wire copy on his desk. He'd find the right one. "The Indians beat the Tigers, four to two," he would say.

We were just that easy to reach—people at home, people in bars, would call the C-J, request the sports desk, and be put right through by the newspaper's telephone operators. They'd want the ball scores. One of the five members of the sports department—six, now that I was there—would give them what they asked for.

There was no television set in the sports department—not even a radio. Unthinkable, today, now that television and sports are inseparable in the public mind, and ESPN is turned on nonstop on nearly every newspaper sports desk. But watching TV in a newspaper office, in those years, would have been considered slacking off. Even when the biggest games were being played—games about which we'd be printing accounts in the morning—we didn't see them, although our readers at home were watching them. We just waited for the wires to tell us what had happened.

"If it's a West Coast late game, just put a little *x* to the sides of the teams in the standings," Pastorius would remind me, reading a dime-store paperback novel as he leaned back in his chair. He seemed very pleased to have me here. Anything to avoid having to look up all those percentages himself. He'd paid his dues—he'd pored over the statistics book and typed up the standings on many nights, for many years.

"The Orioles?" Clarence would say to a stranger on the phone. "Let me see, let me see . . . the Orioles got rained out tonight."

They were World War II guys, some of the men in the sports department—like Bill Moore, they'd spent the 1940s overseas, fighting for their country.

Maybe that's why they liked the feeling of no one on the sports desk appearing to be in charge. They'd taken orders long enough, a long time ago.

At their desks, they didn't even seem that old—but they were veterans of the greatest war in the history of mankind. Later I would hear a story about Tom Pastorius and Woody Hayes—and even though I wasn't present to see it for myself, I would know it had to be true. Each man's part sounded just right.

Woody, when talking to sportswriters after an Ohio State football practice or game, would often shift into long, free-form lectures about military history. Woody was a student of the military, and he liked to draw analogies between football strategies and battlefield tactics. His rambling speeches were usually highly entertaining, if more than a little didactic.

One day after practice, or so the story went, Woody was telling the sportswriters that they would do well to pay close attention to him, and to learn the lessons of one of the epic encounters of World War II—it may have been the Battle of the Bulge.

A few minutes into it, with Woody not having paused to take a breath, Pastorius supposedly stood up, waved his hand dismissively at Woody, turned to walk out of the locker room, and said: "Ah, hell, I was *there*."

I was happy to do the baseball standings for him. To let him read his paperback detective novel in peace. He'd earned it.

When I arrived at work each day—not that I or anyone else thought much about the meaning of this—everyone was typing.

In the sports department, Kess and Pasty and Strode and Stewart would be banging at their Underwoods and Royals (there wasn't a lot of consistency to the office equipment at the C-J—there were different brands of typewriters on every desk, the typewriters felt like hand-me-down clothes); a couple of steps over from sports, in the news department, the same thing would be going on.

The typing—typing by grown men—was something that set newspaperpeople apart. We were decades away from the time when typing would become an egalitarian exercise—when every CEO would have a computer monitor and keyboard. Back then, the assumption in the business world was that clerks typed, secretaries typed—but men who had prestigious jobs did not. If you were a person who had risen to a high and respected level in industry, someone typed for you. Those were just the rules of commerce.

So the fact that everyone at the C-J typed—from Bill Moore to Wink Hess to Kaye Kessler to Tom Pastorius—made us demonstrably lesser creatures than the bigshots of downtown. It separated us from the people we wrote about.

Which was, I thought from my new perch on the sports desk, one more laudable aspect of newspapering. The men and women of the *Citizen-Journal* didn't want to be like the rest of the business world. The aspiration simply wasn't there. The men and women of the *Citizen-Journal* were the way they were by their own choice. They liked it.

The people at 34 South Third Street knew that they didn't make as much money as most of the people they were reporting about (except when they were reporting about stickup men and petty criminals). Not just the business leaders and CEOs—it went without saying that newspaperpeople didn't earn as much as those kinds of executives. But even other, non-executive-level people working in downtown offices—the C-J staff members knew they didn't make as much as those people. Newspaper work was blue-collar work.

Except for the fact that we typed. Kaye Kessler and Tom Pastorius and John Stewart were as traditionally masculine a group of men as you'd ever want to encounter; Tom Keys could have passed for Leo Durocher. They typed—everyone in the city room did. That's what I would see when I arrived at work every day: all of these men, typing.

It helped cement the feeling that we were reporting from below, from a social stratum beneath the one occupied by the subjects of our stories.

That wasn't such a bad thing.

We typed. They didn't.

This snazzy guy would show up in the newsroom early on weeknight evenings.

He would just sort of materialize—we would see him standing by the public service desk inside the glass doors.

The women in the public service department had gone home for the night. The snazzy guy would have talked his way through the lobby.

I say he was snazzy because he dressed like Nathan Detroit. He would have been turned away from, even laughed out of, most downtown business offices. Here, we knew what he had come for.

To take bets.

Our bets.

Scioto Downs was the harness-racing track several miles south of downtown. The snazzy fellow wasn't a full-time bookie; he served, as I recall, some nebulous function at the track. But he was here for one reason and one reason only: to accept our wagers.

"All right, all right!" Clarence Young—that Andy Devine voice like honeyed sandpaper—would call out when he saw the man standing there. "Place your bets!"

And we would. I had to edge my way into it, with some apprehension—two dollars on a horse to show was about as venturesome as I got, I was being paid less per hour than even the minimum two-buck bet. But the night's printed racing program would have been delivered to the city room in the afternoon, everyone would have studied it, and the wagers were made. For the rest of the evening, we would await the results of each heat—they would be phoned in one at a time—to see how we'd done.

It was harmless enough—no one went broke, no one got rich.

But I ask myself now:

What would happen, in an American newsroom today, if the word got out that a tout was showing up every night to take money from the staff members for bets?

I think I know the answer.

It wouldn't be pretty.

Heads would roll.

"All right, all right!" Clarence would yell.

No need to hide it. The bookie had arrived.

"Brownie, you got a horse you like tonight?" Clarence would ask me.

"It's Greene," I would say quietly to the bookie by the city room door, correcting Clarence, just in case I would end up a winner.

"I know," the bookie, snazzy as could be, would say.

I never won.

"You gonna get your feet on the ground, Kess?"

Pastorius would say it—Kessler would be in the office with his suitcase, getting ready to go to Port Columbus, and the running gag would kick in.

"Oh, yeah," Kessler would say, like in a Rat Pack sketch—which, come to think of it, is probably where the sports desk staff came up with the pattern of their patter.

"Kess has got to get his feet on the ground, Pasty," Clarence Young would call over.

"Can't cover a tournament without getting your feet on the ground," George Strode would chime in.

"Can we have a look at those feet?" John Stewart would say.

"I'll call you when I get there," Kessler would say.

"Don't over-exert yourself," Pastorius would say.

Kessler would get to travel—a lot, and to wonderful places. There was one reason he was permitted to do this: Jack Nicklaus. The *Citizen-Journal* had a minuscule travel budget—the rule of thumb was: Don't go—but there were two major exceptions: away games for the Ohio State football and basketball teams (you couldn't publish a newspaper in Columbus and not cover the Buckeyes on the road, no matter how small your budget—your readers would desert you); and big golf tournaments in which Nicklaus was playing. When Jack Nicklaus, the pride of his hometown, teed it up in an important competition, the readers of the C-J expected Kaye Kessler to be there.

He would travel to the Masters, to the British Open, to the U.S. Open, to the PGA Championship . . . Kaye Kessler saw the world, all because of Nicklaus. On the bulletin-board schedule for the weeks when he would be on the road, there would be a notation—*TD*—in the little box that represented the day of that week on which he flew out of Columbus. TD: Travel Day.

"So not only will you be at Baltusrol all next week," Pastorius, taking a gander at the schedule, would say to Kessler. "But while the rest of us are here working, you're going to get paid for your travel day."

"Oh, yeah," Kessler would say, playing his part, Sinatra onstage at the Sands. "A man can't cover a tournament without taking a day to get the lay of the land."

"Of course not," Pastorius would say. "You can't just rush into coverage like that. You've got to . . . *ease* in."

And then, on the travel day, with Kessler gone, and the rest of us there on the mezzanine:

"You hear from Kess?" Clarence Young would ask.

"No, not yet," Pastorius would say with the verbal equivalent of an arched eyebrow in his tone, Dean Martin in a tux sliding down a fire-pole. "I'm sure he'll be calling."

"You think his feet are on the ground yet?" Clarence would say.

"He's working on it," Pastorius would say. "He'll let us know."

What a life. I sat there and I took it all in. Kessler was off somewhere, sleeping in a hotel room, eating in a restaurant, everything taken care of by the company—he was a sportswriter getting a salary from his news-paper even on a day when he didn't have to write anything. A travel day. How could you beat that?

"When Kess calls, tell him we don't want him to wear himself out," George Strode would say from his side of the desk.

"He won't overdo it," Pastorius would say. "He'll take his time get-ting those feet on the ground."

How could you beat it? How could anything be better than all this?

I found myself not wanting days off, even though I had to take them.

Nothing that could happen on a day away from work could match the delights of the sports desk.

I didn't even know exactly how to define my job—no one had told me what it was, other than that I'd be working in the sports depart-ment. It wasn't copyboy work; it wasn't editing work; it was . . .

Well, it was sports-desk work, with all that the phrase implied. And I didn't want to leave it, even on the days I was supposed to.

The very act of picking up the ringing telephone—the single word we'd all say: "Sports!" No one person was assigned to grab the phones—whoever heard the phone first answered it. "Sports!" "Sports!" "Sports!" Sometimes two or three of us would lift different extensions at the same time. We must have sounded like the Mills Brothers in concert, saying that word in three-part harmony: "Sports!"

My shifts were often very late—there were days when I was sup-posed to start at four P.M. and work until one A.M. Downtown, in those years, was a place where you could park your car in the alley next to the *Dispatch* building's presses—if you could find a space, you just stashed your car there and didn't have to worry that anyone would tow it. For those late-shift nights, I was driving downtown; after one A.M., the chances of catching a bus home were slim.

So I'd come to work in the afternoon, and sometimes on my dinner hour I'd wander over to High Street, which got old pretty quickly: there were only so many times that I could walk the narrow aisles of Woolworth's, taking in the musty variety-store smell, or check out the scene inside the dingy little Planters Peanuts shop. High Street wasn't where I wanted to be; taking my dinner hour, even though I was allowed to, wasn't what I wanted to do.

What I wanted was just to hang out on the sports desk, even at dinner, even on my days off. "Sports!" How many people get to answer the phone with that word, every single day? If you've got to say something into the receiver of a ringing telephone, is there a word in any dictionary that speaks more succinctly of good times and grins? "Sports!"

We probably wrote entirely too many "most happy fella" photo captions.

Forget the "probably"—we did write too many of them.

Most happy fella at the Goodale Softball Tournament's final round Tuesday is cleanup hitter Jeff Johnston. . . .

Or:

The most happy fella at the Brookfield Golf Club members-only scramble Thursday is . . .

Occasionally we would go with the "all-smiles" variation:

American Legion Post 122 slugger Ted Grayman is all smiles after hitting the game-winning home run. . . .

And then there was the ever-popular "poses with" caption:

Winding Hollow Country Club ladies match-play winner Sue Harmon poses with the championship trophy. . . .

Our photo captions weren't exactly shining examples of tough-minded investigative journalism; the fact is, we didn't give a lot of thought to the wording in them. If someone appeared pleased with himself in the photo that Dick Garrett or Hank Reichard would bring to the sports desk—and why wouldn't the local athlete appear pleased? He had just won something, hadn't he, he had been instructed to pose and smile by a *Citizen-Journal* photographer—we would reflexively, in the caption, make note of that. He was a most happy fella.

Sometimes we'd hit the photo-caption trifecta:

Most happy fella in the Columbus Jets clubhouse Friday night is Ray Dublonski, all smiles as he poses with the International League player-of-the-month award. . . .

We weren't trying to be ironic; we weren't writing the captions with sardonic intent. What was the big deal? They were just pictures of people having a good time. No need to aim for the Nobel Prize in Literature with every cutline.

Hank Reichard, that lamentive, lachrymose expression on his face, would come grumbling into the sports department after being sent out to cover an amateur baseball game or a public-links golf championship— Hank would look like he'd been sent to shoot the Bataan Death March, so pained would be his countenance—and we'd take receipt of the photo, still wet from the developing fluid, that he brought us, and immediately, in our caption, turn sad Hank's handiwork into something out of *Rebecca of Sunnybrook Farm:*

Dave Jameson, left, and Gary Robinson, right, are all smiles Monday. . . .

We may have had our limitations, working on that sports desk. But no one who was the subject of one of our photo captions ever complained.

Why would they? They were most happy.

Clarence would draw up the sports-page layouts by hand, on sheets of paper divided into empty columns.

He'd do it as soon as he decided which of a night's athletic contests, national and local, should receive the most prominent display, and which were of secondary importance. Clarence would do it with a copy pencil—maybe the allotted space for a big story would be slugged "Jets," in his handwriting on the layout sheet, if the Columbus baseball team was going to lead the sports page, or "NL" for a National League wrap-up, or "Jack" for a story on Nicklaus, wherever in the world Nicklaus (and Kessler) might have alighted that day.

I'd watch Clarence as he'd do it—it was hardly a private pursuit, he would draw up the page layouts almost casually as he gabbed with the rest of us—and it was always a nice feeling, the next morning, to see my father reading the first sports page, and to see all the stories in exactly the place on the page where Clarence had decreed they should be. He'd have sketched out a four-column headline for the Cincinnati Reds game, with a rectangular space beneath it for a wire photo from the game—and there the headline would be in the morning, straight from Clarence's imagination to our breakfast table, there the baseball action photo would be, in the shape and dimensions Clarence had ordained would look most alluring.

There was something about working on the sports desk so late at night. The rest of the city was sound asleep, or getting ready to be, and we were still awake downtown, assembling something to present to the slumbering people. What we were working on, I thought, was better than a late-night newscast, which was there and then gone; what we were doing was coming up with a gift that would be delivered and waiting for all those people when the dawn arrived. Because people liked their sports pages; people eagerly anticipated the gift we were wrapping for them.

At least that's the way I saw it, with midnight on its way. As I would retrieve my car from the alley next to the presses after the sports section had been locked up for the night, I would think of my father coming home from work during all the years of my growing up, of him pulling into the driveway at a conventional late-afternoon time. With the sports section put to bed, I would drive through deserted streets to our neighborhood and steer the car to our house and into the driveway, and all the windows would be dark, not just in our home but up and down the block. Everyone sleeping.

And then, in the morning, Clarence Young's sports page. His name wasn't on it anywhere, but it was his, it wouldn't look the way it did had he not sketched it out on those layout sheets less than twelve hours before. It was like seeing a painting—for me, to see the sports page every day was like looking at a painting I'd seen created from beginning to end, from rough outlines to completion. Clarence, behind those thick eyeglasses of his, had begun with a few tentative strokes, and I'd watched him make them, and now the finished painting, just as he had envisioned it, was on every doorstep, on our block and on every block. I never told anyone how much I liked all of this. Never said a word.

"No *way!*"

That was the phrase, that sports-department summer. Soon enough it would become an ubiquitous part of slangy American discourse—"You're going to California for a month? No *way!*"—and later it would grow so common as to be annoying. But at the beginning of the sports-desk summer I had never heard it, at least not used in that manner.

I think Kessler, coming back from a golf tournament, may have been the first to utter it:

"I asked Doug Sanders if he was using a new driver and he said, 'No *way.*'"

Or maybe it was Tom Keys, on the afternoon following a Jets game he'd covered the night before:

"And these guys think they have a chance to win the International League pennant? No *way!*"

I'm almost certain that the catchphrase began somewhere in the world of sports—undoubtedly somewhere far from Columbus, for we were assuredly not on the cutting edge of American trends. But when it did make it to town, it was in the environs of the *C-J* sports desk that I first heard it.

John Stewart, especially, seemed unable to resist it. For a few weeks it decorated a majority of his spoken sentences, tinged as they were with the twang of Appalachia. George Strode might ask him: "Hey, John, do you want to switch shifts with me next Tuesday?" "No *way*." Or: "John, you feel like going over to Mills for dinner?" "No *way* I'm eating in a cafeteria tonight!" He even started to work it into his stories in the paper; if he was supposed to write, say, the American League wire-service roundup of results from around the league, instead of merely writing that Mickey Mantle had won a game for the New York Yankees by hitting a home run in the ninth inning, he might write: "No way that Mickey Mantle was going to let his teammates down with the game on the line in Yankee Stadium last night."

I felt as if I was being let in on a secret—like I was privileged to be receiving the first faint blips of something on a distant-early-warning cultural radar screen. It didn't matter that the same phrase was probably spreading at the speed of light all across the United States, that it was in fact not specific to the sports department of the *C-J* at all; it didn't matter that we were almost certainly late to the dance, that "No *way*" had doubtless been used for weeks or even months in New York or Los Angeles by the time it reached us.

What mattered was that, in our little patch of the continent, a new and snappy pairing of words was making itself evident, and that of course the place where it would make its entrance was the sports desk of the newspaper office. Why wouldn't it? The sports desk was the snappiest place in town—newspaper offices themselves were snappy as could be, and sports desks were the snappiest precincts in those offices.

Back then, not only did I believe it—back then, it was probably even true. What could be snappier than a newspaper?

Sometimes the words were said deadpan, to convey determined decisiveness:

"Pasty, are you working this Sunday?" "No way."

Sometimes they were said with the second word emphasized, to indicate zest:

"Did you hear that Kessler got upgraded to a suite at his hotel last week, because they were out of single rooms?" "No *way*!"

Sometimes John Stewart would just drop them once again into the lead paragraph of his story in the *C-J*, as if the words needed no supporting verb constructions, no qualifiers:

"No way the Ohio State football team is going to finish anywhere other than first place in the Big Ten this fall, a panel of gridiron experts predicted yesterday."

It was the phrase of the summer. Every summer has one. But that sports-department summer, everything felt original and important; everything sounded special and right. At any rate, it did in the ears of the newest guy on the desk.

The sports desk itself, in a hard-to-define way, was becoming my new best friend, which left open the question of what to do about my real best friends—my old best friends.

I was pretty much out of their lives for the summer, especially at night. During the copyboy job I'd have gotten off work early enough in the evening—a few hours before midnight—that I had been able to catch up with them. But the sports-department hours were so late that, except for on my days off, our paths didn't cross.

And it didn't really bother me. The newspaper was where I wanted to be. I suppose it happens to everyone, when they find the thing in life that they suddenly know they want to do—I suppose a place that is not really home starts to feel like home.

On my two nights off a week I would run into guys I'd grown up with, guys who had summer jobs working for the Ohio Department of Highways—they'd have farmers' tans, sunburned up to the place on their arms where the sleeves of their T-shirts stopped. They'd tell stories about the easy money out there on the roads, about the low-stress requirements of their jobs (mostly holding up signs to slow down traffic while the surfaces upon which they worked were blacktopped), stories about the girls they met, and the lazy lunch breaks sitting under trees and eating sandwiches out of paper sacks. They said they were having the summer of their lives, and I believed them; part of me wanted to be out on the highways with them.

But I knew that I really didn't want that at all; I knew that, endless sun and good times aside, I would have missed the sports desk within five minutes of leaving it. I knew that I was exactly where I was supposed to be. On nights when I would get together with my friends after my shift ended, I would recognize that the narrative of their evenings, the story of their summer, had been forming without me being a part of it. They would talk at length about people they had encountered, places they had gone, and I didn't know what they were referring to; they would laugh at punchlines that meant nothing to me, because I hadn't been around enough to understand the context. That is what I had willingly given up. On the nights when I would meet them after we had locked up the sports page, they would have been together since sundown, and it would be like I was coming into a theater in the middle of the third act of a play.

Sometimes on my nights off my friends and I would go up to a bar on the north side of town, a place called the Sugar Shack. We weren't twenty-one yet, but we could get in because of Ohio's you-can-drink-3.2-percent-beer-once-you're-eighteen law. At the Sugar Shack, every few weeks, a struggling, trying-to-make-a-living local rock band from Michigan would have driven down for the evening to provide dance music for the bar's customers—no cover charge, no minimum. I thought the lead singer was really good—he and I would talk as we stood at the long wooden bar during his band's breaks. He was Bob Seger, a young man on the night shift. That sports-desk summer we were all, in our own ways, at the very beginning of trying to find out who we were, what we wanted to do with the rest of our lives. Not yet knowing that the beginning, in the end, often turns out to be the best and most beautiful place.

Something called the Columbus Invitational Pro-Am—a one-day golf event to benefit local charity—was being played out at Columbus Country Club one Monday, and I went.

Nicklaus was an enthusiastic supporter of the event—he invited many of the biggest stars in golf to attend, and because it was Nicklaus doing the asking, most of them said yes. I wasn't scheduled to work until later that afternoon, so I thought I'd watch as much of it as I could.

Kessler was out there covering it; so was Pastorius. I said hello to them when I saw them near the main country club building, and I heard Kess telling Pasty: "Arnold's in a pretty bad mood—he wanted to fly his own plane here today, but as he was getting into it he saw that the windshield was cracked. So he had to charter another one."

I walked out onto the course to stand among the crowd and watch the great golfers playing in foursomes with an assortment of local businessmen, amateurs and duffers. On an early hole, I saw Arnold Palmer, striding down the fairway, hitching up his trousers just the way I'd watched him do it so many times on television.

I ducked under the restraining rope that separated the fairway from the gallery.

"What do you think you're doing?" one of the volunteer marshals said.

"It's OK," I said. "I'm from the *Citizen-Journal* sports department."

Now . . . that shouldn't have worked. I don't care where you're from—you don't get to go inside the ropes.

But the guy let me keep walking.

And—this was nuts—I walked straight up to Arnold Palmer and began strolling toward the green with him.

He looked at me as we walked.

"I hear the windshield on your plane cracked," I said.

I can't even describe the expression on his face. Let's just say that it was not especially welcoming.

"You hear *what?*" Palmer said.

I repeated what I had heard about the windshield.

"And just where did you hear that?" Palmer said.

"Kaye Kessler," I said.

Palmer shook his head.

"I work with him at the *Citizen-Journal*," I said.

Palmer shook his head again. He looked me in the eye.

And let me keep walking with him.

We walked almost the entire course; we talked after every one of his shots. The marshals, seeing Palmer speaking with me, did not approach to throw me out. They must have thought that if it was all right with Palmer, who were they to interfere? Whether Palmer was silently wishing that they would swoop down and give me the boot, I do not know.

I had to leave before he reached the eighteenth hole; I was due at work.

On the sports desk during my spare minutes that afternoon, I wrote a story: about Palmer, about what he had said to me as we had walked the course, especially about how the gallery—the famous "Arnie's Army"—had reacted to his many well-practiced attempts to get a laugh out of them.

Kessler and Pastorius were busy writing their own stories—their real stories—about the pro-am. They took a break at dinnertime, and went out together to get something to eat.

With Kessler away from the sports department, I went over to his typewriter and—with great trepidation—put my finished story on his desk. I wouldn't have had the nerve to say anything to him about it. (The nerve to duck under the ropes and walk up to Arnold Palmer—yes. To tell Kaye Kessler I had assigned myself to write a full-length story? No.)

Kess and Pasty returned from dinner, sat back down at their desks, resumed typing away at their pro-am stories. I saw Kessler glance at the story I had left on his desk; he kept typing.

I felt foolish. I felt stupid for having left it there.

Just before deadline, he stood up, put on his sport coat to go home for the night, and handed me four pieces of copy paper. "Send this to the composing room," he said. And walked out the door.

I looked at what he had handed me. It had my byline on top of it.

He had cleaned up what I had written, had worked it into the shape he thought it should have, had gotten it ready to go to press, and had put my name on it.

It was as nice—and important—a gesture as I have ever in my life been lucky enough to receive. He would have been quite justified to toss what I had written into a wastebasket, or to use my material as notes for his own story, or to simply ignore it. Who had asked me to write anything?

But instead he had done me the kindness. We all face choices like that every day—whether to help someone out, or not to bother. My first byline. Kessler handed me the pieces of paper and walked out of the room before I had a chance to react or to thank him. The Lone Ranger on Third Street.

He had written my byline as "By Bob Greene," and I changed it to "By Bob Greene Jr.," because my father's name was the same as mine, and I didn't want there to be any confusion in town. I shot the pages up to the composing room through the pneumatic tube, and I went home and had trouble sleeping, and I must have drifted off somewhere just before dawn.

Because when I woke up the lead sports page of the *Columbus Citizen-Journal* had been folded up and slipped under my bedroom door, by my mother. At the top of the page were the two main stories, next to each other. The first—with the highlights and results of the pro-am— was by Kaye Kessler. The one next to it—about the sidelights of the day at the golf course—had the headline:

**ANTICS OF ARNIE
AMUSING TO ARMY**

And, right on top of the story:

By BOB GREENE JR., Citizen-Journal Sports Writer

How long does something like that stay with you? How lasting are the echoes of such a gesture, something seemingly done offhandedly as a man walks out the door?

In December of 1999, in the last newspaper column I would write in the old millennium, I told that story—the story of the day I got my first byline. I said that I hadn't spoken to Kessler in many years, but that if anyone reading the column knew where he was living, to please pass a copy along to him.

The column ended:

Happy new year, Kess. And thanks for the century.

Working on the Fourth of July felt like an honor. Like being part of a club—all of us on the sports desk, all of us in the newsroom, as the rest of the city paused to go to parades, and enjoy picnics, and watch fireworks. As the fireworks exploded, we were getting the morning paper ready. It must be highly essential work—consequential to the town, consequential to our readers—for us to be required to be at the office on a day like this. That's what it felt like, at least to me. Maybe it felt less rousing once you'd worked seven or eight Fourths.

It was a permutation of the Sunday feeling. On Sundays when I didn't have to work the very late shift on the sports desk—on Sundays when I arrived at work around noon—I would see, from the window of my car, people coming out of church in neighborhoods on the way downtown. They'd be dressed up—men in Sunday suits, women in freshly ironed summer dresses, children in their most neatly pressed clothes. Sunday in the city, a day of rest, a day of reflection and prayer—and I was on my way to the sports department. Just fine with me.

It was a self-contained world inside which we worked on the Fourth of July, on summer Sundays. Sunday was always the last scheduled day of professional golf tournaments around the United States—the fourth rounds were played on Sundays, the winners crowned. And early every Sunday evening—right after the tournaments would have ended—a man would call the sports desk and say: "Could I ask you how a certain golfer came out in the tournament?"

The golfer he always asked about was a PGA middle-of-the-packer named Rod Funseth. We knew it was coming—we knew the man would be calling. For whatever reason, Rod Funseth's most ardent fan lived in central Ohio, and was so devoted that he never missed a Sunday call to the *C-J*. If Rod Funseth were playing in our current world, right now, his fan could check the results online, without anyone knowing; that summer his only alternative, other than calling us, was to wait until morning and read the agate type, and he could not bear to wait that long. We could tell, from the hat-in-hand tone of his voice, that he probably thought all kinds of people called the *Citizen-Journal* sports department on Sunday nights, asking about all kinds of their favorite golfers—we could tell that he probably assumed there were dozens, hundreds, of people calling in, wanting to know about dozens of different golfers.

There was only one caller: him.

So it felt like a special club up there on Sundays, working while the city didn't, waiting for the solitary call seeking the sum total of Rod Funseth's strokes. Kaye Kessler only traveled to the most prominent golf tournaments—the C-J's budget could be stretched just so far— and when Jack Nicklaus was playing somewhere in the country in a run-of-the-mill, non-marquee tournament, we relied on the UPI sports wire on Sundays to inform us who had won.

We could usually tell by the first word after the dateline.

Clarence Young would stand over the machine, and as the report of the golf tournament would start to mechanically clatter out he would call to us: "Burly!"

That's how we would know if Nicklaus was the winner.

"Burly!" Pastorius would call back to Clarence, laughing.

The wire stories would begin:

"Burly Jack Nicklaus shot a four-under-par 67 Sunday to win the . . ."

Jack was still a little hefty in those days. The wire service would never want to call him fat.

So "burly" it was. Every day of a golf tournament (meaning, for us, Thursdays, Fridays and Sundays—we weren't in the office Saturdays, for the third rounds), "Burly" was our tip-off that Nicklaus was doing well.

"Burly!" Clarence would yell to us, happy at the absurdity of life on the sports desk.

I don't know if Rod Funseth was fat or skinny, burly or lean. It didn't matter. He was never victorious.

But his faithful fan never missed a Sunday call.

We had no copy desk.

As inconceivable as that may seem, the *C-J* sports department just didn't have one.

The regular city room copy desk, you might think, would have been available to us—the news department copyeditors sat one footstep behind us, they were directly in back of our six shoved-together sports desks. But sports copy went through no one.

"Hey, John, want to give my story a read before I send it to composing?" Pastorius might ask, and if John Stewart had a moment, he'd give it a quick skim. If something blatant jumped out at him as being wrong, Stewart might casually mention it to Pastorius. But the traditional tasks of copyeditors—looking for factual errors, checking spelling and grammar, making certain of logical consistency, getting rid of clichés or clunky phrases—were missing from the sports department, because we were our own editors.

It felt like . . . well, to use a phrase a good copy desk would probably delete because it's so overused, it felt like the inmates running the institution. Which was what was so much fun about it. How serious could all of this be? We were covering games, giving the readers something to breeze through over breakfast. Who needed a copy desk for that?

We weren't exceedingly formal in our writing style; when it's recess on the playground and there's no teacher present, not a lot of rules apply. Kessler, when writing about Ohio State basketball coach Fred Taylor, would often, in second reference, identify him as "Fearless Fred," a construction that likely would not have made it into the *New York Times*. (Kess was also very loyal to his friends; in that Arnold Palmer story of mine that he worked over before putting my byline on top of it, he saw that I had mentioned one of the pro-am participants, an acquaintance of Kessler's named Bob Daniels, who ran a local Buick dealership. Kessler added a word in parentheses to my sentence about

Daniels, so that when the paper came out in the morning he was referred to as "Bob (Buick) Daniels," a juicy plug for his business. A few
days later I received a letter, on Bob Daniels Buick letterhead, from
Bob Daniels himself, telling me what a splendid piece of journalism I
had written. I was so young I didn't comprehend what his thanks were
really for; I thought he truly considered me to be a brilliant and nifty
wordsmith, I thought I had a genuine devotee out there.)

Soon enough the other guys in the department let me start writing
the sports roundup stories from around the nation—the compilations
of game and tournament results, cobbled together from what UPI sent
us. When you wrote the roundups for the morning paper, it wasn't as if
you were pretending to be there—but sitting and writing paragraphs
about big and distant events from all over the world . . . from Wrigley
Field, from Wimbledon, from Fenway Park, from Churchill Downs . . .
was quite a heady feeling.

We would write our own headlines—no copy desk for that,
either—and we tended toward alliteration. If Detroit won a baseball
game, the headline might begin with the words: "TIGERS TOPPLE . . ."
For St. Louis: "CARDINALS CRUSH . . ." For Pittsburgh: "PIRATES
POUND . . ." We thought we were demonstrating the height of raffish
style.

For the first few days when I was doing the sports roundups, I wrote
them, put my own headlines on them, stuck them in the tubes and
shot them to the composing room . . . all this without anyone at all
seeing them first. And the stories got into the morning paper that
way—without any other eye having gone over them.

When Strode or Stewart or Clarence Young realized I was doing
this—I don't recall now which of them it was—they said to me, not at
all angrily, that it might be best if I let one of them take a look before
I sent my stories to the Linotype operators. That's how they did it with
each other's copy, they said—they swapped it back and forth, they let
a buddy have a quick read.

They were almost apologetic about telling me this—they didn't
want me to take it the wrong way. It was just, they said, that it probably wasn't a good idea to have your copy delivered to all those homes

in the morning without anyone in the world but you having read it beforehand.

We were a little short on gatekeepers, there on the sports desk. But we sure could string those headline words together. "WHITE SOX WALLOP . . ." "CUBS CREAM . . ." "DODGERS DUMP . . ." Who needed a copy desk? We had everything under control.

A girl I was going out with that summer sent me a letter in care of the sports department.

When I think about it now—the specifics of the delirious scene that unfolded when the letter arrived—I see, in my mind, George Strode, his head near the acoustic tiles of the newsroom's ceiling.

George, as the youngest sportswriter on the C-J's full-time staff, had kind of taken me under his wing. As for the letter from the girlfriend: I couldn't have been the greatest of dates that summer—getting off work at one o'clock in the morning is not the most seductive of social attributes—but the girl who wrote me the letter accepted my job schedule, and read in the newspaper the sports roundups I was beginning to write, and decided to sit down at a typewriter herself.

A few of the roundup stories had carried my byline; sometimes, on the longer roundups, you would get your name on top of it. And so the girl I was going out with wrote a letter to me—over a fake signature, a man's signature, an important-and-distinguished-sounding made-up name. In the letter the distinguished-sounding man (the girl I was going out with) said that he (she) had read a few of my stories, thought I was a superlative writer, and had decided to do something to recognize this fact.

The purported writer of the letter said that he was a person of considerable wealth, and was going to commission and pay for a statue of me, to be erected at the corner of Broad and High.

It was the least that he could do, the letter said; the statue was being sculpted even now, and would be unveiled on downtown's busiest corner within a few weeks.

I sat in the sports department reading the letter—I hadn't yet figured out its fraudulence—and I passed it across the desk to where Strode was sitting, and he read it. . . .

And he climbed up on top of the sports desk.

It was an all-but-involuntary reaction on his part—he was so amazed, so stunned, that, wearing those Archie comic-book saddle shoes, he climbed first onto his chair and then onto the sports desk itself, and, with reporters and editors all over the city room turning their heads and peering up at him, he stood there on top of the desk, mouth open, and silently read the letter.

"Someone's building you a *statue?*" he called down to me, and I can still see his face, so young and so unguarded.

George would go on to be a not-so-young *C-J* sportswriter, and then he would move from the *C-J* to the Associated Press's Columbus sports operation, and from there he would move to the *Columbus Dispatch*, where eventually he would become the venerable, respected, oldest-man-in-the-department sports editor until his retirement. George: gray in his hair, lines around his eyes, the elder statesman of sports in Columbus.

I would never see his name without thinking of that summer day.

He was so new at all this, and I was even newer, and he all but leaped onto that desk.

"Someone's building you a *statue?*"

(I'm almost certain that John Stewart chimed in with the obligatory: "No *way!*")

George climbed back down from the desk, and we together looked at the letter, and I figured out who had written it.

"Someone's building you a *statue?*"

Anything seemed possible. We were little more than kids.

Whether I was working a two P.M. to eleven P.M. shift, or a four P.M. to one A.M. shift, there was a part of the day I liked the best, an hour during which I would wander for a few minutes over to the windows that overlooked downtown.

It was just after five o'clock, when the going-home commute would be at its peak. The workday for most people would be over—I'd look at Broad Street, and at Third Street, thick with departing automobiles. They were leaving for the night and we were still here—we were just getting started, really. The secret-club feeling of the city room, of the sports department, was kicking in in earnest.

Across the way, on High Street, was the Neil House hotel, where my father ate lunch with his friends almost every day. He would have lunch there even after his company had moved away from downtown, to its new plant on Alum Creek Drive; he would drive down here at lunchtime—downtown was where a businessman dined.

It never occurred to me to go to the Neil House for a meal—that world, the businessman's world, seemed so far from the newspaper world, though geographically they were only one long block from each other, separated by the Ohio Statehouse.

When, that summer, Kaye Kessler would be somewhere on the road covering a golf tournament, he would call in with his dictation early in the evening—he couldn't write his story until the last players were off the course. Many times I would be the one to take his dictation— he would read aloud, word by word, what he had written in the city where the golfers were playing, and I would cock my head to jam the phone receiver between my jaw and my shoulder, and I would take down every word, just as he read them to me.

Kessler would read to me quotes from the famous players—Billy Casper, Julius Boros—and even as I typed I would picture him sitting around a bar with them after their rounds, picking up their comments. I didn't yet know about press tents and mass press conferences; I still today, in fact, have no idea if, back then, all the sportswriters at a tournament got their quotes at the same time in the group press-tent setting, as is common now. If Kaye Kessler was quoting golfers for the *Citizen-Journal*, I assumed that he must be friends with them—that the golfers and the sportswriter were pals, hanging out. Maybe they were, that year—maybe the antiseptic comments-made-from-a-conference-table way of obtaining quotes from athletes had not yet commenced.

One thing I never once thought about as I took Kess's dictation— my neck starting to hurt as the phone pressed against one ear and I typed with both hands—was the possibility that this way of newspaper life would ever disappear.

How could you improve on this? A man—Kessler—sat down at a manual typewriter in a faraway city, and wrote his story on pieces of copy paper; then the man placed a long-distance telephone call to someone—me—back in his newspaper office. Slowly, one short burst of words at a time, the newspaperman on the road, pausing between phrases, spelling out proper names, saying "comma" each time a comma was supposed to appear, saying "period" at the end of every sentence, saying "new paragraph" when it was time for that, read his story aloud, while the other man at the other typewriter—me, not technically a man at all—took it all down.

(*"Hold, on, Kess, there's something wrong with this ribbon"; "One second, Kess, I have to put in a new sheet of paper."*)

The man in the newspaper office sent the story to the composing room, where a third man would do the keystrokes all over again, setting the words in hot lead type. . . .

I never thought about that way of newspapering as something that would soon be gone.

Laptop computers, when they arrived, would give the writer of a newspaper story on the road the ability to, essentially, set type; a reporter could go to his hotel room, craft his story, plug his computer into the phone, hit a button, and not have to hear another human voice. A much more efficient way of doing things.

Yet when I think of sitting on the mezzanine after the summer sun had dropped behind the downtown buildings, listening to Kaye Kessler over the miles, knowing he was counting on me to be the middleman between the words he was dictating from the road and the people in central Ohio who would read those words in the morning . . .

What it felt like was teamwork—what it felt like was being a member of a team of which you were proud.

The team surely didn't feel like one that would be dead by the time a new century rolled around.

We didn't think that far ahead, anyway—we couldn't, we were too busy thinking about the next edition. If we had looked around us, we might have understood that so much of what we were in the midst of would die before long—not just the *Citizen-Journal*, but Paoletti's, down the block (the people in their cars heading for the suburbs at five o'clock—they weren't going to be lingering downtown just to eat dinner at an old Italian family restaurant); and the Neil House; and Woolworth's; and the Deshler Hilton; and Mills Cafeteria; and the Lazarus department store. . . .

All of those places, like our newspaper, seemed that summer as if they would be there forever. They were part of the structure, the very constitution, of the city's life.

If we had looked around us, we might have sensed how fragile, how transitory, all of this was.

Or maybe not—maybe we wouldn't have sensed a thing.

We were busy.

"Hey, Greenie," Clarence Young—he had figured out, for a second time, that Brown was not my name—would call to me.

"Kess is on the phone. You want to take his story?"

"Sure," I'd say. I'd pick up an extension, tilt my head and trap the receiver next to my ear, say, "Kess—you there?"

"Oh, yeah," he would say, and he would start dictating—a few words at a time, carefully matching the pace of his voice to the speed of my fingers on the keys as he listened over the miles to the sound of my typewriter.

Outside the windows, downtown would be more deserted than when the sun had been out.

"Go ahead, I got it," I would say to Kessler, and he would keep reading his story to me, one burst of words after another, and why should either of us have thought that this would ever die? This was the way a newspaper sports page was born every night. How could it die?

I would save my stories. I'd go out and buy them.

It was a five-minute walk from my parents' house to Rogers' Drug-

store on Main Street in our community, and on mornings when I had a
sports roundup in the paper I would go over to Rogers', buy five or six
extra copies of the C-J, take them home, and store them on a closet
shelf in my bedroom. There were never all that many spare copies lying
around the newsroom by the time I'd arrive for my late-starting sports
shift, and at seven cents a shot, purchasing them at the drugstore was
something I could do for a couple of quarters, and get change back.

I did it because . . . well, because if I didn't, it would all go away.
There were no electronic databases; public libraries kept microfilmed
copies of the local newspapers, but you had to use a viewing machine
to read them, and the microfilms looked like photo negatives. It gave
you a headache to try to find a particular story as you slowly rolled the
film from spool to spool—and besides, it could take months for an edition of the C-J to make it on microfilm to the Columbus Metropolitan
Library.

So I purchased extra papers whenever they contained my words,
and one day at work I mentioned this to Kessler and Pastorius, and it
was like I was telling a joke or something—they looked at me with grins
on their faces, as if I had delivered a punchline.

"You buy 'em all?" Pastorius asked, incredulous.

"Yeah," I said.

"Why?" Kessler said.

"To save my stories," I said. "You don't save your stories?"

They each laughed.

"No," Pastorius said.

"Why save them?" Kessler said. "We're just going to write new ones
the next day."

I suppose I shouldn't have been surprised; I would seldom see the
C-J sportswriters even briefly scan their own stories in the paper the day
after they'd written them. I would stare at mine; I'd sit in the newsroom
on days when a story by me made it into the paper, and I would read
that story five or six times, thinking about how twenty-four hours before it hadn't existed, thinking about how I had decided in what order
the games in the national sports roundup should appear, and what
words to use to begin each account of each contest . . . I'd look at my

story in the paper the next day, and I couldn't take my eyes off it. The headline I had written on it, now in big black type on the broadsheet newspaper page in front of me: "RED SOX ROUT . . ."

Kess and Pasty and the others never stared at their work. I didn't even know, when they woke up in the morning at home and brought the C-J in to their breakfast tables, if they read their own stories. Maybe they didn't; maybe they figured they already knew what was in the stories, because they'd written them.

So it shouldn't have shocked me that they thought it was funny that I went out and bought extra copies of the paper to save. They'd been doing this for a long time. Maybe, to them it had become just a job.

That thought, though, seemed impossible.

And one day Kessler said to me:

"I used to do it, too."

"Do what?" I said.

"Buy extra papers to save," he told me. "When I was just starting out."

"When did you stop?" I asked him.

"I don't know," he said. "You just do. You'll see."

"Do you still have any of the papers you used to save?"

"I'm sure I do," he said. "In some box in the basement somewhere, or in some attic. I doubt that I ever threw them away."

It wasn't just a job. That was the whole reason for being here. Just a job? Never.

12

There were never any *Citizen-Journal* parties. The day at the paper was the party. The reporters didn't have to get together after work to enjoy each other's company—the unspoken thought seemed to be: Why gather outside of this place? We know we get to do it again right here tomorrow. Same cast of characters, same stage.

Kessler and Pastorius and Keys and Strode and Stewart and, sometimes, Clarence Young, began to invite me to eat dinner with them at Paoletti's (Clarence, a solitary soul behind those spectacles, chose most of the time to eat at his desk; he joined the others at the dinner hour only rarely). Those commuters hurrying away from downtown each evening may have been abandoning the old Italian restaurant on Third Street after the sun went down, but the owners of Paoletti's, optimism in their hearts, kept its doors open for whoever might choose to wander in. Who chose to wander in was us. Some nights we had the place to ourselves.

For me, the fine feeling of dining with the stars of the C-J sports page each night was almost beyond explicating, after a lifetime of eating dinner with my parents and my brother and sister. Sometimes, at our family dinner table during my growing-up years, my father and I would discuss something that had been on that day's sports page—a column by Keys, a game report by Kessler. So to be eating supper each night with the sports staff, at a downtown restaurant . . . Kess and Pasty may have been, in my mind, Sinatra and Dean Martin, but had Frank and Dean somehow come to Columbus and invited me to join them for a meal, I might very well, given the choice, have elected to eat dinner with Kessler and Pastorius instead.

"What are you going to have tonight, youngblood?" Thelma, the Paoletti's dinner-shift waitress, would invariably ask me, and I loved this, loved being "youngblood" to her (even as I sensed, underneath conscious thought, that George Strode must have been "youngblood" at this table not so many years ago, before I came along). Thelma had the same abandoned-anthracite-shaft grit in her voice that John Stewart did— she even looked a little like him, with her red hair and strong eyes she might have passed as his older sister—and all of this, the emptied-out downtown, the newspapermen at their customary table, the uniformed waitress with the dirty jokes she wasn't afraid to tell in cultivated company because, being from the local paper, we weren't assumed to be company all that cultivated . . . all of this made dinner in the middle of our sports-page shift something to look forward to all afternoon.

In my memory of those dinners, there was very little moaning about office politics, about who was or who wasn't getting ahead in the newsroom—very little of the hall-monitor-like sniping about colleagues, and backbiting about the world of journalism in general, that I would see in other newsrooms in later years. Or maybe I'm dead wrong— maybe it just seemed that way to a neophyte at the Paoletti's dinner table, sitting with those sportswriters, men who (there could be no faking this) genuinely liked each other, as those men swapped stories and maybe had a beer with their pot roast and peas and accepted into their midst the new guy who, at so many other dinners past, would have talked with his father about the words these very men had written. A guy who not long ago, in his copyboy incarnation, had stood at the counter at Paoletti's and placed sandwich and coffee orders for these men—and who now, contrary to all plausibility, was joining them for dinner every night.

They didn't look at their watches; no one was going to bawl them out if they were a few minutes late walking back to the paper, because as long as the sports pages got put together by the end of the night they were on their own about how they did it. "I'd bring you a martini, youngblood, but I think I'll refill your Coke instead," Thelma would say, and why should there ever have been any *Citizen-Journal* parties? This was the party, and I have a feeling that, if anyone at the C-J had ever announced to his fellow staff members (not that anyone at the C-J ever did): "I have been awarded a Nieman Fellowship" . . .

I have a feeling that if anyone had ever said that, the response from the others would have been, "Don't let the door hit you on the way out." Ambition and hopes for upward mobility aside, who would ever want to pack up and go study advanced journalism at Harvard, when you could be here, doing this, instead?

I invented a beat for myself, which was a necessity if a person who wanted to write about sports hoped to get regularly read—a necessity that, today, no longer exists for aspiring writers.

Analysts of our current media world have a phrase that sums up the change: "barriers to entry." It's an economics term, but the way it applies to newspapers, according to those who study such things (Andrew Cassel of the *Philadelphia Inquirer* chief among them), is this: There was a time when, in order to become published, you needed to know someone who owned a press. That was the barrier you needed to get past if you wanted entry to the cosmos of those writers who were reaching readers with their words. Today the barrier to enter that cosmos has been all but obliterated: You don't need a printing press at all, you just need a computer and the will to send your words off in search of an audience.

That sportswriter summer, the barrier was still firmly in place. And while I did not know anyone who literally owned a press, I knew someone who had daily access to one: Tom Keys. One night at Paoletti's I mentioned to him that his sports pages never covered local tennis tournaments.

"You really think people want to read about tennis?" Tom asked me.

Having no idea at all if it was true—in fact, I doubted it; Columbus was not exactly a hotbed of tennis enthusiasm—I said: "I know they do. People in this town are crazy about tennis."

He bought it. As the C-J's sports editor, he had a tight news hole and a limited staff, but he told me that if I wanted to go out and try to find some tennis stories, that would be all right with him.

Thus it was that, although I was only there for the summer, I became the *Citizen-Journal*'s tennis writer. The idea had been the product of a process of elimination on my part. The municipal-tennis-courts job of the past summer notwithstanding, I didn't really care about tennis one way or the other by this point in my life, although when I was younger I had liked the game so much that I fantasized about making a career of playing it. That was over, but I wanted to be in those sports pages on a regular basis—I *really* wanted to be in those sports pages on a regular basis—and so I checked off in my mind the summer sports that were already taken. The Jets, Tom covered himself. Major-league baseball, we took from the wire service. Big golf tournaments, Kessler was assigned to. Local golf and amateur baseball and softball went to John Stewart, who also intermittently covered harness races at Scioto Downs. High school football preview stories were George Strode's. Ohio State sports were split between Pastorius and Kessler.

No one had thought to do tennis. If there had been dogsled racing in central Ohio in July, I would have lobbied to be the dogsled correspondent. Anything to get in the paper.

The barrier to entry: if you wanted to write for the public, someone standing sentry at the barrier had to wave you through. Keys waved—he probably distractedly said yes to me while Thelma was fetching him a piece of pecan pie with vanilla ice cream—and I within days found a Junior Davis Cup training camp up at Ohio State. One of the players in attendance was Bobby McKinley, whose older brother Chuck had been Wimbledon singles champion in 1963. I located Bobby eating his lunch in a university residence hall cafeteria.

The lead paragraph may not have been much:

Bobby McKinley gulped at his milk to wash down the last
bite of a hot dog and laughed. "Sure, I'm just 'Chuck McKin-

*ley's kid brother' to a lot of people," he said. "But I'll beat
him one of these days—he's getting a little fat, you know."*

Not much, but it was sufficient—it got me past the barrier. It is impossible to overemphasize the importance of that in those newspaper
days: if you couldn't persuade someone with access to a press to print
your words, then you might as well sit in your room, type up your stories, and read them aloud to yourself. You had to be an entrepreneur of
sorts—you had to sell yourself to someone who was manning that barrier.

On the tennis beat I tended toward narrative leads that, often con-
fusingly, promised to take the reader to an eventual plotline payoff by
story's end (if, that is, Clarence Young, short on space and short on pa-
tience for ornamentation or flourishes, didn't decide in the composing
room to chop off the last few paragraphs):

> *Dave Snyder made a joke during the warmup session for
> Sunday afternoon's Central Ohio Tennis Doubles Tournament
> finals, but it wasn't until an hour and a half later that Jim
> Criswell and John Thomas discovered the punchline wasn't
> so funny.*

It could have been dogsledding. It could have been sumo wrestling.
What mattered to me was that it was getting me onto the sports pages
any time I could find a contest to cover.

And the reward for making it past the barrier was almost immediate.
We were sitting at dinner at Paoletti's one night—I'd by now had a few
of my tennis-beat bylines in the paper—and Thelma said to Kessler
and Pastorius:

"You better watch out. Youngblood's sneaking up on you. I see more
of his stories than yours."

"And I'm sure he's buying five copies of each of them," Pastorius
said.

It mattered. It truly did. Make it past the barrier, and maybe people
will read your words.

There were nights when the RKO Palace was three percent filled.

I saw the empty seats myself. The movie theater, with its decks of soaring balconies, its plush velvet seats, its ornate ceiling painted to mimic Michelangelo, was built to hold 3,500 filmgoers. But by the summer of 1967, the men and women who for decades had been counted on to buy tickets and settle into those seats had decided, as if by a silent vote, to stay away. They were in the suburbs, where newly constructed movie houses—including some with more than one screen—were more convenient. They were many of the same men and women who fled from downtown each dusk, leaving the center of the city to the likes of us on the C-J sports desk.

On my nights off from the paper I would sometimes take a date to the RKO Palace. When there are only a few dozen people in a single-screen theater intended to accommodate thousands . . . well, when you are one of the few dozen, craning your neck at the echoing void around you, certain questions begin to form in your mind.

I knew that my parents, in the years just after World War II, would regularly take in a movie at the Palace—theirs was a downtown of flashing neon lights, and crowds on the sidewalks deep into the evening, and lines to get into restaurants. I had seen photographs of my father and mother on a downtown night out, he in a business suit, she in a party dress. When you went to the RKO Palace, in the era of their young adulthood, you dressed appropriately. The assumption was that the whole town was going to be seeing you.

They would also go to the Maramor, the Stork Club–knockoff nightclub a few blocks east of the Palace on Broad Street. It was still there during my sports-page summer; headliners from out of town continued to be booked into the Maramor's showroom: George Shearing, Peter Nero, the just-pre-controversy Smothers Brothers. In the pages of the *Citizen-Journal*, Ron Pataky would critique the first-run movies at the RKO Palace, would attend opening nights at the Maramor and evaluate the singers and musicians and comedians. If you read the re-

views in the morning paper, you would think that Columbus was stylistically only a few steps removed from Broadway—the reviews made
it sound as if downtown at night was still the hub of the city's life.

But I would look around the yawning interior of the Palace—
seeing the underused ushers in their jackets with the braided epaulets,
observing that the balconies had been sealed off because they weren't
needed, noticing that where the theater's seats had commenced to fray
and tear, no one had spent the money to mend them. Downtown—as
I recall those nights now—was beginning to have something of a last-
gasp feel to it. The big movies continued to be booked exclusively into
the Palace for their inaugural weeks in Columbus, the theatrical
agents in New York continued to send their clients to the Maramor for
three or four days of belting out tunes or tickling the piano keys before
the dwindling crowds—it was as if downtown was operating mostly on
muscle memory, going through the brawny motions the way it always
had, when its brawn was present-tense.

Years later, when every single lively thing had fled to the outlying
suburbs and to the sprawling new shopping malls, civic drives would be
announced with the professed intention of bringing people back downtown. That sports-page summer there was no talk of bringing anyone
back downtown, because the thought had not yet fully sunk in that
downtown was being forsaken. It was right in front of everyone's eyes,
but they—we—chose not to see it. In the RKO Palace I would look at
the rows upon rows of empty seats, and I would think that perhaps the
movie was a dud—that's why no one was there. I wouldn't consider—
not yet—that perhaps the movie itself had nothing to do with it.

Our newspaper was a part of that downtown—as big a part of it as
were the Palace and the Maramor. The Night Green was no longer
on sale on the street corners of downtown in mid-evening; the nights
of Harold Schottenstein, my friend's father, driving down to Broad and
High just to pick up an early edition of the next day's paper were over.
Had it made any sense for the *Citizen-Journal* to hire hawkers to work
the downtown corners under the streetlamps, the paper's management
undoubtedly would have done it; we could have used the circulation.

But any nighttime hawkers, by then, would only have stood disconsolately. It would have been a waste. There was no one to sell to after dark. We worked away in our downtown office. From certain deserted intersections, you could see our lights blazing in the mezzanine windows.

The localness of what we did defined everything. It was a localness not confined to the geographic scope of our coverage—it went without saying that the *Citizen-Journal* wasn't about to send its reporters to Africa or France (or even to Kentucky or Indiana). The men and women in the city room arrived at work each day knowing that they weren't going to be assigned to anyplace from where they couldn't drive back to the office by deadline.

The localness extended beyond that, though, and infused the very feel of the place. One night the phone rang and I picked it up with the customary: "Sports!"

The person on the other end said:

"Now, that's no way to answer a telephone, is it?"

"Who's calling?" I asked.

"To whom am I speaking?" the caller said.

"This is Bob Greene," I said.

"Now, I've seen your name in the paper," the caller said. "It's Bob Greene Jr., isn't it?"

"Yes," I said. I thought I recognized the voice from somewhere.

"Now, I believe I know your mother and father," the caller said. "Are your parents Robert and Phyllis Greene, from Bexley?"

"Yes," I said.

"I know they didn't raise you to answer a phone that way," the caller said. "When you answer a business telephone, the proper way to do it is to tell the caller your name first."

"All right, sir," I said.

"I know your parents are fine people, and I'm sure they taught you good manners," the caller said. "You don't want to disappoint them by giving a bad impression of yourself on the telephone, do you?"

"No, sir," I said.

"Good," the caller said. "Now, this is Woody Hayes. I was calling to speak with Tom Pastorius. Is Tom there, please?"

And, my hands shaking, I connected him with Pasty.

I knew it really was Coach Hayes because of that phrase early in his lecture to me—"To whom am I speaking?" His grammar was always scrupulous—no "Who am I speaking to?" from Woody Hayes.

The localness was all around us. Woody had met my mother and father on a few occasions, he remembered them, and he was setting their son straight. He may have been the most nationally famous person in the community, but he was first and foremost a member of that community—during all his years as head football coach at Ohio State, Woody kept his home telephone number listed in the Columbus phone book: W. W. Hayes, on Cardiff Road. That made for a lot of late-night crank calls from a lot of insulting or drunken people, but he thought that if he was going to represent the community, then he should be as available as any other man or woman in town.

Once, years later, I heard a story—I'm almost certain that it was Kessler who told it. It seemed that early in Jack Nicklaus's golf career, Nicklaus's father, Charlie, a Columbus pharmacist, was following him on tour, and Woody Hayes offered to travel with Charlie Nicklaus to keep him company and provide moral support. Apparently at one tournament someone in the gallery kept referring to Nicklaus as "fat Jack"— no "burly" for this golf fan. And, the way I remember the story, either Woody Hayes had to physically restrain Charlie Nicklaus from going after the fan, or Charlie Nicklaus had to restrain Woody. (I have a feeling I know which one was which.)

It was all part of the localness. Woody Hayes and Charlie Nicklaus were two Columbus residents on the road to cheer for a local golfer; the fact that the local golfer would become the greatest ever to play the game was incidental. And we—in the eyes of our readers, and in our own eyes, too—were, proudly, the local paper. That was all, and everything, we aspired to be. Just like the proud local papers in a thousand other American towns. "I know they didn't raise you to answer a phone that way," Woody said. He thought, by saying it, he was doing me a favor. He was.

The non-local aspects of the C-J—the parts of the paper that undertook to be resolutely national—were a bit of a store-bought hodgepodge, almost an afterthought.

There was the syndicated columnists' page—the first page of the second section. We didn't have a Walter Lippmann–level pantheon of distinguished Washington voices—ours were mostly Scripps-Howard lifers whose work the C-J got for free, or close to it—and the columnists ran stacked on top of each other in two vertical rows on either side of that section front. So you'd have Inez Robb, musing on politics and national affairs, on top of Norton Mockridge, doing his best to deliver the Broadway scoops that the much more famous Earl Wilson (whom the *Dispatch* printed) might have deemed not worthy of his attention. Those national commentators were trimmed mercilessly to fit the little boxes to which they were allotted—however long their columns may have been when they arrived via wire in the C-J newsroom, they were chopped like butcher-shop rump roast and jammed into the snug holes laid out for them. It probably wasn't the syndicated columnists' fault that what appeared under their names in Columbus was occasionally close to indecipherable; a leg or an arm had invariably been whacked off the body of what they had written, and sometimes, it seemed, the head had been whacked off, too.

So local were we, in the strictest definition of the word, that the C-J's staff reporters usually didn't even get to cover state politics, although the Statehouse was directly across Third Street—we could look right at its white cupola (which it featured instead of a dome) from the windows of the sports department. What went on in the Statehouse was covered by the grandly named Scripps-Howard Ohio Bureau, which consisted of a small coterie of longtime political writers who worked out of a separate building from us, and who also serviced (that was actually the word that was used) Scripps-Howard papers in Cleveland and Cincinnati. I never even knew where their office was—I think they rented space on Broad Street, so as not to sully themselves by being associated too closely with us—and occasionally one or another of them (they tended to be stuffy-acting men who smoked pipes) would deign to come into our city room, and when they did they looked as if they were encountering an unpleasant odor. Ohio government and politics was the biggest continuing story in the state, and even though the governor and the legislators worked within eyeshot of us, the unspoken message was that we at the *C-J* were not fit to cover them. We should stick to city council meetings and police stories.

The *Citizen-Journal* printed a State Edition; it came off the presses early, and all that the phrase—State Edition—really meant was that those early-run papers were going to be tossed into trucks and driven to Bucyrus and Newark and Millersport and Circleville, in the hopes that someone in those smaller towns might want to plunk down some change to see what the morning newspaper from the state capital had to say.

There was no dedicated reporting staff assigned to state news; other than the State Edition designation, it was pretty much the same *C-J* that people in Columbus were seeing, except that it almost always had splashier headline display, to attract hoped-for street sales in the outlying counties. How else were you going to deliver your news to faraway villages and hamlets but to print it early and put it in a truck? The Internet was decades off in the future, and a pedal-to-the-floor truckdriver was the preferred method to get the stories that had been written by the *Citizen-Journal*'s reporters to their more remote audiences.

There was the daily horoscope, and the crossword puzzle and the comics page—that was non-local. In sports, we ran no nationally syndicated columnists—no room. There was, however, one nationally generated feature that ran on the front page of the *Citizen-Journal* every single day. Called "Today's Chuckle," it was just that—a one-sentence joke, mainstream as could be so that it was guaranteed not to go over the head of even one reader. It wasn't produced in our newsroom—we certainly didn't have the budget for a gag writer, even part-time—so my assumption is that the little jokes were provided by one of Scripps-Howard's feature-syndication subsidiaries, probably the Newspaper Enterprise Association. But there was, in fact, one thing that was local as local could be about "Today's Chuckle," something that few readers may have noticed: the little standing logo that ran on top of it.

The logo had been drawn, in some year past, by Al Getchell—I knew his script style, I knew the look of his pen. It was just those two words—"Today's Chuckle"—and the joke beneath it may have been shipped in from New York, but the person who had drawn for daily publication the two words in the logo was Al, a man who seldom smiled, who seemed always to have a sour stomach, who, in the entire time I knew him, never came close to emitting anything that in the least bit approximated a chuckle. Yet, each day without fail, on the front page, were those happy, joshing words: "Today's Chuckle." Drawn by a man who wouldn't laugh if you had held him down, taken off his socks, and rubbed feathers across the bottoms of his feet.

We, the writers in that room, didn't aim to be national. We were waiters delivering local news and local sports, and national wasn't our table.

And yet . . .

A foot or two south of our six pushed-together sports desks—next to Tom Pastorius's right shoulder—sat the *New York Times* News Service wire machine.

I don't know why it was there, abutting the sports department; maybe that was the only place where there was room for it. The *Citizen-Journal* was a subscriber to the *New York Times* News Service, and one of the things this meant was that a special teletype machine, which carried only stories from the *New York Times*, had been installed.

Throughout each afternoon and into the evening, the machine would type out the same stories that would be appearing in the next morning's *New York Times*. Because the machine was so close to the sports department, I would sneak a look. Stories from Washington, stories from London, stories from Warsaw, stories from Rome . . . I would finish writing one of my tennis-beat stories:

> *Tall, tanned, quiet Mark Conti took all the cannonballs powerful Chick Hawley could fire at him Monday and answered them with the sharp, sure-fire accuracy of a machine gun to win the Ohio State Men's Singles Tennis Championship 6–4, 6–3.*

And then I would step behind Pasty's chair and go over to the *New York Times* machine to see how the real pros were covering the world beyond our town.

One of the features the *New York Times* News Service provided to its client papers was, early each evening, a description of what the *Times's* front page was going to look like in the morning. This was before graphics were easily transmitted from one newspaper to another—there was no photo or drawing of the *New York Times* front page. It was done with written words: an editor in New York would describe what the various Page One stories were about, which ones would receive the most prominent display, which front-page stories would be above the fold, and which would be below. . . .

The assumption was that newspaper editors around the country would read which news events the editors of the *New York Times* considered to be the most salient of the day, and would model their own front pages after that of the *Times*—that if the editors of the *New York Times* decreed that, say, a story about a mutual-arms-reduction meeting in Paris would lead the front page of the *Times*, then editors all across America, being given that advance notice, would consider putting that story on their own front pages, too.

Standing next to the sports desks, looking at the *New York Times* News Service wire machine, I was sometimes tempted to send the editors of their news service a message back—to tell them what was going to be on the front page of the *Citizen-Journal* the next morning. "Well, we had a robbery at the Big Bear supermarket, and that's definitely going to be on Page One of the *C-J.* Governor Rhodes cut the ribbon to open the Franklin County Fair, and Hank Reichard took a picture of it that we're going to run above the fold on the front page, with a story inside. Today's Chuckle is about a cat who found a dog trying to eat its cat food. . . ."

I never did any such thing, of course—I never sent the editors of the *New York Times* an advance description of our front page. But, standing at their machine, I wondered what would happen if I did. If I said to them: Since you're nice enough to tell us what you're putting on your front page, here's what we're putting on ours. Would they laugh— would they think it was funny? Would they wire me back a message? Would they just throw my note out?

We were local, first, last, and always—but I guess we could dream, if only in silence, of what lay out there beyond Third Street. Years later, I was on tour with the Alice Cooper rock band during the time they were the number one concert act in the United States, when their albums were topping the charts. Their bass player, a pleasant and soft-spoken young man named Dennis Dunaway, told me that when they were younger and living in Arizona, and their first record had been released—a record that ended up doing nothing at all in sales—they were so excited to have an album in stores that they thought the most important and famous musicians in the world were all rushing out to buy it and take it home to play on their turntables.

"The day that record came out, we thought the Beatles were listening to it," he said. "We were so young."

It was an understandable hope. I would write another tennis story:

Red-haired, red-faced John Thomas, who never stops smiling, and pretty, 20-year-old Marmee Fry, who never cracks a grin until she's won her match, combined Sunday to breeze to the second annual Prudy Gray Memorial mixed doubles tennis championship at the Swim and Racquet Club.

And, secretly, I'd think of someone in Times Square in New York strolling up to an out-of-town newsstand, browsing through all the papers, picking up a copy of the *Columbus Citizen-Journal*, thinking it looked interesting, and buying it. I'd picture in my mind the person taking the paper back to his or her office, and approving of the way I put my words together. Or a person in Washington, at an out-of-town newsstand near the White House, seeing a *C-J* there, carrying it down Pennsylvania Avenue. In my imaginings, the people picking up the *C-J* by sheer chance were influential figures in the news business— Chet Huntley, David Brinkley. I'd write those sports stories in Columbus, and wonder just how far the bottle cast into the water—the bottle containing my words, the bottle that was the morning paper—might float before someone, somewhere far away, would see it and reach down to retrieve it and read what was inside.

We were local—as local as the Broad Street bus. We weren't supposed to think things like that.

And because thinking things like that was not something you talked about out loud, I still don't know if I was the only one who did. My guess is that I had company.

Management, what there was of it, was largely invisible. Don E. Weaver, when he was editor of the paper, had spent much of his time in his private office near Miss Allison's protective desk, and Charles Egger, as Mr. Weaver's successor, mostly did the same. It wasn't that the editorship of the *Citizen-Journal* was an intrinsically standoffish position—the newsroom floor was small enough that we saw Mr. Egger every day, just as we had seen Mr. Weaver before him. But they didn't hang out on the floor with us.

Our ultimate management, the Scripps-Howard corporation, the owner of the paper, had its headquarters in another city. I always did like that lighthouse logo of theirs, the line drawing that ran next to the nameplate of every Scripps-Howard paper; I always thought that the "Give Light and the People Will Find Their Own Way" slogan was sparely and elegantly inspiring, just the right words to define a newspaper's rightful mission. We never saw the out-of-town Scripps-Howard executives, and we understood that even if we had seen them, they really didn't run things in the building where we worked. The *Dispatch* did. The *Citizen-Journal*, and, by extension, Scripps-Howard itself, were just tenants, journalistic sharecroppers on the *Dispatch*'s land.

There was one manager, though, who we saw every day and every night. Jack Keller, the managing editor of the *C-J*, was out in the city room with the rest of us. He had no office, only a newsroom desk.

The assumption among some of the staff had been that when Don Weaver retired, Jack Keller would be given the editor's job and the editor's office. He knew the workings of the *C-J* like no one else. He made the place run.

But he didn't get the promotion. Scripps-Howard brought Mr. Egger in from another city for the top job, and Jack Keller remained out in the city room, reporting to a new man. He was tall and rangy with slicked-back hair and a stolid expression that somehow spoke of sadness; he had a deep, resounding voice—it was he who would call over toward the sports desk late at night: "Clarence—twenty minutes until we lock the pages up"—and the look on his long and narrow face was that of a self-conscious man who you sensed didn't like to have his picture taken.

I had heard something about him, something that was a rumor in the city room. The rumor went like this: Jack Keller, as a young man, was a world-class track athlete who, in a long-ago Olympics, tripped on a hurdle and lost his chance for a medal. No one at work ever mentioned it to him, and I could find no clips about it back in the *C-J* library. But in the newsroom it was said that he had been very close to achieving the goal that would have meant everything to him—very close to winning a medal in the Olympics—and he had stumbled.

Years later—when, because of the Internet, it became easier to look into such things—I did.

I found nothing specific about Jack Keller tripping. But what I did find was, in a way, even worse—especially for a man who would go on to have his presumptive editorship of the paper he loved snatched away from him and given to someone else.

In 1932, the Olympic Games were held in Los Angeles. According to the historical accounts I read, because the United States was in the midst of the Depression the grandeur of the Olympics was especially welcome. Among the Hollywood stars who were in attendance were Will Rogers, Gary Cooper, Clark Gable, Mary Pickford and Douglas Fairbanks.

The world-record holder in the 110-meter hurdles, going into the Olympic Games, was Jack Keller of Columbus East High School and the Ohio State University. In the Olympic hurdles final race, Keller finished third, and was awarded a bronze medal.

Whether or not he stumbled as he leapt over a hurdle, I do not know. But even though he had not finished the race as champion, he had won the one thing every athlete dreams of—he had won his Olympic medal. The ceremony was held, the medal was placed over his neck, and he had it.

The 1932 Olympics was the first in which the technology for photo-finish results was approved for use in the races. The device utilized for this, according to the historical records, was known as the Kirby Two-Eyed Camera.

After the 110-meter hurdles competition was completed—after Jack Keller had been presented with his medal—officials of the Olympics developed the film from the Kirby Two-Eyed Camera, and decided that another athlete—Donald Finlay, of Great Britain—had finished just the slightest bit ahead of Keller. The judges on the scene at the race had ruled that Keller had come in third—but the camera, which had never been used in an Olympics before, seemed to say that Finlay had crossed the line ahead of him.

And here is what Jack Keller, in Los Angeles, was directed to do:

He was told that, in the interest of sportsmanship, he should go to the Olympic Village, find Donald Finlay, and give to Finlay his medal.

Which he did. Jack Keller took from around his neck the medal he had worked all his life to win, and he walked up to Finlay and he gave it to him. Because it was a bronze medal, and because there are no medals for fourth-place finishes, that left Keller with nothing. After handing his medal to Finlay he returned to Ohio and went on with the rest of his life.

He'd won. That's what he had thought; that's what he had been told. And then it had been taken from him.

Now, thirty-five years later, he worked with the rest of us out in the city room, the editor's office having been denied him although everyone had assumed he would receive the promotion. He was a hard man to warm up to; he didn't show much of himself to anyone. "Clarence," he would call over to Clarence Young on our sports desk, even though Clarence didn't need reminding, and we would know that deadline was upon us.

13

In that American summer the air was no longer quite so saturated with the sounds of Beatles singles. Just a few years earlier it had seemed that a new Beatles record was being released every three or four weeks. But by 1967, as I drove downtown each afternoon for my sports-desk shift, hoping even before I got to Third Street that there would be an empty parking space in the alley next to the presses, mostly other voices came out of the dashboard radio.

It wasn't that the Beatles had disappeared entirely. By late July their one summer release, "All You Need Is Love," had gone to number one on the WCOL Hitline survey in town. But maybe they were getting tired, or too wealthy, or both; they evidently didn't feel the same urgency about constantly making music.

So from the car radio, as I headed for the city room, Every Mother's Son sang "Come On Down to My Boat," and Stevie Wonder sang "I Was Made to Love Her," and the Monkees sang "Pleasant Valley Sunday," and I would go from this—from fresh sounds drifting down from the summer sky—to the loud room where under fluorescent lights I would sit at an old Royal typewriter.

If the Beatles were increasingly AWOL from the radio, they were mostly gone from Ed Sullivan's television show, too. He was still, by the way, Ed Sullivan of the New York *Daily News*—to the rest of the country he might have been defined by his Sunday evening CBS-TV show, but the reason he had been given the show in the first place was that he was an items columnist for the *Daily News*. That was still his day job, and in his head, or so it was said, that was still who he was: Ed Sullivan of the *Daily News*, a working newspaperman who happened to have a freelance TV job on the weekends.

His attitude about that—the reflexive confliction over the relative importance of his two roles, even as his mind must have told him one thing while his heart told him another—emblemized a world of mass communications that was not only on the tip of transformative change, but a world in which the change, in many ways, had already come to pass. Young people had grown up accustomed to having their entertainment and news delivered instantly to them out of the ether—the Beatles on Mr. Sullivan's Sunday show, the news of the day from their car radios or from their parents' television sets. Yet even as the change had immutably taken over, there was a reluctance to let go of the old ways—and, just as salient, to let go of an ingrained belief in the endurance of the old ways. Ed Sullivan continued that summer to tap out the column for the *Daily News*, because a newspaperman is what he was, and I drove each day toward the alley next to the printing presses, with "A Girl Like You" by the Young Rascals and "Fakin' It" by Simon & Garfunkel as my companions inside the car.

Their voices were conveyed so cleanly, seemingly effusing from nowhere, and then I would be inside the newspaper building and up on the mezzanine, wearing a shirt and tie and business slacks like we all did, working inside walls that contained the lingering smell of decades and decades of barrels and barrels of industrial-grade ink. Whatever I wrote that day would by midnight be set into type by the Linotype operators, the words in the story taking form one letter, one metallic click, at a time. There was something about what the Linotype men did—the very act of it, the physical fact of them sitting there at their machines and looking at the reporters' stories and converting, by hand and gears and heat, the reporters' words into something metal . . .

There was something about it that made our work seem that it had value. From the perspective of today's technologically sophisticated new era of computer-generated handless typesetting, what the Lino-type operators did may have been economically inefficient. Yet there was something about it—if these men were being paid to turn our words into newspaper type, if their lives and their livelihoods and the support of their families depended on their mastery of this craft, then what we were doing had to be worth something. Didn't it? The Tremeloes sang "Silence Is Golden" out of a million car radios that summer, and Ed Sullivan thumped out his column in New York, and on Third Street in Columbus the clicking in the composing room never stopped, which made it seem that it never would.

"Hey, Tom, were you going to be writing a column tonight?"

Keys looked over at me. "I was planning to," he said. "Why?"

"Oh, just because I wrote one this afternoon, and if it's not in the paper tomorrow, it's sort of outdated," I said.

A *how-did-I-let-myself-get-into-this-mess* smile appeared on Keys's face.

"So you'd like me to hold my column so we can run yours," he said.

I just looked back at him. I didn't even need to shrug.

I had talked him into letting me write a semi-regular tennis column—different from my stories about specific tournaments, more of a notes-and-comments column. A place where I could put bits and pieces of tennis news that didn't, on their own, warrant entire articles.

He probably should have said no to my original request to be al-lowed to write the column. I was summer help—that was all. I'd be back in school by the time the leaves fell. Just what was I doing, asking to be given a column?

But he'd said yes. I think it was because he may have looked at me and remembered what it had been like for him when all of this was new—when wanting to write for a newspaper every day was a hunger that had overwhelmed him, when every morning that the paper came out without him in it was an empty morning.

As the sports editor and sports columnist, he saw new classes of teenage football and basketball stars joining the varsity teams at Ohio

State every year. I'd noticed that he—and Kessler, and Pastorius—seemed to interview the Ohio State coaches much more often than they interviewed the players. Maybe it was because, once you've seen fifteen or twenty classes of nineteen-year-old quarterbacks and forwards take to the gridiron or the basketball court, you begin to feel that you have very little in common with them. You're getting one year older, every season, yet they remain nineteen. Maybe it's easier to talk with the coaches, who are growing older each year just like you.

And maybe, when the new kid standing in front of you is not someone on an athletic field, but someone who works for you—maybe when the new kid shows up every day in your sports department—you allow yourself to feel not like the covered-too-many-games-to-count-them-all-up sports editor. Maybe, when the new kid is asking for your help, you give it to him, because it makes you feel something good and welcome. It makes you recall the days when you were him.

Whatever the reason, Tom Keys had said yes—he had said that if it didn't interfere with my other work, I could from time to time put together a column called "Tennis Volleys."

But space in the *Citizen-Journal*'s sports pages was sufficiently tight that only one column per day of any kind could run. There were too many game reports that had to be in the paper; there was not room for two sports columnists in any day's edition.

So: "Were you going to be writing a column tonight?" I asked him.

Which really meant: Would you mind delaying your column for a day so we can run my tennis column?

He was such a good guy; I wasn't so much worried that he would yell at me as that he would laugh out loud.

"I suppose mine can wait a day," he said. He'd only seen about ten thousand of his columns in newspapers over the years.

"Thanks," I said. "Mine just can't hold."

(I still have a copy in an old scrapbook. The subject of the column wasn't exactly something that absolutely had to appear the next morning: *The United States may be knocked out of Davis Cup competition, but here in Columbus team tennis action is still hot. Eight 10-man aggregations from local courts are entering into the final rounds of play in a league spon-*

sored by the Greater Columbus Tennis Association, and the crown is still up
for grabs. . . .)

I think Tom knew that being in the paper the next morning meant
more to me than it did to him. We were at that stage in our respective
lives.

"Sure," he said. "Go ahead and run yours."

I was going to be in the next day's newspaper. This day had been
worth living.

"Clarence," I said to Clarence Young, who was drawing up the page
layouts, "I'm going to have a tennis column tomorrow instead of the
one Tom was going to . . ."

"I heard every word," Clarence said, not looking up.

And then, to Keys, Clarence said:

"So I should sub Greenie's column in for yours?"

"Might as well," Keys said to him.

"You don't mind that I check with the boss, do you?" Clarence said
to me, trying not to laugh himself. "I mean, when you tell me that
you're going to run in the sports editor's space, you don't mind if I ask
the sports editor?"

"No, I don't mind," I said.

"That's nice of you," Clarence said. "Thank you."

It was worth it. It was worth hearing the little jab.

When the presses rolled, my words would be on them.

Was it deserving of all that—was what I was in love with deserving of
that kind of emotional investment?

I think the answer is: Yeah. It was.

Many nights when I had written and the shift had ended, I would
take home my dupes—the carbon copies of my stories.

Before I went to sleep, I would give that evening's effort one more
read:

> *Jake Schlosser's words came back to haunt him Sunday*
> *afternoon in the form of a shaggy-haired, wiry whirlwind*

from Worthington. The result was the 1967 Central Ohio Men's Singles Tennis Championship for Mike Jeffries, captured in a fiercely fought fracas, 9–7, 4–6, 6–3.

The payoff would come in the morning, when I would read the dupes again one final time—but in the morning I would read them against the newspaper itself, I would look at those carbons and at the same time look at the sports page of the C-J, and the words would match, every word would be the same; those Linotype operators and composing room makeup men and press foremen and loading-dock guys and truckdrivers and paperboys had taken my words from the night before, and had gotten them to my family's home, and I would place the dupes next to my story in the newspaper and read the words, and I would think: This is unbelievable.

And it was. It defied belief. How did this happen?

The knock—the centuries-old joke about newspapers—was that it was all fishwrap, that yesterday's news was good only for lining birdcages. We didn't have a bird at home, so I never saw a C-J at the bottom of a parakeet's cage, but I saw the paper in trash cans all the time—in my family's house, on city streets next to bus stops, just about everywhere garbage was collected. It was a common sight: our yesterday's effort, today's trash.

And that didn't matter—it didn't matter at all.

Because the other side of the newspaper knock, the antidote to the old newspaper joke, was that yesterday's news might be forgotten by our readers, but we who had written it had discarded it already, too—or, if not truly discarded it, we had filed it away in our memories and moved on to the next edition. We got to start over—our subscribers might be throwing our work away, yes, but even as they were, we were telling ourselves: Well, yesterday's done, better do it again.

Unbelievable, all right. I would read my dupes, before turning out the light in the room where I'd slept since I was a boy, with my parents in their own room right down the hallway, and I wouldn't have believed any of this, except for the fact that proof would be arriving as the sun came up. I would hurry downstairs with the dupes in my hand, and read them against the newly delivered *C-J*, and nothing seemed beyond believing, because it was right in front of my eyes.

The localness in which the men and women of the *Citizen-Journal* took such pride masked a certain ambivalence toward the world of big-time journalism outside of central Ohio, or so it seemed during passing uncomfortable moments when the two worlds clashed.

One of the eighteen-year-olds whom Keys and Kessler and Pastorius and the other sportswriters got to know when he enrolled at Ohio State was Jerry Lucas, the immensely talented basketball center who, during his sophomore year, led his team to the NCAA championship. Lucas arrived toward the end of the college basketball era in which going to the NBA after graduation (graduation itself was assumed) was not every player's automatic goal; there was seen to be something pure about a college player taking the position that professional sports were beneath him. This was the same era in which dunk shots in college basketball were illegal (the rule prohibited the player touching the rim); if a tall man like Lucas stuffed the ball into the hoop, the basket did not count. There was a vestigial remnant of Victorian prissiness presumed both in the rules of the game, and in the personal aspirations of the young men who played it.

Jerry Lucas made it clear, in numerous interviews with Columbus sportswriters over the years, that when he graduated from Ohio State he intended to become a businessman, not a basketball player. The writers regularly reminded the hometown readers that Lucas had vowed not to become a "play-for-pay boy." The very phrase synopsized the supposition that there was something akin to prostitution in a bright, university-educated player going to the pros instead of venturing out into the world of suit-and-tie commerce.

Lucas was a steady and settled presence in town even as a college student; he was a married man while he played at Ohio State, and one longtime local sportswriter—Dick Otte of the *Dispatch*—was so friendly with Lucas that, it was said, Otte and his wife regularly played bridge with Lucas and his wife at Lucas's apartment. (If, today, the thought of a college All-American athlete and his wife getting together for regular evening games of bridge with an older newspaper sportswriter and his wife sounds like something out of outlandish fiction . . . well, both couples, the Lucases and the Ottes, probably watched *My Three Sons,* too. The cultural stimuli in the land were somewhat different then.)

Lucas may have played bridge with the Ottes, but a basketball play-for-pay boy he would never be. That's what he told Otte, that's what he told Keys, that's what he told Kessler, that's what he told Pastorius—not just once, but many times.

So, when Jerry Lucas decided to turn pro, and when he made his announcement not in the pages of the *Columbus Citizen-Journal* or the *Columbus Dispatch,* but instead in an exclusive story in *Sports Illustrated* . . .

This was confounding to the men on the *C-J* sports desk, but more than that, it was something they saw as verging on treacherous. Yes, *Sports Illustrated* was the most powerful sports chronicle in the United States; yes, *Sports Illustrated* was the categorical authority on all things athletic. But for Jerry Lucas to give his story to *Sports Illustrated,* and not to one of his Columbus sportswriter friends—for Lucas not only to become a play-for-pay boy, but to tell the world about it in the pages of *SI* . . .

When he did that it confirmed a thought—a truth—that mostly went unuttered on the sports desk. That thought—that axiom—was: We have our perimeters here. What we do is fun and it's fulfilling, but our influence doesn't necessarily extend much farther than the county line. A person like Jerry Lucas will move on, will move past us—and when he does, and he wants the world to know about it, we are no longer the ears he will turn to when he tells his story. Nothing against us. Nothing personal. The bridge games with the Ottes may have been harmonious, but when it was time for Lucas to leave Columbus he confided in a writer from *Sports Illustrated.* The bang, Lucas knew, would be bigger.

Sports Illustrated, as a matter of fact, had a network of local stringers around the country—people in towns where the magazine did not have full-time staff assigned. The stringers—often they were local sportswriters in the towns, stringing for *SI* part-time—were supposed to keep the *Sports Illustrated* news desk in New York informed of developments in their smaller towns. The stringers were listed, in agate type, on the masthead of each week's *SI*; the stringers were listed by city and were referred to as "correspondents," and to readers of the magazine—especially young readers of the magazine—it was a pretty impressive sight, to see the name of a writer in their town as a *Sports Illustrated* "correspondent."

The Columbus, Ohio (the "Ohio" was part of the listing in *SI*), correspondent was Kaye Kessler, and as a boy I guess I had imagined Kess as being an integral part of the *Sports Illustrated* team. But once I met him, and joined him on the *Citizen-Journal* sports desk, I saw what the part-time job really meant. Mostly it consisted of sending background material and statistics to New York for the *Sports Illustrated* writers to scan as they prepared to write stories that included references to Ohio State—sort of research work, from the middle of the country. And then there were times when a teletype message would arrive addressed to Kessler from *Sports Illustrated*'s offices in the Time-Life Building in Manhattan. One of the magazine's famous writers—Dan Jenkins, perhaps—would be coming to Columbus to write a story about Ohio State football. Would Kessler please call the best local hotel and make a reservation for Mr. Jenkins?

Kess once told me that he got five dollars for doing that—for picking up the phone and calling the Sheraton-Columbus on behalf of *Sports Illustrated*. He didn't seem to mind. When the magazine broke the news that Jerry Lucas would turn professional, Kessler was as much in the dark about it as anyone else—he hadn't been told that the story was coming. That was a matter between Lucas and *SI*'s editors in New York. We liked our localness, most of the time. But there were moments, or so I sensed, when it stung a little.

Those moments were mitigated, though, on nights like one Friday at Franklin Park, where I'd driven to cover a doubles tournament on deadline.

Nothing could be more local than matches like these: there was practically no crowd present, the only way anyone in the city would even be aware the tournament was taking place was by reading the *C-J* coverage. The *Dispatch* wasn't reporting on tennis that summer—Tom Keys may have bit at my questionable assertion that Columbus was a tennis-crazy town, but whoever was running the *Dispatch*'s sports department evidently understood that no great public clamor would arise if his paper ignored tennis. The television and radio stations weren't expending even a second of airtime on local tennis.

So I was it—if I showed up to write about a tournament, the city (or at any rate the portion of the city that read the *C-J*) would know, and if I didn't, the city would have no idea. On that particular night I looked up at the lights that surrounded the public courts—they were tennis court lights that you switched on using a metal box attached to one of the wooden lightpoles, it was done on the honor system: you turned them on when you wanted to play, and turned them off when you went home. I looked up toward the lights, seeing swarms of bugs flying near the banks of electrified bulbs, and I thought: these matches aren't over yet, but whoever wins them will get their names in the paper tomorrow morning, and their pictures (the *C-J* had sent a photographer), and people all over town will be reading about it. It's late at night right now, and I don't know who will win the matches being played on all the courts, but the paper is trusting someone—me—to get back downtown on time, and write all of this up before the presses roll, they're trusting me to get it all right and make our deadline. It's local through and through—and my paper is counting on the story getting written.

What an exceptional feeling. What I recollect about the next morning is my father, on a summer Saturday at the breakfast table, reading the sports section and smiling as he looked at the lead on my story. He'd been asleep in his bed while, downtown in the *Citizen-Journal* newsroom, I had written it, but here it was, under the byline I never tired of seeing because of the second line of it, the little descriptive line under my name:

By Bob Greene Jr.
Citizen-Journal Sports Writer

What Bob Greene Sr. was smiling at was the way I had played around with the words in the first paragraph. I was doing that a lot, as the summer wore on: trying to fool with the cadence of the words, to make them sound special. I had gotten used to seeing my words in the morning paper; now I wanted to try to make them dance a little.

That Saturday morning the lead was:

> *Twenty talented tennis twosomes try to topple each other today as three divisions of the Central Ohio Doubles Championships turn to Franklin Park, amid the thunder of nearby locomotives and shouts of softball players, for the meet's quarter and semifinal rounds.*

"That's onomatopoeia you're doing there, right?" my dad said.

He may have meant alliteration; if he was referring to the "twenty talented tennis twosomes" line, that's probably what he intended to say. Or maybe not; maybe he thought that the thunder of locomotives or shouts of softball players qualified as onomatopoeia, which, technically, they didn't. What mattered to me was that he was reading it, and that he was noticing what I was trying to do.

It may not have been *Sports Illustrated*. It may not have been read all over the country.

But my dad was carefully taking in the words that I had typed while he had slumbered. "I had to write it fast," I told him. "I didn't really think about what I was writing."

Sure. Right.

There were advantages to the tacit truth that no one but us was in charge of ourselves on the sports desk.

One evening we were short-staffed—Keys was out at Jet Stadium covering the ballgame, Stewart and Strode both had the night off, Kessler had worked early and was about to go home—and Pastorius said to us:

"You know, my wife's really feeling bad. It's our wedding anniversary, and she's sitting home alone."

Kessler said, "Why don't you take her to dinner?"

"Can't," Pastorius said. "I've got to do the baseball roundup tonight, and I've got to take the Scioto Downs dictation when it comes in."

"Go home," Kessler said. "Greenie will do the baseball for you—won't you, Greenie?"

Kessler flashed me a look that indicated his question really wasn't a question—his eyes said to me: You're going to do the major-league roundup so Pasty can be with his wife. Not that I needed any persuading—I relished writing stories for the paper as often as I could.

"I'll be glad to do it," I said.

"And I'll stay down until the race results from Scioto come in," Kessler said.

"You don't have to do that, Kess," Pastorius said to him. "You're done for the day."

"I don't have anything planned for tonight anyway," Kessler said. "I'll just stick around here. Now get out of here."

And Pastorius said that he would. I still remember the color of his sport coat—it was light blue. He stood up, took the coat from where he had draped it over the back of his chair, put it on, and said to us—to Kessler, to me, to Clarence Young, who was drawing the page layouts:

"Thanks."

It's one of the moments I recall most fondly about that summer—just the sound in his voice as he said that one short word. We were a team, and no one hovered over us, and we made our own rules. The *Citizen-Journal* didn't give its employees the day off on their wedding anniversaries, but no one in management had to know about this. It wasn't their decision. It was ours.

"Thanks," Pastorius said to us, and walked out the door to take his wife to dinner, and Kess and Clarence and I looked at each other and we didn't have to say a thing. No matter what else might happen during the evening, this was already a good night at work.

Not that, on other nights, we weren't reminded that there was, indeed, someone in charge of the city room as a whole. Late that summer the last episode of *The Fugitive*—the David Janssen television series based on the Sam Sheppard case—was scheduled to be broadcast on ABC. This was only a few summers after I had been sent to look for Dr. Sam at Benny Klein's; now the TV show had run its course, and was going off the air.

There were no television sets around the newsroom, but it was a slow night, and everyone in the country was guessing about how the series was going to end up. We knew there was a television set in Charles Egger's private office, and he had gone home hours before.

So, just as *The Fugitive* went on the air for the evening, some of us from both the sports and news departments walked into Mr. Egger's office (the door was not locked), turned on the television set, and stood there to watch.

We lasted only a minute or two. Jack Keller noticed that few reporters were on the floor, looked around, found us in Mr. Egger's office (which, had he received his expected promotion when Don Weaver retired, would have been his office) . . . and blew up.

"Get the hell back to your desks!" he yelled. "What do you think you're doing? We're trying to put out a newspaper and you're watching television?"

He was genuinely angry—this wasn't measured professional pique, he was enraged and offended. Today a newspaper would assign a reporter, perhaps more than one reporter, to cover the events related to the end of a long-running television series, to go out and interview fans, maybe to watch the show with them—today newspapers, desperate to take advantage of any cultural trends that might interest their readers, would treat the events surrounding the end (or the season-ending cliffhanger episode) of a popular television show with the same degree of attention granted to real news. Think of *Seinfeld*, and *Sex and the City*, and *The Sopranos*—those shows, once editors figured out that readers cared about them, sometimes received more coverage on a given day than did the local county commission.

But that's now. Then, there was supposed to be a line between what working newspaper reporters cared about, and what happened on a television program. In all probability the line had already been long-erased, but some in the news business still held on to the old beliefs. "Get back to your desks!" Jack Keller shouted, and we did, we turned off *The Fugitive* and went back to work. The whole country was watching the television show, millions of people would be talking about it the next day, but that was not supposed to include us. We were a newspaper, after all.

I hadn't yet tried to use the pages of the *Citizen-Journal* to make any particular editorial point—alliteration and onomatopoeia were daunting enough without my also attempting to make alterations to society—but at a tennis match one day I found myself sitting next to a guy who inspired me to give it a shot.

I had arrived at the courts where the tournament was to be held, and the organizer said to me: "Bob, you know John Havlicek, don't you?"

Gulp. I tried to be as cool about it as I could—I tried to act as if standing next to Havlicek was the kind of thing I did every day—and he and I shook hands, and the organizer said, "I told John that he could sit next to you at the card table we've set up next to the court. That way people in the crowd won't be as likely to come up and bother him."

Havlicek, by this time, was playing basketball for the Boston Celtics; he had been a star at Ohio State on the Jerry Lucas team, he had been known by his nickname "Hondo" to every fan, and he had gone on to the Celtics (with no apparent angst or distaste at the thought of being a play-for-pay boy; he was proudly a professional basketball player), and this weekend he was back in Columbus visiting some friends, and had decided to come out and watch the tennis tournament.

He, of course, had not the slightest idea who I was. Sitting at the little card table taking notes—sitting next to Hondo—felt like nothing if not a dream.

In one of the matches that day a player named Dave Snyder had severely injured his ankle before the first set began, but tried the best he could to get through it anyway. His opponent—a stocky kid with ferocious groundstrokes and a disagreeable, bellicose on-court attitude—toyed with Snyder. He ran him mercilessly, he laughed when Snyder lunged for shots, he jibed at him and in general did everything he could to take advantage of Snyder's injury, even though the outcome of the match was never in question. He seemed to be enjoying Snyder's anguish.

Havlicek, sitting next to me, saw this going on, and said to me: "What a . . ." He used a descriptive term that was not, in that era, often uttered publicly.

It was as if Havlicek's comment gave me permission to write something about it. I probably wouldn't have, otherwise; I probably would have just reported the score of that match, and let it go. It hadn't occurred to me that I had the mandate to let readers know what the player was doing to Snyder.

But Hondo had been disgusted by what he'd seen, and that made me feel as if I had backup. I might not have possessed the seniority or the authority to make a judgment about what constituted permissible conduct on a field of play, but if anyone did, Havlicek did.

So, seven paragraphs into my story about the tournament the next morning, I wrote briefly about what I'd observed. I smile when I look at the old clipping now; in our current overheated era of incessant Internet invective, where the most insulting and crudely defamatory comments are not only encouraged, but routine, what I wrote that day seems like nothing. It seems timid, stilted, too cautious. But I wasn't writing for an Internet site, because there was no such thing—I was writing for a morning newspaper in the capital city of Ohio, and I knew that I had to be careful. If Charles Egger or Jack Keller were to be displeased with my use of the *C-J* to make an accusation about an athlete's behavior, I wanted to make sure I didn't step over the line.

Here is the paragraph that I slipped in:

> *There's no sportsmanship award in this tourney, but they ought to make one just for Dave Snyder. The No. 1 ranked player in the Southwest was crippled by a badly twisted ankle and could hardly maneuver around the court, but he didn't utter a word of complaint while dueling an insufferably childish opponent, who could take a few lessons on the meaning of the word "gentleman."*

That was it. I didn't even mention the name of the player who had derided Snyder; any reader who wanted to know would have had to go down to the agate results of the matches that ran at the end of my main story to see who had defeated Snyder, and figure it out. I was that prudent about staying within the boundaries of newspaper decorum.

But, mild as the paragraph was, at the tournament it caused a sensation. It was all anyone was talking about that next day. The player about whom I'd written the paragraph, I was told, was looking for me; he was infuriated and he wanted to have a little talk with me. I knew he had a hot temper; I'd seen it on the court. A few minutes after arriving for the day's matches I could see that, across the way, someone was pointing me out to the player.

He came up to me, loud and red in the face, and lit into me. He was much bigger than I was, and was standing way too close. He was livid—he said I'd had it all wrong, that if I wanted to say something to him I should say it right now, that I wasn't going to get away with what I'd written. . . .

I was beginning to think that maybe this complete-candor-in-tennis-reporting wasn't such a great idea, after all. People were gathered around, to see what would happen next.

And then someone said to the guy:

"I thought the story in the paper was exactly right. If anything, I thought he was too easy on you."

John Havlicek.

The tennis player looked up at Havlicek—the tennis player was a large guy, but Havlicek was NBA large, and more important than that, he was *John Havlicek*. . . .

And the guy walked away to play his match.

I suppose, if you want to be resolute about it, there were two lessons to be taken from having written that story. One: When you write something about someone, you should anticipate the moment when you will have to look that person in the eye. Two: If you were correct in what you wrote, you won't have to worry when the person's eyes meet yours.

That's what you could take away from it if you were being resolute. Me, the main thing I took away from it was the memory of Havlicek.

I sat down to resume covering the tournament, and Havlicek sat down next to me. I'd thought that watching the match with him the day before had felt like a dream? This, what had happened today, was better than a dream. A dream, you wake up from.

On my last night at the newspaper that summer I went into the little room with the bamboo-rod binders, and I leafed through every paper—through every sports page.

I hated for this to end. The sports department was already gearing up for Friday nights in autumn—there would be no days off for anyone on Fridays, because Saturday morning papers during the fall were one time when the *Citizen-Journal* had a built-in competitive advantage over the afternoon *Dispatch*. Readers would want to know as quickly as possible the scores of the Friday night high school football games, and the C-J always obliged their desires, running the final scores of the fifteen or twenty biggest games across the top of the paper's Saturday morning front page, higher on the page than whatever the biggest news story of the day might be. As I was getting ready to go back to Evanston, Illinois, for a new college year, the sports desk was getting ready for football—making certain that they had people in place at every school to call in the scores and game highlights, so no reader would be disappointed on a Saturday morning.

I wanted to be there for that—to help out with it, to hear Pastorius and Stewart and Clarence Young calling out "Sports!" into the telephone dozens of times late on Friday nights, to see them jamming the phone receivers against their ears as they typed it all up. I wanted to be there to watch George Strode hurry into the office—he would have been assigned to cover the night's biggest game in person—and to see him write the lead football story in one take; I wanted to greet Dick Garrett and Hank Reichard as, right on top of deadline, they carried across the city room the action photos from the games and handed them to Clarence, who would fit them into the layout. . . .

Who would ever want to leave this?

I didn't, but I had to. In later years, I would see newspaper sports departments turn into operations almost as stern and furrowed-browed as news departments, with sports reporters learning to cover police-blotter matters involving star athletes, and financial matters involving agents and owners, and courthouse matters involving free agency and contract disputes and stadium-construction bond issues. The sports departments expanded into that kind of coverage because they had to; sports, somehow, ceased to be all about fun, and maybe sportswriting did, also.

Which is why I am eternally grateful to have been a part of those six shoved-together desks in the *Citizen-Journal*'s sports department for the brief period I was allowed to be there. It was, unapologetically, fun and games—that's all it was, and that was all the people at those desks wanted it to be. On my last night there I heard it all once more—"Sports!" "Pasty, can you take some dictation?" "Sports!" "Kess, toss me some paper, will you?"—and the rest of them, on that night, had no idea I was listening quite so closely.

But I was taking it all in, one last time, because I wanted to remember the sound of it, wanted it to stay with me. And it has, for all these years. "Sports!" they called out, their voices intermingling, and it was like a floor show, I would have paid money to watch and listen some more, to make it linger a little longer in my life. The phone rang; "Sports!" I said, picking up the receiver, not wanting the clock to run out.

14

Because I wanted to hold on to what I'd had to leave, that year at college I paid for a mail subscription to the *Citizen-Journal*.

I was sharing a house with three friends that school year in the Chicago suburb of Wilmette, a few miles from the Evanston campus. We were daily subscribers to both the *Chicago Sun-Times* and the *Chicago Tribune*; this was an era in which one of the first things college students did when they rented off-campus housing was to make sure they arranged for home delivery of the local newspapers.

So we would read the Chicago papers each morning—papers with up-to-last-night's-press-time news of the metropolitan area in which we were temporarily living—and, three or four or five days late, the mail carrier would bring me the *Citizen-Journal*, sometimes two or three rolled-up copies in one day's delivery.

The C-J, I couldn't help noticing, was much thinner than either Chicago paper, its news was woefully out-of-date by the time it was stuffed into our mailbox, and within weeks I realized, with something close to sadness, that at least for now it had nothing to do with me. I liked seeing the bylines of the sportswriters with whom I had worked all summer, I liked seeing the pages that Clarence Young had laid out, but the C-J came tardily to the town where I was living, its reference points were suddenly not my own reference points, and it made me understand just how perishable and place-specific the contents of a local newspaper are. The mailing wrapper that covered each *Citizen-Journal* was light green in color; by October there were weeks when I would let three or four editions of the *C-J* lie unopened on a table near our front door.

I didn't like that feeling; I didn't like acknowledging the distance I felt from the *Citizen-Journal* just because I was living hundreds of miles away. I felt disloyal. At Christmastime I returned to Columbus for vacation, and I looked up John Stewart's number in the phone book and decided to call him to see if he wanted to get together. He'd had this phrase he always used on the phone in the *C-J* sports department, whenever someone who'd previously called the paper was calling in again; "Hey, *I* know *you*," Stewart would say with bright enthusiasm, a welcoming slogan of his that had a smile built in. The call could have been from the man who phoned in results from Scioto Downs, or from a country club golf pro phoning in news of a hole-in-one by a member; "Hey, *I* know *you*," John would say, and there was something agreeably easygoing about it, something I liked.

So, for whatever reason, when I was home for Christmas I looked up John's number and I called his house, anticipating the "Hey, *I* know *you*" that would greet me.

A woman—John's wife—answered.

I asked if he was there.

"Who's calling?" she said.

When I identified myself there was a pause, and then the woman said:

"John's not living here."

He had separated from his wife. This was a concept totally foreign to the world my parents and their friends lived in; no one separated, no one divorced. I had known John only in the context of the sports desk; I had never thought about what his home life might be like.

I thanked her and hung up. There was a minor-league ice hockey team in Columbus that winter—I believe they may have been called the Checkers—and they played their games at the Ohio Fairgrounds Coliseum. I saw in the paper that the *C-J* sportswriter who covered their games was Tom Pastorius.

So one night I drove up to the fairgrounds and bought a ticket, and I climbed up to the rickety press box and found Pasty and a sportswriter from the *Dispatch* sitting there. Tom was surprised to see me—not displeased, not pleased, just surprised—and I sat with him during the game, wondering the same thing he must have been wondering, which was: What was I doing there? It was a dreary contest in a dreary setting, with few people in the stands; Tom was expected to file an account of it on deadline for the morning edition, and one of the things I recall about that night was that at the end of the game, after I climbed back down to the main floor, one of the hockey players was crying.

He was very young, probably in his late teens; this was undoubtedly his first professional team, and he had been involved in a fight on the ice as the game concluded. He wasn't crying because he had been hit; rather, a player on the other team had knocked him to the ice and had pulled this player's jersey up over his head so that he could not see or breathe. This, the claustrophobia of it, unmistakably had frightened the player terribly—being restrained on the ice with his face trapped by the opposing player holding his jersey. It was the last thing I had expected to see at a professional hockey game—a player sobbing—but that is what I saw, and what I heard, as I left the arena, while Pastorius, high above the ice the week before Christmas, typed his story for the *C-J*.

That was wintertime, though. When summer came around I returned to 34 South Third Street, having been invited back via a letter from Mr. Egger. He had said that this time he'd like for me to work as a reporter on the city desk.

That whole sports summer I'd seen the news reporters working just a few steps from the sports desk, but the invisible wall that separated the two departments served as a barrier. We on sports said hello to them, they said hello to us, our work was delivered to the same subscribers every morning. Nonetheless, there wasn't much contact.

I knew most of the reporters from my time as a copyboy. Now I was supposed to be one of them. Turnover in the department had been minimal; most of the faces were the same. Wink Hess, I would almost have sworn, was wearing the same too-heavy-for-the-season business suit he'd worn four summers before—it reminded me of the suits that certain high school algebra teachers wore day after day, year after year, chalk dust all over the teachers' sleeves. Wink's suspenders appeared to be the same, his fatigued face looked to be unchanged—he was the oldest newspaperman in the room, still, and as I saw him working the keys of the same typewriter at the same desk, I would have been tempted to believe it if someone had told me he hadn't moved from his chair since I'd departed the sports department the previous September.

I was assigned to sit next to a reporter named Stan Spaulding—face like a tomato, florid and full; physique like a loading-dock worker, stocky and squat; accent out of the Grand Ole Opry. He had joined the C-J staff during my sports-desk summer, and I had liked him instantly—I had no idea how he had ended up as a reporter in this room, everything about him was as punch-the-clock as a bread-truck driver, but such a thing wasn't uncustomary, back then. Newspaper reporters, especially outside of the biggest cities, weren't expected to have advanced university degrees, or necessarily any university degrees at all. What mattered was being able to produce on deadline, to be willing to walk into any situation and ask whatever questions needed to be asked, to work for relatively low pay, and—mainly—to hustle. It sounds simple, and part of it was. There was no special premium on elegant writing—in the same sense that a sanitation worker was a garbage collector, a reporter was, at his nucleus, a news collector, and Stan had proved to the editors of the *Citizen-Journal* that he was just about tireless at collecting as much news as he was told to. I don't know if he could get hired today.

"Stan Spaulding," he had said to me on the day we'd met, extending his hand, which was at the end of a beefy arm encased in a one-size-too-small white-rayon short-sleeved shirt, and I'd said I had seen his byline, which seemed to catch him unawares and please him. If he blushed, there was no way to notice; his face was already too constantly crimson for that to show.

The biggest change in the newsroom was on the city desk itself.

Bill Moore was gone, replaced on someone's whim by Sam Perdue, a longtime reporter for the old *Citizen* and the *Citizen-Journal* after that. He'd covered everything: cops, courthouses, politics. He had a mane of grayish-white hair and a hint of a haunted look, and several years would pass until I found someone else in the world who reminded me of Sam both in appearance and in manner. It would be a movie character—also named, by pure coincidence, Sam.

Sam the Lion—the owner of the dying pool hall in the dying Texas town in the movie *The Last Picture Show*, the character portrayed by the actor Ben Johnson . . . that was Sam Perdue, down to the shock of hair with almost all of the color drained out of it, down to the dry-voiced compassion mixed with pained resignation at the world's many cruelties, down to the lifetime of bittersweet memories and private disappointments, some of them stretching back to when he was a young man, buried not very deeply beneath the skin of the older man's body. It would take me several months to figure Sam Perdue out—but three years later, when *The Last Picture Show* was released, I sat in a movie theater in Chicago and saw the Sam the Lion character framed in the doorway of his doomed establishment, and I thought: How did they know? How could they know Sam Perdue?

In the city room he was like the dealer in a never-ending card game; it was Sam's job to distribute the cards to the various players—to dole out assignments to the *C-J*'s reporters—and it was up to each reporter to make the most of the hand he was dealt. The jackpot was front-page display the next morning.

This room felt more like home to me, by now, than my own home did; I was so glad to be back. "Stan, you up?" Sam called out to Stan Spaulding, and Stan leaped to his feet—no easy trick for a guy carrying around all that weight.

"I'm up, Sam, what have you got?" Stan said—meaning that he was available, he had completed his previous assignment, he was always ready for whatever Sam had in store for him.

"Got a little yarn here," Sam said, selling the story even before he told Stan what the subject was. Stan stepped over to the city desk to be dealt his hand—to find out where he would be spending the rest of his day—and I hoped that Sam would see fit to toss me some cards today, too. You couldn't win the pot if you weren't in the game.

It was Stan Spaulding who showed me the *Citizen-Journal*'s way of collecting the news even when the news—or the newsmaker—didn't feel much like being collected.

There was a bank robbery on one of my first days at work; C-J photographer Herb Workman had walked into the emergency room of St. Anthony Hospital, had seen an assistant bank manager lying on a gurney with an ice pack resting against his head, and had snapped a photo of the man. Herb had not talked with any hospital public relations people, had not asked anyone's permission to enter the emergency room, had not requested the bank manager's consent before taking the picture. Such niceties were not a part of the daily work regimen—not at the C-J, and not at other papers around the country in those years.

So we had in the city room a dandy photo of the bank manager groggily looking toward Herb's lens; we were told, late in the afternoon, that the bank manager's name was Paul McLeod, and that he had been released from the hospital after treatment. Sam Perdue beckoned me over to the city desk and said: "We're working on a main story about the bank robbery. Why don't you write us something about what it felt like for the bank manager who got knocked around?"

"Sure," I said, having no idea how I was going to do that.

There was one Paul McLeod in the Columbus phone book, but his number rang busy for a half hour straight.

Stan Spaulding, sitting next to me, said: "The family's probably taken their phone off the hook to duck calls. Go to the criss-cross and find their neighbors' phone numbers."

The criss-cross directories were thick volumes that enabled you to locate phone numbers in ways different from the customary technique of looking up a name. If you knew a street address, you could find the phone numbers of the houses near the house you were interested in; if you knew a phone number but not a name, you could find out to whom it was registered.

"Call the guy's neighbors and have them go get him and bring him next door to their phone," Stan said.

"You think they'll do that?" I said, not quite believing it.

"Tell them you're a reporter for the *C-J*," he said. "They'll do anything you want."

So, after consulting the criss-cross, I called the bank manager's next-door neighbors, I said it was very important to our newspaper that they go to his house and bring him back to their phone. . . .

And they said they would. They seemed excited about the whole process.

Within a few minutes Mr. McLeod—sounding tired, but not especially annoyed—came to the phone. He said that his family had, in fact, taken their own phone off the hook.

And he proceeded to tell me the whole tale.

The next morning—right next to Herb Workman's emergency-room photo, under the headline BANDIT KNOCKS OUT BANK BRANCH AIDE—my account ran:

> The last thing Paul McLeod remembers about Wednesday's robbery of the Main-Miller branch of the Ohio National Bank was a man who said he wanted a loan.
>
> After that McLeod, 64, of 899 Kenwick, was knocked out by the would-be borrower. The next thing he knew, he was lying beside an open safe.
>
> "All I remember is sitting at my desk," McLeod, the bank's assistant manager, told the Citizen-Journal Wednesday night. "This fellow walked up and said he wanted to find out about a loan. I told him, 'Sure, sit down.' Then he must have knocked me out. . . ."

That was how the card game was played. You could fold your hand if you wanted—you could tell Sam that the bank manager's home phone number rang endlessly busy—but then you'd be out of the game.

Sam would either run the main bank-robbery story without a sidebar, or, more likely, he would send another reporter out to the man's house to knock on the door until someone answered. Which is why folding one's hand was never a good option. If you weren't prepared to win the pot, someone else in the room would be.

We didn't cover many press conferences—there didn't seem to be many. The city was easy to navigate, and we tended to just go out and talk to people one-on-one instead of waiting for someone to set up tables and chairs for some sort of news conference. There would be crimes and emergencies, I would learn soon enough, when you would beat the cops to the scene. Sam would hear something on the police-radio scanner he kept next to his desk, he'd tell you to hurry to where the commotion was, and some days you'd find yourself walking up to some front door side-by-side with the police officers or ambulance drivers who had been sent to the address.

We didn't have any training about how to do this—certainly no training about the ethics of any of it. That first week, Sam sent me to a fire in an office building just to the west of downtown. All he did was call the address over to my desk, and tell me to go there. When I arrived I could see the flames and smoke pouring out of a third-floor window. I didn't discern any other reporters around, so I just walked in the door and started climbing the stairs.

A fireman, encountering me on the stairwell, said: "Who are you?"

"I'm from the *Citizen-Journal*," I said.

"What are you doing here?" the fireman said.

"Covering the fire," I said.

"You don't cover a fire from inside the building," he said. "You stand outside. Go!"

No one had told me.

And it made for some nice, colorful touches in the story when I got back to the office to write it.

"How'd you get this?" Sam Perdue said, reading my description of the interior of the smoky building.

I explained.

"This fireman said you're not supposed to go inside a burning building," I said.

"Yeah, that's right," Sam said. "Don't do it again. Good story."

In the city-room-assignment card game we doubtless weren't supposed to notice that the dealer, at certain moments, was not all that sure of himself. Sam kept a poker face.

But every time he would assign a "local angle" story, I would sense that maybe he was vamping. It was Sam's job—just as it had been Bill Moore's job before him—to come up with enough central-Ohio stories to fill each day's paper. And if he was short on ideas on a given day . . .

Well, there was always the local angle to fall back on. Take a big national story, figure out a way to tie it to Columbus in even the most tenuous way, and you've got another niche filled in that day's city desk rundown. It was almost too easy.

How else do you explain the assignment that sent me to the Ohio Osteopathic Association's annual convention at a downtown hotel, all to inquire about the condition of Robert F. Kennedy?

Senator Kennedy had been dead for weeks—shot to death in Los Angeles. But Sam thought it would be a good idea for me to ask a local osteopath what he thought of Kennedy's bullet wound.

So I walked to the hotel ballroom and corralled a Columbus osteopath, who told me—this was not exactly astonishing—that the bullet that had struck Kennedy had killed him.

It was right there in my story in the next day's *C-J:*

> *The bullet that entered Sen. Robert Kennedy's brain caused an "obviously mortal wound," and surgeons operating on the senator had no chance to save his life, a Columbus osteopath said Monday.*
>
> *"That bullet lodged where you really 'live,'" said E.J. Rennoe, D.O., chairman of the division of neurology and neurological surgery at Doctors Hospital.*

*"The vital centers are all there. I'm sure there is nothing
the doctors could have done." Rennoe is attending the 70th
annual meeting of the Ohio Osteopathic Association at the
Sheraton-Columbus. . . .*

Now, there was undoubtedly only one person in the country who had
any interest at all in what an osteopath in Columbus, Ohio, might have
to say about the gunshot that had ended the life of Robert Kennedy the
month before, and that person was Sam Perdue. And if there was anything that was destined to surprise readers of the *Citizen-Journal* less than
the revelation that the bullet that had killed Senator Kennedy had really and truly injured him severely, it may have been the headline that
the C-J copy desk put on top of my story:

KENNEDY DOOMED,
OSTEOPATH SAYS

What would have been news was if Dr. Rennoe had informed me
that Robert Kennedy was going to be just fine. But the local angle is
what Sam wanted, and the local angle is what he got. In the hotel ballroom just down the street from the C-J, the doctor announced to me
that the dead senator was doomed, which was good enough to get me a
byline in the morning, and good enough to get Dr. Rennoe's picture in
the paper.

Deaths elsewhere of prominent Americans gave Sam plenty of open-
ings for local angles that summer. A man named Marty J. Rosen, who
owned a store he called J-Mart's, taped photographs of the late Senator
Kennedy and the late Reverend Dr. Martin Luther King Jr. on the wall
above his cash register, the photos on either side of a hand-lettered sign
that said: SORRY! WE NO LONGER CARRY HANDGUNS AND HANDGUN AM-
MUNITION. THE MANAGEMENT.

That was enough for Sam to send me out to Westerville Road with
a photographer named Tom Wilcox so Tom could get a photo of Marty
Rosen carefully positioned between the photos of Senator Kennedy
and Dr. King, and so I could dutifully record a quotation from Mr. Rosen:

"It's a sad state of affairs when a man can come in a store like mine and buy a lethal weapon."

Actually, that wasn't a bad local angle at all. Sam Perdue was doing his best. If his job title had been national editor (a job title that didn't exist at the *Citizen-Journal*), then maybe he wouldn't have had to contort himself to find Columbus tributaries flowing from the grand river of stories with nationwide impact; if his title had been national editor, maybe he would have sent his reporters to the airport to fan out across America.

His job title was city editor, and we didn't go to airports, at least not with our bags packed. We went to Westerville Road.

Many newspapers that summer ran photographs of Robert F. Kennedy and Martin Luther King. But only one paper—I would bet on this—had Marty J. Rosen posed between then.

"I ran into Huge DeMoss out on a story today."

The speaker was George Roberts, a *C-J* reporter, and he was addressing the city room at large, looking for a laugh. Everyone knew to whom he was referring; Hugh DeMoss was the anchorman at WLW-C, the local NBC television affiliate, and DeMoss had the requisite leading-man good looks, the telegenic face made up of flat planes intersecting at sharp angles, the booming baritone, the full head of glistening hair. His name wasn't Huge; it was Hugh. But George Roberts, upon whom nature had seen fit to bestow a weak chin, a reed-thin voice and a nervous tic, and who, or at least it was said around the office, lived by himself in a single room at the downtown YMCA, felt perfectly at ease mocking "Huge" DeMoss in the *Citizen-Journal* newsroom because . . .

Well, because Hugh DeMoss was on television, and newspaper reporters, without spending too much time considering why, deemed themselves to be above that. It was false bravado, mostly; behind George Roberts's high-pitched voice as he made fun of DeMoss was the unspoken knowledge that, even in the *C-J* city room, there was a certain cachet to be had for having run into DeMoss and spoken with him. Hugh DeMoss was a genuine luminary in Columbus, he was Gary

Cooper to George Roberts's Arnold Stang, and one thing was sure: now that the news story the two men had covered had wrapped up, Hugh DeMoss wasn't back in the WLW-C offices telling everyone—or anyone—that he had run into George Roberts today.

The pecking order, across the country, was being established; television was well on its way to local dominance in the delivery of news. In newspaper offices the hired hands didn't dwell too openly on just what that was going to mean for them in the long run. Better to make fun of Huge DeMoss, behind his back.

DeMoss's handsome countenance was beamed into homes all over central Ohio; he couldn't walk down the street without being stopped and asked for his autograph. Meanwhile, we hoped for bylines.

They weren't automatic; the city editor had to think you had done an especially good job on a story for him to put your name on top of it. Otherwise your article ran in the paper unsigned. A reporter would never have the temerity to type his byline on a story before handing it in; the byline, when granted, was written by the city editor with a thick copy pencil. It was a reward; everyone knew that. You'd turn your story in and try not to be too obvious as you peered across the room to see if Sam would scribble your name at the top before passing the first sheet of paper to the copy desk.

So, even as Hugh DeMoss's full-color face was floating out of the blue and into all of those houses, I would go to the composing room and look at my byline, upside down and backward in a page form, before it was sent to the presses. I wanted to run my fingers over the metal, although I never did. The words beneath the byline would be in a hundred thousand homes by morning. That seemed better than anything television could promise.

And when each new day Sam, from behind his desk, called out, "Are you up?" . . .

Well, it felt like being on a baseball team. The very words had a batter-up quality to them. Are you up? Are you ready to play?

Sometimes Sam would say, "Garrett's going to swing around the front of the building to pick you up," and what had seemed like an unattainable fantasy the copyboy year—the thought of running out to cover stories with Dick Garrett or Hank Reichard in the *C-J* press cars—became a regular occurrence. We would make our way through the city—usually bound for someplace where something unhappy had happened—and, riding down unfamiliar roads (unfamiliar to me—no roads in central Ohio were unfamiliar to Garrett and Reichard), looking at street signs, checking addresses against the one Sam had handed to us on a piece of paper. . . .

We had been sent to intrude on something, and the intrusion felt almost legitimate, because the city editor had said it was.

The lead paragraphs that resulted may not have been anything to stand the test of time, or even to be especially proud of:

> *Police narcotics squadmen raided the North Side home of a vacationing Ohio State University professor of economics Friday night, uncovering marijuana in various stages of preparation. . . .*

On evenings like that one, it was probably best not to ponder too deeply what the professor might think if he knew that a newspaper reporter and photographer were standing around his house with the cops as the cops picked their way through closets and drawers. It didn't occur to the cops not to let us in; it didn't occur to us not to enter. Sam had heard about it on the police radio in the newsroom, and that seemed enough to give the whole queasy enterprise permission.

A hint of heroism always helped get a story better play:

> *Because Skip Adams could see his buddy's yellow swimming trunks, Jerry Miles is alive this morning.*
>
> *Miles, 18, of 724 Wilson-av, dived into the deep end of the Marion-Franklin Swimming Pool, 2699 Lockbourne-rd, about 9:15 P.M. Friday night. He did not come up.*
>
> *Adams scurried up the high diving board and went down after his friend. . . .*

We were news collectors, all right, creating the daily scrapbook from blank sheets; zipping around town in those boxy press cars, we were collecting the scraps of news that would constitute tomorrow morning's paper. Often you would climb into a press car to go wherever Sam had sent you, and the scattered effluvia of the last reporter's news-collecting foray would still be in there—hamburger wrappers, and discarded notepaper, and overflowing ashtrays. Whatever the last story had been, the residue of its pursuit would be all over the front seat.

You'd brush it aside and go.

Driving around town like that, it felt as if you *were* the newspaper—it felt, as you drove down streets you had never been on before, that you were the embodiment of the *Citizen-Journal.*

At home the next day I would see my father working the crossword puzzle. That, to him, was as important a part of the *C-J* as the news stories were. If his morning paper were ever to have been delivered without a crossword puzzle in it, that would have been more upsetting to him than if a news story or two were missing.

The crossword puzzles arrived in the *Citizen-Journal* newsroom by U.S. mail, sent by a national syndicate. The puzzles, in the form we received them, were imprinted into an egg-carton variety of soft gray cardboard, which in some way or other could be used in the composing room to make metal plates for the newspaper. In the press cars we may have believed that we were the *Citizen-Journal,* but a newspaper means different things to different readers, and to my father the *Citizen-Journal* meant the daily crossword. And I couldn't help noticing—his son's front-page tales of marijuana raids and valiant swimming-pool rescues notwithstanding—that he, like many other people in town, was starting to get his local news, maybe the preponderance of it, from Hugh DeMoss.

Yet thoughts like that—thoughts about the value, and the popularity, and the ultimate future, of the newspaper we put out every day—were momentary and soon forgotten.

Hugh DeMoss might materialize out of thin air, smiling his way into people's homes—"I hope your news was good today" was his show-closing tagline—but then he was gone. Nothing remained once his face left the glass screen at eleven-thirty each night, to be replaced by Johnny Carson's. What we did was permanent. You could hold it in your hands. It endured.

At least that is what we told ourselves.

One day I was sitting at my desk in the city room, between assignments, and Sam Perdue called over to me: "What are you working on?"

"Nothing," I said. "I don't have anything to write."

He stared at me. I might as well have just cursed at him, to judge from that stare.

"Nothing to write?" he said.

He stood up and motioned for me to follow him. He walked to one window of the newsroom—a window that overlooked Broad and Third.

We stood together and he pointed out at the city and said to me:

"Nothing to write? There are *people* out there!"

What we did on the pages of the daily newspaper may or may not have endured. But what Sam said to me that day has. I can hear his voice now.

When we printed something in error, it did not precipitate a crisis in the newsroom—certainly not a crisis of conscience.

It's not like we made the mistakes on purpose.

Just because there was no corrections column did not mean we were oblivious to or uncaring about our missteps. Each night, about half an hour before the presses rolled, several proofs of the front page would be sent down from the composing room, and whoever was available— editors, reporters, anyone on the floor—gave the page a careful read, to do all we could to make certain the *Citizen-Journal* would not land on those hundred thousand doorsteps with a glaring error on Page One. It felt like prom night every night, like those last moments in front of the mirror before leaving the house to pick up your date—making sure we were as presentable as possible, with no bits of potato chips stuck between our teeth, no stains on our tuxedo shirt. We may not have been beautiful, but we wanted to look our best.

When mistakes did slip through and make it into the newspaper— mistakes flagrant enough that the C-J had to deviate from its usual no-need-for-corrections stance, and admit that we had blown it—we typically did so with a "very-much-alive" style of rectification. The very-much-alive correction was printed with an implicit grin, even a wink—its wording said to our readers: We're all in this together. We know that you know we didn't foul up intentionally.

The very-much-alive kind of correction was published when someone did something like . . .

Oh, to use an example from much-too-close-hand experience, the very-much-alive kind of correction was published when someone did something like saying in a story that Hattie McDaniel, who in 1940 had won an Academy Award for her role in the movie *Gone With the Wind,* was "the late Hattie McDaniel."

Which certainly would have been news to her.

How could such a mistake get by? As the person who made it, I can tell you that it could get by when someone you were interviewing referred in passing to "the late Hattie McDaniel," and you dull-wittedly took it on faith that the person knew what he was talking about, and you put the information into the paper. Only to have the city desk be informed by phone callers the next day that . . .

You know.

What we would do on days like that was prepare a little paragraph for the next morning's C-J that said:

> *A story in yesterday's* Citizen-Journal *referred to actress Hattie McDaniel as "the late Hattie McDaniel." We are happy to report that Miss McDaniel is very much alive.*

It was such an amiable way to acknowledge our imperfections. We were *happy* to report them. We who on deadline read the Page One proofs to head off errors wanted everything in the paper to be clean

196

and without blemishes. It bugged us when the blemishes evaded our detection.

When they did, though, we didn't lower our eyes in shame. When you made a mistake you'd see it the next day and either silently or out loud go "Ahhh . . . ," and you'd give yourself an imaginary little slap of chastisement on your forehead. You'd shake your head at your denseness, and maybe field a joke or two about it from other reporters.

But it didn't ruin your day. You hadn't done it deliberately. Most of our stories had no preconceived agenda, other than to be part of the scrapbook. A typical morning's lead paragraph, from the same guy who thought Hattie McDaniel was dead:

> *Three-foot-tall kids chomping down foot-long hot dogs . . .*
> *the smell of pigs, horses, sheep and cows, hanging heavy in*
> *the air . . . the giant Ferris wheel churning up dust as it grinds*
> *around . . . fair season, unmistakable in its outward dress,*
> *came to Hilliard Tuesday.*

That was our standard output. We weren't trying to elevate mankind and we weren't trying to get things wrong. In later years many newspapers would appoint ombudsmen, also called public editors or readers' representatives, to examine the news product on a daily basis and make sure that what had been written adhered to the straight and narrow. We thought—we really did—that *we* were the readers' representatives. That's what a reporter was there for—that was the whole point of the job, the point of going out and reporting stories: to represent the reader.

We truly believed it. When we made mistakes and they got into the paper, we felt dumb, but the remedy seldom had to be spoken aloud. The remedy was a version of what every coach has ever said to a losing team after a bad game: "We'll get 'em next time." And there was always going to be a next time—always going to be a tomorrow's paper. That, we believed more than anything else.

15

Sometimes I think about what the staff of the *Citizen-Journal* would have done if someone had told them about Web logs—about blogs.

If someone had said to them that, somewhere off in the hazy distance, the day would arrive when every newspaper reporter would have a computer on his or her desk—and that many newspapers would empower their reporters to launch random thoughts around the world, under the newspaper's nameplate, any time they wanted. That a C-J reporter musing at his desk—about, say, the quality of that day's fried-egg sandwich from Paoletti's—could type those musings onto a screen, and instantly have the musings available for reading everywhere from Mississippi to Moscow.

I think the reporters, hearing that, would have deemed the proposition so loony, they would have done pirouettes—they would have placed their fingertips on the tops of their heads and twirled around on their toes like ballerinas. It just would have struck them as deranged—to think that a reporter (not to mention anyone else who owned a computer) would have the ability to reach the world, and without having to wait for an editor's approval, or for presses to roll.

We had one foot—usually both feet—in another time. The interstate highways were relatively new; some were still being constructed. For many stories that we were sent out to cover, we drove on two-lane roads. We knew no one was ever likely to see a word we wrote if they lived outside our circulation area.

When we were told to venture somewhere outside of Franklin County, it was with the explicit understanding that we would drive there, report the story, and drive back the same day to write it in the city room. There were no sleepovers in hotels; if a story couldn't be done in a round-trip commute on a single day, then we didn't go.

And when we did go—and were given an out-of-town dateline— we were inclined to overwrite. The dateline was what did it—the very act of typing as the first word of our story the capital-lettered name of a city other than Columbus made us feel as if we had to commit literature. The dateline made us feel like *correspondents*.

So when Sam sent me down to Athens, Ohio (with Hank Reichard and his camera in tow), to cover the opening session of a convention of high school boys who would be leading their student governments come the fall, I might as well have been deployed to Athens, Greece. I couldn't just write it straight; I knew the story would take a dateline (my first), so I felt compelled to work into the lead paragraph allusions both to anti-war protests at American universities and to recent floods in southern Ohio:

> *ATHENS, O.—The student demonstrators have gone home for the summer and the flood waters have subsided, and Thursday 1370 delegates to the 31st annual Buckeye Boys State quietly took over the Ohio University campus here.*

The "O.," I always thought, was a nice touch; that's how Ohio was referred to in all *Citizen-Journal* datelines, as if we couldn't spare the space for the "hio." Even on datelined hard news stories, when grandiloquent leads would never have made it past the copy desk, the instinct was to write with a certain portentous gravity. When there was a disturbance among inmates at a state prison facility in the nearby Ohio town of London (Athens, London . . . the datelines were pretty cosmopolitan), and I was sent in a press car to cover it (with instructions to have the car, and myself, back in Columbus by nightfall), I felt as if I were an International News Service war ace writing about the Blitz, so powerful was the sight of that dateline. If you squinted your eye and sort of blurred out the "O.," that is:

> *LONDON, O.—Four hundred inmates at the London Correctional Institution staged a sit-down strike that turned into a near-riot Monday, with two prisoners shot by guards and another escaping.*

The banner headline the story received—stretching all the way across the top of the next morning's *C-J*—entranced me, because looking at it allowed me to pretend that I was filing breaking stories from Europe:

LONDON PRISON STRIKE QUELLED

But the fact is, it didn't matter that it was London, Ohio, instead of London, England; being on the road for a few hours for the *Citizen-Journal* was reward enough. Our newspaper universe had boundaries that we knew better than to challenge. Every time any of us would prepare to roll blank pieces of copy paper into our typewriters, and place a sheet of carbon paper between the pages, we would see, on the carbon paper, the leftover words and letters from stories that had come before.

Each piece of carbon paper in the office was used over and over; we threw a piece out only when it became so thin and beaten-up that it was beginning to disintegrate. So, as we got ready to write each new story, we would see, on the old carbon paper, remnants of stories that our *C-J* colleagues had written in the days and weeks before. All their false starts, all their X-outs—it was there on the carbon. Our fields of view, both literal and symbolic, were rather constricted. We shared the carbon paper and never slept in a hotel and wrote mostly for the readers of the town.

A blog?

To tell Stan Spaulding, methodically hammering out his assigned articles, that he could step to a computer and write anything he wanted, on any thought or subject that popped into his mind, and shoot it off, instantaneously and without prior approval, to the far reaches of the planet?

He probably would have looked over to Sam Perdue for guidance.

And then said: No, thanks.

He was on deadline. Sam had told him what his story was today.

The front page was everything. People didn't have scores of different ways to get their news every day—the front page was the home-delivered oracular authority, it was the official announcement to the town, every morning, of what was most important. So to have a story on Page One . . .

The front page was everything.

To walk past a vending box, on the day you had a bylined story above the fold on the front page of the *Citizen-Journal,* and to see it looking out at you—the words you'd written, your name on top of those words—seeing that behind the glass of the newspaper box was a better feeling, or so I believed, than being on television must be. Television images moved around and flickered; your story in the vending box stood still, so you could stare at it. And to go to Rogers' Drugstore in my family's neighborhood to buy the customary five or six copies (I was still doing it, Kessler's and Pastorius's smiling admonitions the summer before notwithstanding), to hand my money for the papers across the same counter where not so long ago I had handed Joanne, the longtime cashier, my money for Elvis Presley bubble gum cards . . .

The second line of the byline was different from what it had been on the sports desk; I was no longer "*Citizen-Journal* Sports Writer," I was "*Citizen-Journal* Staff Writer," which sounded, in print, like a very substantial thing to be. The papers were tossed onto the doorsteps of all the neighbors on either side of my parents' house—the Dormans, the Fenburrs, the Kayneses, the Baases—people who had seen me on the block since I was a baby. Now here I was, in that blackest-black byline type, a *Citizen-Journal* Staff Writer. On the front page.

And the best thing about it, in retrospect, is how quickly it went away each day. You'd feel proud for a few minutes—looking at your work on Page One, knowing that Lew Dorman and Herb Fenburr and Bob Kaynes were reading it at their breakfast tables up and down Bryden Road—and you would realize: Oh, yeah. I have to do it again. If I don't do it again today, that front page is going to come out tomorrow without me on it.

It was a built-in lesson on what ambition is. If you didn't try anew every day, what you had already achieved would all be gone. You have to do it every single day—ambition isn't a once-in-a-while thing. That allurement—half promise, half dare—was waiting for you each morning. Your story's on the front page. Good for you—and so what? If you don't find a way to do it again today, you won't be feeling so good tomorrow.

Not that ambition was ever mentioned in the *C-J* newsroom—not by name. "Good yarn today," Sam might say to a reporter, or one reporter might say to another: "Nice." But to speak of ambition? Not here. Not out loud.

Charlotte Curtis had made it out of here—that was the word. She had started at the old *Columbus Citizen*, had absolutely shined as a writer at the *Citizen* and then at the *C-J*, had gotten herself hired by the *New York Times*, and was by now well on her way to becoming the first woman in history to be listed among the senior editors on the *Times*'s masthead. Everyone in the room knew it: Charlotte Curtis got out of here. It can be done.

No one discussed it. But it was all the proof anyone needed of just how much the front page mattered; the front page had propelled Charlotte Curtis to the very top. The phone would ring in our house that summer; it would be Sam Perdue or Bill Keesee, asking my parents to call me to the line. "We've got a couple of guys who called in sick," Sam or Bill would say. "I know it's your day off, but would you mind coming in? We're sort of short."

There was never any question. Stay home, and the paper comes out tomorrow without you in it. Go to work on your day off . . .

The news boxes were waiting, more tantalizing than a TV screen. Maybe, tomorrow morning, you'd be in those boxes again.

Ambition was one thing. Pride was quite another.

While neither was spoken about aloud, whatever ambition may have lived within the men and women of that city room remained not only silent, but hidden. Whoever may have been feeling it kept it under wraps: invisible.

Pride, though, on days when there was reason to be proud, was easy enough to see.

There were reporters on the staff who had a much smoother personal style than Stan Spaulding did—tall and taciturn John Milton and stubby and speed-talking Stan Wyman were two of them. They had the social skills to maneuver among Columbus's political, business and social elite, if their assignments took them to places where the elite were gathering. Milton and Wyman were men who, in a crunch, could affect a certain polish, could assume a studied refinement, at least until they rejoined the rest of us in the city room.

Stan Spaulding couldn't. He was ever the reporter-as-dumptruck-driver, earthy and full of pungency and looking like he spent his off-hours at drag-strip races. Because of this, his utter newspaper professionalism sometimes went unnoticed; when the cornpone comedian at the country-and-western dance hall tells his jokes to warm up the audience for the hard-charging main-event band, people don't pay much attention to the particulars of the comic's adroit sense of timing—they just see him as the funny and familiar, if well-worn, opening act.

One night—this had been during my sports-desk summer—we received, after 11 P.M., a call in the newsroom. It didn't seem like it could be right.

A commercial airliner bound for Port Columbus had supposedly, for some unknown reason, landed instead at Don Scott Field—the small private airstrip at Ohio State University.

This was unheard of—and, if it was true, it was dangerous. The university field was not intended for full-size jets.

Stan took the call, and started working the phones, and from across the room I watched him. This was one of the few cases when a breaking news story would be absolutely exclusive to us in the morning—it was developing too late to make the late local television newscasts.

The plane, as I remember it, was from one of the once-great airline companies that are now out of business—it was either from TWA or from Eastern Airlines. And it would turn out that the big passenger jet had, in fact, landed by mistake at Don Scott—the pilot had seen landing lights, he evidently had been confused, and he had put the plane down not at Port Columbus, but on the little university airstrip.

No one had been injured. But—in our town, and in any town—a jetliner landing where it wasn't supposed to was a big story.

There was a look in Stan Spaulding's eyes that night—a fierceness of belief in himself, mixed with palpable nervousness about pulling the story off in time for the presses; his face got even ruddier than usual, his feet began to tap beneath his desk, he met one of the photographers at the side door and hurried down the stairs to grab a press car. . . .

The big bosses had gone home. Stan was either going to pin down this story in time and get it into the paper, or he wasn't. There was no confirmation yet that the plane had really landed at Don Scott, it was just a telephone tip, and if Stan could get himself out there and find out, in time, whether it had happened, and, if so, how it had happened, and why, then in the morning the people of Columbus would read about it. If Stan couldn't do all of this before the presses rolled, the people in the morning wouldn't. It was that fundamental.

After midnight, when Stan returned from the airstrip to the newsroom, running, I walked over from the sports department, sat with him and fed him background facts from the clips in our library as he sweated and banged away at his typewriter and looked at the clock. The expertise and aptitudes of the men and women in this room may have been, by their own admission, limited—this was what they knew how to do: find things out and write them up under pressure—but the aptitudes, and talent, that allowed them to do this were something most of the population didn't possess and never would.

The government officials who worked across the street in the Statehouse, the business executives who occupied the top-floor suites of the downtown office buildings, my father and his friends who ate their lunch in the Neil House's lobby-level restaurant—they couldn't do this. Not on deadline—they couldn't be told what Stan had been told, and go out and gather the facts and have those facts be right, and in one sitting put it in a clear and understandable form that would stand up to scrutiny in the morning. Maybe it was a skill those other people wouldn't even want to have. But Stan had it, the men and women in the *C-J* city room all had it, and on certain nights, when stellar demonstration of that skill was needed, they proved what they could do.

Our main home-delivery edition had already come off the presses; Stan would only be able to get a brief account of the errant landing into a replated edition for street sales in the morning. His longer piece, with all the color and follow-up and details, would run the day after. On this post-midnight he wrote and looked at that clock and checked his notes and wrote some more; he was drenched with perspiration when he was finished—I thought he might pass out. He sent his story to the desk, looked at me with raised eyebrows and an expression that said, *Whew*, and we waited for the edition to be brought up from the pressroom when those presses, right on time and not a sweep of the second hand late, rolled.

There it was, in the newborn newspaper—the account of the airliner sitting at the wrong airport. By Stan Spaulding, *Citizen-Journal* Staff Writer.

Stan—his scrawled notes still on his desk, scattered around the base of his typewriter—read his story, the story he had crafted from those notes.

Ambition wasn't something you could see in that room. The people who worked there wouldn't let it show.

But pride?

I looked at Stan with the new newspaper in his hands. Maybe there were things in life that he could not do.

But he could do this. I watched his eyes as they read his words.

The women on the *C-J* staff, or so I thought, must have lived in perpetual resentment that an "our gal" story might always be just one assignment away.

It was the era of our-gal stories in American newsrooms. Female reporters weren't exactly plentiful—they were around, but there weren't all that many of them. At the *Citizen-Journal*, Gail Lucas and Pauline Taynor were writers back in the women's department, and Sherry Woods and Betty DeBold were reporters on the city staff, but that was about it. And, unlike the male reporters, they always had to live with the possibility that they would be called upon to write an our-gal story.

When Ringling Brothers came to town, some editor might decide to send one of them to ride on an elephant in the parade, and label the resulting account "Our Gal at the Circus." If an old-fashioned steam engine was hauling a train through Columbus as some kind of promotional stunt, an editor might be inspired to send one of the women reporters to do an "Our Gal Rides the Rails" feature. It was like that in just about every city. The very presence of this exotic species of reporter—a woman—apparently caused male editors to be overcome with visions of our-gal stories.

There was never an our-guy story. The phrase wasn't used. And if there was a conspicuous dichotomy in the newspaper-business state of mind that, on the one hand, would allow Doris the copygirl to be hooted at, to suffer catcalls, in the composing room that first summer I was there, and on the other hand was ever ready to publicly deem any female reporter as "our gal," with all the self-congratulatory warmth and cloyingly paternal protectiveness the term implied . . .

Well, the world had yet to change. There was a board game being sold in department stores that year, marketed toward families. It was called *What Shall I Be? The Exciting Game of Career Girls*. It encouraged young girls, playing the game with their mothers and fathers and sisters and brothers, to choose among six careers toward which to aspire:

Teacher. Actress. Nurse. Model. Ballet dancer. Airline hostess.

That was it. That was the entire range of possibilities. Some of the game cards inside the *What Shall I Be?* box listed the skills a girl must learn to assure herself of success in one of those careers: how to use makeup; first aid; hair styling; stage techniques; good posture.

That was the larger world in which the women in the *Citizen-Journal* newsroom were making their way. "Our gal" was the least of it. Sizable segments of society still seemed primed to wonder why our gals weren't models instead of newspaper reporters.

Betty DeBold, especially, whose attentive face seemed locked into an expression of constant curious challenge, was just a superlative reporter, with an unfailing eye and an ever-alert ear, able to break your heart with stories like one she did about local military personnel whose daily job it was, in central Ohio during the Vietnam war, to knock on the doors of families and tell them their sons had been killed in action. But even Betty knew that an our-gal story might, at any moment, be brewing in some male desk editor's fertile mind.

Even Betty? How about Charlotte Curtis?

You'd think that she, of all people, would be able to escape that patronizing syndrome—she was a star of stars on the *New York Times*.

Yet here is how a 1965 story in *Time* magazine chose to praise her:

"The *Times*' girl on the beat studies her subjects with the detachment of a sociologist."

Our gal was a sociologist.

Charlotte Curtis, in 1965, was thirty-six years old. The girl on the beat.

If there had been "our guy" stories, I could have written a somewhat sheepish one about the whole experience of being thrown into downtown side street life after dark. *Our Guy Steps Into a Noir Movie*. Not that I would have written it; I'd have been embarrassed.

The life of the city I was immersed in downtown was quite different from anything I'd been a part of prior to my *C-J* days. There were evenings when, taking my dinner hour alone, a little tired of Paoletti's, I would find some bar or other on a street near the paper, and duck in for a cheeseburger. There'd be down-on-their-luck guys, and pinball players who seemed to have been standing around these shadowy rooms since the end of World War II, and bartenders who looked like Tugboat Annie's ill-tempered older brother. If I didn't work for the *Citizen-Journal* it never would have occurred to me to walk through any of these doors, but because I worked there, these were logical places to dine. Some of the bartenders began to know my name. I was still the kid who had quit the Epsilons baseball team to work for a newspaper; I was a second baseman, not a downtown tough guy sitting in a seedy tavern. Except I was. Sitting in the tavern, that is. I was about the furthest thing there was from a tough guy.

It was a summer of racial tension in American cities; Dr. King had been murdered in May, riots and arson had broken out around the nation, and just about every town of any size asked itself the question: Is it going to happen here?

Rumors would come in by phone: this or that black neighborhood was going to erupt on a given night. Who knew where such rumors started? Rioters presumably didn't adhere to schedules, like sports teams. But on several nights, Sam sent Dick Garrett and me out in a press car, just to spend the evening cruising the city's roughest neighborhoods, looking for trouble. If we saw anything brewing, we were immediately to call in from the car's two-way radio.

We never spotted anything especially volatile. "What do you think?" Garrett would say to me. "I don't know," I'd say back. "Nothing on this corner." I wasn't even really certain what we were supposed to be looking for. And there was something ineffably sad about the whole exercise—two white guys, one barely old enough to vote, driving warily through black neighborhoods with no interest in finding out what the lives of the residents were like: what they aspired to, what they were upset about, what frightened them, or gave them hope. Our assignment was not to get out of the car and talk to them. Our assignment was to look for fires, and listen for gunshots. It felt like being cops—not especially good cops, at that—and I'm certain that the residents of the neighborhoods where Garrett and I cruised, seeing us prowling up and down their streets in our light blue car with the skinny radio antenna sticking out of the roof, must have known without really having to think about it that we weren't their friends, that we were there for insulting reasons. I can't say that they were wrong.

There was a night that summer when I did ride with police officers. It had nothing to do with rumors of racial turmoil; Sam had no story in particular to send me out on that night, so he told me to drive to a certain nearby municipality and "just go out with the cops to see what you find."

I don't know if reporters still do things like that, even in smaller towns; the legal liability that would be involved today, and the distrust between the police and the news media, probably prevents it from happening much.

But that night, in that year, there was no resistance at all from the local police department in a less-than-prosperous neighboring town. I said I was from the C-J, I said my editor had told me I should ride around with them, and they said to hop in. I don't even recall having to sign a release.

This, like the dinners in the grungy downtown Columbus taverns, was very different from anything I was accustomed to; I had observed, in the C-J city room, the seen-everything, heard-everything demeanor that some reporters affected—it was as if you couldn't be a newspaperman unless you could do a creditable imitation of a burned-out homicide detective.

It was an interesting pose to strike, for those reporters who chose to do so, and maybe, for some of them, it even became real. But for me these were still first-time experiences, I was about as jaded as a Dairy Queen chocolate soda, and that night in the police cruiser the cops got a radio call to go to a corner where a robbery was reportedly taking place. The cops turned on the siren, and we sped through darkened streets, hearing other sirens coming from other directions. We reached the intersection just as other cruisers were getting there, too; the citizens who were being rounded up and questioned were not the most savory-looking bunch, certainly not fellows who were likely to join my dad and his friends for a noontime meal at the Neil House any time soon.

My immediate thought was: Gee, we should get out of here.

That was my instinct: to tell the police that we should probably drive to somewhere else. These were rough guys, outside on the corner.

I didn't say anything, naturally enough; on a rational level, I knew: it's the people on the *street* who should be scared, not you. You're with the police. The guys on the corner are the ones who are being handcuffed and arrested—what do *you* have to be nervous about? You're with a bunch of cops with guns, who are going to take the guys on the corner to jail. Why are *you* so jittery?

The answer probably was: because, *Citizen-Journal* Staff Writer or not, I was a fish out of water. This wasn't really my world.

I could have pumped up a story:

Our Guy Helps Make an Arrest.

But I couldn't have, really—not with a straight face. And anyway, there were no such things as our-guy stories in the C-J.

When I got back to the office and the night staff asked me how it had gone, I did give some world-weary version of: "Pretty quiet—a couple of arrests for attempted robbery."

As if it was something I encountered every night.

As if I hadn't wanted to be as far from that corner as possible.

Our Guy Gets Stomach Cramps at a Robbery in Progress.

Some stories are best left unreported.

Jay Anderson didn't talk much as he sat at the copy desk.

He was the *Citizen-Journal*'s only African-American copyeditor. If it was not the most opportune time to be a woman trying to find work on a newspaper, it also was not, by all appearances, the most welcoming time for aspiring black journalists. Ed Colston was the sole black reporter; Jay Anderson was the sole black copyeditor.

I'd met him my copyboy summer; he was one of the people whose food orders I would seek several times each day, and he wasn't the most heartily congenial of guys. If he was too busy working to talk to me when I was asking for orders, he would send me back later on a special trip just for him. He never seemed to interact much with the other *C-J* copyeditors; he came in and did his job and left, without excessive bantering or small talk. He wore a white shirt and a tie just about every shift.

That summer when Dick Garrett and I would be sent on surveillance missions to Columbus's all-black neighborhoods, I found myself wondering what Jay would make of it. If it was obvious even to me how slighting to the residents those *C-J* drive-throughs of ours were—just checking to see if everything's all right here, ma'am, just taking a look from our car—then Jay must almost certainly have had his own opinions about it. Not that he would have expressed them in the office. He was a man on the copy desk earning a paycheck.

The summer before—the sports-desk summer—a story had come across the news wire one night. NASA had announced that it was commissioning its first black astronaut—an Air Force test pilot named Robert H. Lawrence Jr. Lawrence, who also had earned a doctorate in physical chemistry from Ohio State, would begin training so that he could be in line to be sent into space.

Because, in the sports department, we sat so close to the news copy desk, I could see and hear what was going on that night when the UPI story came across.

Some of the copyeditors—white men, sitting side by side with Jay Anderson—were passing the wire copy about Robert Lawrence back and forth, laughing and talking about what headline they should put on top of it for the next morning's paper.

I remember their words exactly, because the words sent a chill through me.

" 'The Jig's Up,' " one of them said.

" 'Coon on the Moon,' " said another.

It was supposed to all be in fun. They evidently didn't worry about saying what they were saying in front of Jay Anderson, because they expected him to see the humor in it. They didn't mean anything by it—therefore, why should they be embarrassed about saying it out loud?

It must have been quite a feeling, to be a woman on an American newspaper in those days, to be an African-American in one of those all-but-all-white newsrooms. Perhaps they were supposed to feel lucky to be there. Perhaps that was the assumption. These jobs weren't easy to get; just look around. Perhaps they were supposed to feel grateful.

No one ever checked on how the stock was doing.

I don't think anyone was even aware of whether the *Citizen-Journal*'s parent company, Scripps-Howard, was a public corporation, with stock for sale. If it was, no one in the room owned any. The newsroom staff of the *C-J* weren't exactly securities-owning folks.

Today, how a newspaper corporation's stock is doing seems to be just about the whole caboodle (until private equity firms take over the operation, that is). The dictum is drummed into employees' heads: the company that issues your paychecks is in business to provide a good return to its stockholders. Otherwise: layoffs, expense reductions, cutbacks in travel, skimpiness with newsprint. At many newspapers, the staff is invested in the stock, either through employee-purchase programs or stock-option grants. The stock—its fluctuations, its valuation—has become part of the daily life of the newspapers and their reporters and editors. They may not like it—they may, in fact, hate it. But the stock, and what it means, is always with them.

And so they check up on it, which is easy: look on the computer screen—the same screen on which you write your news stories—as many times a day as you like. Take the temperature of your company. By four o'clock on a given afternoon you may have written about a highway resurfacing project that will tie up traffic in your town for months to come, and seen your newspaper corporation's stock drop by a point and a half. All on the same computer monitor on your desk.

Not at the newspapers of that era; not at the C-J. We put the stock listings in the paper every day (and, Bob Moeckel's mispasting of the numbers that one time to the contrary, they usually were the correct numbers), but that was for the benefit of the businessmen and investors of our town. The people who worked in the city room were indifferent to the Dow Jones, as far as it applied to their own lives, because basically it didn't.

Even if they had wanted to follow the stock market, there was no easy way to do that. The only means of keeping track of how the market was doing during the day was to walk over to one of the big brokerage firms' branch offices—Bache and Company; Merrill Lynch, Pierce, Fenner & Smith—and sit in comfortable leather chairs next to well-to-do investors, and watch the ticker. That's how it was done, then—a daily, club-like gathering, in brokerage offices, of men with the wealth and spare time to sit around together observing the numbers come across. Maybe with a cocktail in their hands as they did it.

The staff of the *Citizen-Journal* wasn't a part of that—they didn't give a thought to how the national market was faring, just as they didn't give a thought to entering their work in national journalism contests. No boss at the C-J was going to give any reporter any shares of stock, and no boss at the C-J was going to enter any reporter's work for a Pulitzer Prize or a National Headliner Award. There wasn't money available for the former—give stock options? To reporters?—and there wasn't time or manpower for the latter. Who, in a room always short-staffed and always on deadline, had time to sit around dreaming up long-term special projects meant to impress journalism judges, or to paste clippings into scrapbooks and fill out contest-entry forms?

There was something very freeing about that attitude—it wouldn't have occurred to the staff in quite those terms, but there was something liberating about not doing what we did for the stock, or for contests, about not caring about the approval of Wall Street or of a writing-competition jury composed of faraway strangers. We did what we did for tomorrow—for tomorrow morning's paper—and it truly didn't seem any more complicated to us than that.

We would type up our stories about, say, Fourth of July celebrations;

those stories made Page One because . . . well, because they were important to the town. The readers would want to know how to plan their holiday, and if we didn't tell them in a place where they could find the information right away—the front page—who would?

It may not have been poetry:

> *Independence Day is still five days away, but already various Columbus area civic groups are completing plans to commemorate the Fourth of July with gala celebrations.*

But on the day that story ran, on the front page under my byline, it made me feel useful to see people in town reading it—the story was heavy with mundane details, timetables of events in Whitehall and Hilltop and Linden and Reynoldsburg, museum hours and fireworks schedules, information we figured our readers desired.

Not that we were always letter-perfect. Without computer databases to check particulars, we did the best we could on names and titles, but on certain things, we probably blew it, and probably often. The same way we would swarm over the front-page proofs before the presses rolled—everybody looking for typos and misspellings, everybody taking one frantic final nightly gander, hoping nothing wrong got in—so, too, did we do our best to make the information in the stories we wrote flawless. But of course we failed—and likely we failed more often than reporters do today.

As for our opinions, the *Citizen-Journal* didn't have an editorial writer on its staff—not even one. The great majority of editorials in the *C-J* were canned national commentary from Scripps-Howard's main office, delivered to us over the wire.

Maybe Scripps-Howard thought it was helping to set the national agenda by piping those editorials into each of its newspapers. The company owned many papers in many cities during that time: papers in El Paso, and Denver, and Pittsburgh, and Birmingham, Alabama, and Evansville, Indiana, and Albuquerque, and Memphis . . . two papers in Memphis, the *Press-Scimitar* and the *Commercial Appeal*—a newspaper publishing company in that era could run two separate papers in a city like Memphis and be certain that each could find a loyal readership and each could turn a profit. Who didn't read newspapers?

Copies of all the Scripps-Howard papers, from those cities and every other city where the chain published each day, would be mailed to us—all the newspapers in the chain were expected to mail their daily editions to all the other papers, as if the papers were brothers and sisters dispersed about the country, ordered by their parents to write to each other regularly. The papers, wrapped up tubelike, often unopened and, eventually, thrown out by the cleaning ladies, would sit back on a shelf beneath the C-J staff's cubbyhole mailboxes.

So we would run the Scripps-Howard editorials that were wired in from headquarters, while the corporation seemed to have nothing to do with us on the city room floor as we put out the paper each night. And maybe the most significant shift in the wind, just beginning to materialize—significant to Scripps-Howard, significant to the newspaper industry, significant to those of us who merely wrote the stories and snapped the photographs and laid out the pages—was one that I only intermittently noticed:

For all the work that we put into each morning's paper—all the care, all the double-checking of facts, the same kind of care and checking that the staffs of all those wrapped-up Scripps-Howard papers back on the mailbox shelf were endeavoring to provide in their own cities—there were many days when I would see my best friends before I went to work for the night, guys my own age, and these were days when I'd had a story on the front page of the C-J . . .

And they wouldn't have seen it.

The front page—and these guys, on the cusp of adulthood in America just like me, wouldn't have seen my stories because newspapers were not as big a part of their lives as newspapers were of their parents' lives.

Why this didn't strike me as being more important, I don't know. But I had grown up believing that newspapers were beyond essential, that they were imperative, that people in town devoured them as soon as they hit the doorstep. This, in fact, had been true, for a very long time.

Now my friends, on certain days, apparently didn't see Page One, apparently they didn't see any of the paper, and maybe I thought it was just them. Maybe that was it—maybe I didn't understand that they might be a part of something that was beginning to form, something that would turn out to be as meaningful to those of us who loved newspapers as anything we put on our front page, the front page that, as the clock ticked, we proofread each night, wanting everything to be perfect for the people we believed were counting on us.

16

One night my friend Chuck Shenk came down to the newspaper office because he needed some help with a summer-school paper for a class at Ohio State.

Apparently he'd not done well in a course during the spring semester, and had been required to take it a second time. He had a paper due, and he wanted me to assist him with it.

Actually, he wanted me to write it.

I would like to say that I expressed strong and deeply held moral objections to doing such a thing, and that I angrily cast him out onto Third Street with a burst of outraged indignation. But I didn't. I thought it was funny: sitting in the *Citizen-Journal* city room, at the same typewriter where I wrote my news stories, pounding out a college paper for Chuck based on a brief and murmured description he gave me of the assigned topic. I wanted to see what grade I'd get.

So Chuck, in a pair of Bermuda shorts and a T-shirt, stood among the reporters and editors on deadline—Wink Hess on one side of him, Stan Spaulding on the other, Sam Perdue across the way reading copy— as I banged out three or four pages for him. Chuck had an older brother named Bill who regularly used to rant to me about how "the press always gets things wrong," and about how "the press decides how it wants to slant the news." I would automatically defend the press—all of it, not just the *C-J*—to Bill Shenk, telling him that there was no intentional lack of accuracy, no purposeful twisting. He never bought it.

But I have a feeling that Chuck, as he looked around the newsroom that night while I wrote his college assignment, sensed that I was right and that his brother was wrong. Not that he was beholding any paragons of virtue in that room—or any paragons of anything. It wasn't that he peered around him and saw unsullied goodness and rectitude.

Rather, what he saw was a roomful of rumpled mutts—the oddballs that we were. Sam, pacing and running his hand through his hair as he muttered something to himself; Wink, wearing down the threadbare seat of his old business suit as he sat in his chair one more night; Stan, his grin and his corny jokes more attuned to a beer-fueled bowling league than to a dark and secretive journalistic cabal. This assemblage of struggling humanity was conspiring ways to distort the news? It was hard enough for us just to make sure we got the street addresses right, and the correct names with the correct faces in the photo captions. Skew the coverage for some abstruse and nefarious purpose? We wouldn't have had the time for that even if we'd had the inclination— who had enough spare hours to coordinate grand plans about how to distort what went into the *C-J*?

Chuck looked around as I quickly wrote his paper, and what he must have perceived, on some level, was a total absence of grandeur. The power of the press, the majesty of the Fourth Estate? Not here. Not by a long shot.

Which may have been the single best thing about the place. Today there is much talk about the public's disdain for the news media— sometimes a disdain bordering on hatred.

But who could hate the people in this room? Not Chuck. Were these the kind of people to connive ways to twist the news? Please. We were way too life-sized for an undertaking as big as that.

I could always see, in the eyes of outsiders who came into the newsroom, that they were surprised to find us working in such close quarters. It doused any of their preconceived notions of vastness. An immense, almighty news operation? The physical distance between the reporters and the city editor was approximately the same as that between customers at a pizzeria and the guy behind the counter taking orders.

Sam didn't even have to raise his voice, although sometimes he did, just for effect. He'd usually say a reporter's name in a regular speaking voice—"Bob?" "John?"—and we'd walk over to find out what he had in mind for us. We were accustomed to the cozy scale of the room; visitors—like Chuck, in his shorts and T-shirt—weren't. The bustle, they always thought, was cool. But they almost uniformly said, afterward, that the place wasn't as big as they'd imagined.

So we were life-sized in a lot of ways. The newspaper—the finished product—may have seemed big. Not us.

And our readers didn't despise us—it never even occurred to us that they might. Whatever assumed characteristics today's public, in its antipathy, associates with the press—arrogance; vanity; condescension . . . take your pick—was nowhere to be found in the city room of the C-J, and probably not in the city rooms of most papers in those years. The *Citizen-Journal*'s reporters weren't capable of being snooty or snobbish; knowing that they were working stiffs, they couldn't see themselves as anything else.

There was no television camera positioned in the newsroom, the way cameras are set up in many twenty-first-century newsrooms to broadcast live interviews with reporters over affiliated stations. That has been a fairly recent development: local newspapers asking their reporters to be debriefed on TV, to help promote the paper.

If anyone had mounted a live camera in the C-J newsroom . . .

Well, no one would have. And if a camera had magically materialized one day, the reporters probably would have run away from the lens, giggling. If an editor had ordered them to sit in front of it while an unseen anchorman—Hugh DeMoss?—asked them questions from a studio miles away, the instinct of the reporters in all likelihood would have been to ham it up for the amusement of their colleagues in the city room. I can visualize it:

"Stan, Hugh DeMoss, live on the Channel Four six o'clock news. What can you tell us about that shooting on the west side?"

"To *beeeeeee,* or not to be, that is the question. . . ."

"Stan? Can you hear me? We're live on the air."

[Laughter is heard in *C-J* city room.]

"Yeah, Hugh, I can hear you. As I was saying to your fine audience: To *beeeeee,* or not to be, that is the . . ."

No one ever asked the reporters to make speeches, paid or otherwise, because . . .

Because, what would they possibly talk about?

I can hear their reaction now—not that they ever had reason to react to the nonexistent invitations:

"Make a speech? You mean—like, a speech?"

They covered speeches—they didn't make them. Why would a newspaperman deliver an address? Among the city room reporting staff, there were no celebrities, and no one aspiring to be one. Elite? Pompous?

Chuck Shenk sat on the edge of a desk that night, as I finished his college paper for him. He wasn't intimidated at all to be there. In that room, these were just a bunch of guys.

You couldn't hate them. And, if somehow you had, they'd wonder why, and feel bad about it.

If there was ever a day when being a newspaper reporter seemed like the only job a person would ever want to have, it was the afternoon when the state highway patrol and the Columbus police blew a hole in the wall of the Ohio Penitentiary.

There had been minor disturbances at the pen earlier in the summer. The prison was a dreadful, almost medieval place—it had been constructed on Spring Street, on the edge of downtown, in 1834, and, incomprehensibly, the same structure was still in operation more than 130 years later, Ohio's main penitentiary. It was crowded to the bursting point—by the middle of the twentieth century its inmate population had grown to 5,235 felons—and, far from being hidden from sight, the gloomy, forbidding-looking stone complex was right where thousands of Columbus residents entered and departed downtown each day.

On a Tuesday morning at approximately ten-fifteen A.M., word reached the C-J city room that prisoners on the C and D cellblocks had taken guards hostage. They reportedly had seized the guards' keys, had freed other prisoners from their cells, and were setting fires and looting the prison commissary and hospital. As the flames fed upon themselves, the rioters said that they had captured nine guards—and that unless their demands for improved conditions, and amnesty, were met, they would burn the guards alive. There was one shouted threat from inside the pen that the prisoners would cut off the head of one guard and throw it into the prison yard.

Columbus firefighters arrived with Ohio Highway Patrol escorts and were able to contain the flames; negotiations began, but broke down at sunset. One of the demands from the prisoners—quaint, from the perspective of today's media world—was that the guards would be released only when the prisoners saw copies of the Columbus newspapers with their grievances printed for the people of the city to read.

Just about the entire *Citizen-Journal* city staff spent the day and night outside the walls of the penitentiary; the next day began with no progress. By the second afternoon, Ohio law enforcement authorities had devised a plan. We who witnessed it could scarcely believe its audacity.

At virtually the same moment, two huge explosions were set off. One was on the roof of the cellblock where all the hostages had been moved; one was in the outside wall of the prison. Highway patrolmen and Columbus cops dropped into the hole in the prison roof, and separate squads stormed through the outer wall; guns blasting, they made their way through the cellblocks, trying to get to the guards who were being held hostage.

What a sight—what a sound. The wall of the Ohio Penitentiary blown apart, lawmen charging through the hole like infantrymen on a battlefield; the rat-tat-tat of ammunition being discharged deep within the cellblocks . . . and all of this in an American city in the middle of a workday.

We didn't know quite what to do—the last we had heard, negotiating teams were being formed, and then came the explosions. We would learn later that five inmates had been killed in the onslaught. But what we would observe first was the hostages—the guards—being carried out to safety. They were all alive.

They were rushed to Mount Carmel Hospital downtown. And . . . this is the part that would never happen today, this is what made that afternoon such a newspapering knockout—no one kept them from us, or kept us from them. At the prison, C-J photographer Herb Workman ran to his car, I ran with him and hopped in, we raced to Mount Carmel and double-parked outside . . .

And walked right into the emergency room to find the nine guards receiving treatment—and willing to talk to us. They hadn't been debriefed by the police or by prison authorities yet—we were the first people they spoke to, other than the doctors and nurses. No one at the hospital thought to stop us, or them; no one set up a press conference or an official briefing. This was going to be the first word.

Oh, it was great. The adrenaline . . .

I was scribbling notes as fast as I could. One of the freed guards—his name was Paul Freshour—told me, "One minute they'd say they were going to burn us, then the next they'd say they weren't." An older guard named Harley Reeves—still wearing his official-issue patrolman-style billed cap—said, "We had conversations, some about their troubles, but mostly just about things in general. They played the radio, and they had one copy of the *Citizen-Journal*."

Just minutes before, over at the prison, these men to whom I was talking had thought they were going to die. A guard named Stephen Huffman told me that as the police had rushed to rescue them, the prisoners tried to set the cellblock ablaze, but couldn't reach their gasoline cans in time. A guard named Don Dilley—stripped down to a white T-shirt in the emergency room—described to me what it was like when the police were shooting their way in: "We couldn't see the police, but we could hear them. The corridor is so narrow, and we heard shots and saw prisoners falling everywhere. They were shot just as they were going to set the place on fire."

Herb was snapping away with his camera, and when we were fin-

ished we sped to Third Street, told Sam what we had gotten—his eyes
lit up—and I started writing while Herb went to develop his film.

I got the solo byline on the front-page story about the guards. But the
biggest kick—the thing that gave me the most pride the next morning—
was a little box that accompanied the *Citizen-Journal*'s coverage. Most of
the paper that day was filled with stories and photos from the prison riot
and rescue; this is what the one-column box said:

RESCUE STORY
TEAM EFFORT

Coverage of Wednesday's rescue of nine hostages at the
Ohio Penitentiary and related stories are the combined effort
of a team of *Citizen-Journal* reporters and photographers.

Reporters were Stan Wyman, George Roberts, John Milton, Bob Greene, Sherry Woods, Wink Hess and Dave Scheen,
along with photographers Dick Garrett, Phil Long, Tom Wilcox
and Herb Workman.

It was a swell team to be on—especially on days like that. It was my
father who pointed out the team-coverage box to me at breakfast; I
hadn't known about it. He didn't even comment that they'd inadvertently, in their rush, left the "Jr." off my name in the little box.

There had been so much energy in the city room that day and
night, so much camaraderie as we hurried to put together the best newspaper we could. . . . Why, after a day and night like that, would you
ever want to do anything else with your life?

That morning, the morning after the rescue, our phone rang at
home, and it was Bill Keesee, calling for me from the city desk.

"Did you forget something?" he said.

I felt my innards clench. Had I screwed up some facts?

"Is there something wrong with my story?" I said.

"Nope," he said. "Story's great. Congratulations."

"Then what did I forget?" I said.

"How did you get over to the penitentiary yesterday?" he said.

"I drove a press car," I said.

"Right," he said. "And do you mind telling us where that press car might be?"

Standing in the little hallway off my family's kitchen, I held the phone and winced.

In the excitement of running with Herb Workman from the blown-apart prison wall to his car, I'd forgotten that I'd driven a C-J car to the prison. After writing my story on deadline I'd gone home for the night without giving a thought to the fact that the car was still where I'd left it.

"The car's over by the prison," I said into the phone.

"Would you mind telling me where at the prison?" Keesee said.

"There's this little alley just to the side of the east wall," I said.

"Would you mind stopping at the prison on your way to work today, and bringing our car back to us?" he said.

"I can take the bus there and do that," I said.

"Thank you, Bob," he said.

The team was swell. As swell as could be.

One day Wink walked into the newsroom looking so upset that it seemed he might cry.

He never showed any emotion about anything. As the longest-serving member of the reporting staff, he had covered just about every kind of story for the paper. But on this day he was shaken, and not a one of us missed it. We said nothing.

He walked up to Sam and, his voice trembling—with anger, with hurt—he said: "I'm not going back there."

The national convention of the Congress on Racial Equality—CORE—was being held in Columbus that summer. With racial unrest such a dominant American story, the one-week convention seemed that it would make national news. Militancy was in the air; African-American leaders were publicly espousing a much harder line than in years past, and some of those leaders—Roy Innis, Wilfred Ussery,

Maulena Karenga and James Farmer among them—were supposed to be in town.

The *Citizen-Journal* wanted to cover it as a major event, with probable Page One display for the main stories each day. Sam had assigned his most experienced reporter: Wink.

So Wink, in that vintage business suit and suspenders, had walked over to the Sheraton-Columbus for the opening session—and had been blindsided.

There was a certain style that was favored by some of the more uncompromising black leaders that year—they often were aggressively dismissive of white journalists at press conferences, sometimes even purposely contemptuous. The message was: What would you know about our problems? The posturing was mostly an act for television cameras; the black leaders may have been sincere in their goals and beliefs, but their stagecraft—the belligerent sparring with white journalists—was mainly good theater. The white reporters in these situations were props, symbolic punching bags; it played well on home screens.

It wasn't difficult to figure this out. And in non-public settings, the same leaders who all but jeered white reporters before the cameras were many times quite cordial and friendly to those same journalists. It was a game, of sorts; no one was supposed to take it personally.

Wink Hess didn't know that. He was from a different era, just a meat-and-potatoes, try-to-get-all-the-facts-right reporter; Sam sent him to the Sheraton and apparently, at that opening press conference, he had asked a bland enough question and Roy Innis had all but jumped down his throat. I wasn't there—I didn't hear the exchange. But evidently, in a room full of reporters, Innis, the associate national director of CORE, had mocked and demeaned Wink—he had used him as an example of unknowing white journalists, and he had scorched him and patronizingly dressed him down in front of the others.

And it appeared to have upset Wink to his very soul. He was a mainstream older man, nearing retirement, visibly tired much of the time . . . and in his own town, when he wasn't expecting it, he had been publicly humiliated.

So when he appeared in the city room, ashen and unsteady, and said to Sam, "I'm not going back there," it was a serious thing. In the setting of that newsroom, seeing Wink Hess so pained was a very big deal. Sam didn't question Wink's request even for a second. There was no way Sam was going to make him return.

None of us wanted Wink to know how distressing this was for us—to see him brought low. We pretended to ignore what was going on right in front of us, and Sam, as close to inaudibly as he could, called me over and said, "Do you think you're up to covering this thing?" I said I didn't think it would be a problem; I would read up on the background material and go right over.

The news that came out of the convention—the stories that ran on the front of our paper—were not what I remember about that week. News stories come and go. What I remember is Wink's voice, and his face, when he had been made to feel small. And it wasn't until years later that I found out something about Wink—about what he had been through before coming to the *Columbus Citizen*, and then the *Citizen-Journal*.

I happened upon his name by chance; I was doing some research on World War II, and I found a story about combat correspondents in the Pacific. I was reading about an Australian reporter named Keith Palmer, thirty-seven, of the *Melbourne Herald*, who had been killed on November 7, 1943, when a Japanese bomber had demolished a press tent on the island of Bougainville.

The account said that five other men in the press tent were with Keith Palmer when he died; the five suffered injuries, but survived. They were, according to the story, Rembert James of the Associated Press; Captain Patrick O'Sheel, a military press relations officer; Ted Link, formerly of the *St. Louis Post-Dispatch*, assigned by the United States Marines as an official combat correspondent; Paul Ellsworth, a Marine artist; and Willard (Wink) Hess, assigned to the Office of War Information.

The Japanese plane had dropped a five-hundred-pound bomb. Some of the other men who had been with Palmer in the tent, and who had seen their buddy die, helped to bury him in a makeshift cemetery near the beach.

That was where Wink Hess, as a younger man, had been: under sudden bomber barrage on a distant Pacific Island as he served in what he and the nation believed was a noble American cause. Now, twenty-five years later, no longer young, he trembled in the city room. He had been singled out to be debased and belittled in his own country, in his own city. It had come out of nowhere. "I'm not going back there," he had said to Sam Perdue, and Sam told him that was all right.

We didn't have all that many celebrities passing through town.

The Kenley Players would occasionally have big-name guest stars in their summer theater productions—usually actors and actresses well known from television. That would guarantee a bigger box office at Veterans Memorial than if the Kenley Players had imported a Broadway luminary; Helen Hayes almost certainly wouldn't draw as well in Columbus as would Roy Rogers.

The all-time perfect Kenley Players guest stars, in terms of local audience appeal, had to be Ozzie and Harriet Nelson. I don't recall the name of the play in which they were acting, but I was quite young the summer they came to town—this was before my *C-J* years—and Regene and Harold Schottenstein (my friend's father who would drive in the evening to Broad and High to pick up a Night Green) invited my sister and me to go to the play with them and their sons and daughter. Afterward there was a reception, which Mr. and Mrs. Schottenstein were invited to attend, because Harold was the local RC Cola franchisee, and RC was a sponsor of the Kenley Players.

So we went to the reception—backstage at Veterans Memorial—and it was disorienting to meet Ozzie and Harriet because, somewhere in the back of all of our minds, in the middle of Ohio in the middle of the century, we symbolically believed that Ozzie and Harriet Nelson, and Ward and June Cleaver, were as much our parents as our real parents were. With Ozzie and Harriet it was even more befuddling—at least on *Leave It to Beaver* Ward and June Cleaver were fictional characters played by actors Hugh Beaumont and Barbara Billingsley; on *The Adventures of Ozzie and Harriet*, the character named Ozzie Nelson

229

was played by the real Ozzie Nelson, and the character named Harriet Nelson was played by the real Harriet Nelson. Were they genuine people? They had the same names and faces as the characters they played, but where did truth end and make-believe begin? I stood in front of Ozzie and Harriet as if they were not humans, but a legendary mountain. Like they were the Matterhorn.

It didn't help that Ozzie Nelson had the largest head of any man I had ever met in person. He looked exactly like Ozzie Nelson, but with this enormous head. Harold and Regene Schottenstein introduced us children to Ozzie and Harriet, and at that time in my young life I was still aspiring to be a tennis player, so I said to the Nelsons:

"I know that David plays tennis."

Harriet Nelson, very cordially, replied: "No, it's our son Ricky who plays."

I said: "No, I think it's David."

Ozzie Nelson said: "Ricky is the tennis player."

I looked at Ozzie and Harriet and said to them: "I'm almost sure it's David."

Harriet Nelson's smile became so frozen that I thought her face might crack. I was a reader of tennis magazines, and I was quite convinced that I had the right Nelson son as the budding tennis champion. Even now, I can't be sure; I'm reconstructing the conversation from memory, so it's possible that Ricky was the one I mistakenly thought was the tennis player, and David was the one that the boys' own parents insisted I was thinking of. But, after years of watching *The Adventures of Ozzie and Harriet*, I felt I knew the Nelson family so well that it didn't occur to me that Ozzie and Harriet Nelson might have a firmer knowledge than I of which of their sons spent his spare time on tennis courts.

So . . . we didn't have all that many celebrities passing through Columbus, and when, at the CORE convention, the leaders announced that Muhammad Ali was flying in to make an appearance at their event, it was a newsworthy moment.

When Ali arrived, he had a new miniature tape recorder with him, and he said to us—we were gathered around him, this was not a formal ceremony—"One of these days, I'm going to put out an album of all these interviews."

He was recording us. He held the microphone from his recorder up to his mouth, and said in that Ali voice—the voice was smooth and undamaged, his physical decline had not begun, his face was young and unmarked—"This interview will be conducted by some big-shot press people. I'm in Columbus, Ohio. . . ."

Everyone has to be somewhere. Ozzie, Harriet, Muhammad Ali . . . everyone, every day, has to touch down. I went back to the city room from the CORE convention and told Stan Spaulding that Ali had tape-recorded the Columbus reporters. Wink Hess, at his desk, was typing away, not looking up.

Because the city room was a self-contained and collegial place, sometimes it was easy to forget just who was on the other end of what we did every day—who was out there reading it.

Lew Dorman and Bob Kaynes and Herb Fenburr, I could comprehend—because I could actually see the newspapers hit the front stoops of their houses on my parents' block, I could accept the fact that what I wrote at ten o'clock the night before, they read at seven o'clock the next morning.

But the idea that the bigshots in town—the mayor of Columbus, the governor of Ohio, the president of the Lazarus department store— might be reading it over their breakfasts . . . that was a more difficult concept. Up there on the mezzanine, we typed happily away like the riffraffish band of buddies we mostly were; that the leaders of the town would pick up their cups of coffee come the dawn and with genuine interest take in the words that had come out of our typewriters . . .

We knew it was true, I suppose, but it almost didn't register.

With all the turmoil at the Ohio Penitentiary that summer, I came up with a series of stories that, even now, I think weren't so bad for a person who had just turned twenty-one and was due back in school in September.

The prisoners' complaints about conditions in the penitentiary, everyone knew about. But the general feeling around the city seemed to be that prisoners are always going to complain. Why spend any time thinking about it?

I found some prison guards who told me that the prisoners were correct; they told me that the assurances from state corrections officials that things were being run in a humane way in the state penitentiary were lies. The guards said that the way the prisoners were being forced to live was so brutal as to border on being criminal itself.

I found the first guard on my own; no one had assigned me the story. I interviewed him at length and told him I would not write the account unless I could use his name—and his address. He said yes.

I turned the story in and waited to see what the reaction from the editors would be.

> A detailed list of "animalistic, inhumane" practices used in handling prisoners in the Ohio Penitentiary was outlined for the *Citizen-Journal* Sunday by a former prison guard.
>
> The guard's disclosures came in the wake of an announcement by Gov. James A. Rhodes that "no probe of the Ohio Penitentiary or its management is either under way or contemplated."
>
> John Chester, of 518 E. Town-st, was a prison guard for four months before quitting last Friday, because "it was just too depressing." He said conditions at the ancient penitentiary include:
>
> —Solitary confinement cells with only a bare cot and a hole in the floor for toilet purposes.
>
> —Drinking water in cells "that makes you sick just to smell it" . . .

The list of particulars went on: the beating of mentally ill prisoners by fellow prisoners assigned to be "nurses"; sick prisoners being forced to miss meals; petty offenses punished by solitary confinement and the loss of visiting privileges; fights between prisoners ignored by guards.

After I spoke with Chester and the first story appeared, more guards came forward to tell me what they had observed. I would talk with them in a *C-J* conference room; Dick Garrett would come in, tell them to look toward his camera, and snap their pictures. We weren't looking for great and artistic photography—we just wanted to show the faces of the men making the charges.

That first Sunday night, when I turned the story in, Jack Keller was in charge. He read what I had given him, slowly, page by page. I hovered nearby.

He glanced at me and half muttered:

"It's not supposed to be a country club."

But he ran it—he ran it as big as you could run a story in that newspaper. All the way across the top of the front page, with a headline in dominating typeface:

EX-GUARD TELLS OF INHUMAN TREATMENT AT PEN

The next day—the Monday the story ran—was my day off. At dinnertime, my father was watching the local news and I heard him call to me:

"Come in here."

I did. Chet Long, on WBNS television, which was owned by the *Dispatch*'s parent company, was leading his broadcast with official government reaction to the story. Long was the top newscaster in Columbus, more popular even than Hugh DeMoss. On the television screen in our house, he was speaking of "a news report about alleged problems at the Ohio Penitentiary," and he had comments from the governor, from the head of the state's corrections department, from law-enforcement officials, all saying that the story was wrong. That conditions in the prison were acceptable.

They weren't telling the truth; the story I had written was on the money. The Ohio Penitentiary would soon be closed and eventually torn down.

But here was the thing:

My dad said, "They're talking about your story."

And I said, "I don't think so."

Whatever "news report" Chet Long was referring to, my first instinct was that there must have been a second news report that had caught his eye—nothing I could possibly write would be important enough to engage the attention of Chet Long. Never mind the attention of Governor Rhodes.

I had grown up watching Chet Long—*Looking With Long*, that was the name of his newscast on Channel 10. He had read what I'd written? And was getting the governor of Ohio to tell him that I'd gotten it wrong?

It wasn't that I was angry, or upset—I knew that my story was right, and would be proven right. It was just that it didn't sink in. What we did in that room every night—Stan and Wink and Dave and John and all the rest—Chet Long was reading it in the morning? James A. Rhodes was getting agitated about it?

"It has to be your story Chet is talking about," my father said, and we both watched the television set in our home.

As pleasing as it was—as gratifying, while more than a little perplexing, to consider the local ramifications of something like that—there were other moments.

Such as when Nelson Rockefeller arrived in Columbus.

He was trying to defeat Richard Nixon for the Republican presidential nomination. Rockefeller was destined to fail.

But on the summer day he arrived at Port Columbus—on a full-sized chartered jet, with a cabinful of national press on board—he believed he still had a chance. Sam sent me to cover his visit.

Rockefeller was in town for four hours, and the feeling of riding the press bus from the airport with the national reporters, being shepherded past rope lines with them, moving through the city with the United States Secret Service—it was a little bit like being inebriated in broad daylight, so heady and out of the ordinary was the experience.

There was a press room set up in a ballroom of the Neil House, with typewriters and phones, and I watched as the traveling correspondents from the major papers and wire services and broadcast networks phoned their offices with updates on their day in the Midwest. We were escorted across the street to Governor Rhodes's office in the State-house; there was Rockefeller, there was Rhodes, just a foot or two away from us. All my life, in the Columbus papers, I had seen Rhodes striking that certain pose of his, a tilting of the head evidently intended to show off his "good side"—the profile he thought photographed most attrac-tively. Now, with Nelson Rockefeller at his elbow, I saw him almost in-voluntarily lock his head into that position as soon as the cameras came out—it was like watching a long-running Broadway play where the ac-tor hits his mark every time.

There was a rally on the Statehouse steps, with thousands of people gathered in the noonday heat to see Rockefeller and Rhodes; I talked with a political reporter from *Time* magazine as we took notes in the sun, and he treated me like a colleague, he didn't talk down to me as we struggled to make ourselves heard over the amplified voices of the politi-cians and the cheers of the crowd and the music of a campaign band.

The story I would write for the early edition was, I see as I read it now, wide-eyed and politically naïve to the extreme:

> *Nelson Rockefeller brought his presidential drive to Columbus for four hours of hand shaking, smiling, eyebrow twitching, and straight talk—the kind of campaign with which he hopes to keep the GOP nomination away from Richard Nixon. . . .*

Eyebrow twitching aside, the story offered no meaningful insights into the behind-the-scenes nuances of Rockefeller's visit and what his real chances in Ohio were—I included such groundbreaking sentences as: "Security was extremely tight"—but for that one edition my story got the banner headline:

ROCKY PLEDGES U.S. LEADERSHIP

(The pipe-smoking men of the Scripps-Howard Ohio Bureau, who had also covered the visit, came to the newsroom to complain that their story, not mine, should lead the *Citizen-Journal* in the morning; they prevailed, probably by pointing out passages in my story such as this one, about an appearance Rockefeller made separate from the main rally: *About 200 supporters were on hand, from teenage girls in mini-skirts and Rockefeller hats to the "Housewives for Rockefeller" under their banner.* The Scripps-Howard men wondered how such observations advanced the public's understanding of the race for delegates or of the complicated relationship among Nixon, Rockefeller and Rhodes. It would have been difficult to argue that they were wrong; by morning their story was leading the paper, with my eyebrow twitches and mini-skirts relegated to a sidebar.)

But what stays with me about that day is not anything that appeared in the newspaper. What stays with me is the feeling I got when I rode the press bus back to Port Columbus as Rockefeller prepared to depart for his next stop.

There was chatter in the bus all the way from downtown to the airport—the national reporters talking about the speeches they had just heard, and the places they'd be flying in the days to come—and as the bus pulled up to the American Airlines charter waiting on the runway, the guy from *Time*—the guy who'd been nice enough to treat me as an equal, even though I wasn't—said:

"You coming to Cleveland with us?"

That was the next stop—that was where they were going.

"How would I do that?" I said.

"Just get on the plane," he said.

Maybe it would have been as easy as that—maybe had I silently followed the others onto the airplane, I would have taken off for the next city, no questions asked.

But I didn't know how I would get back to Columbus, and I knew Sam would be furious—I wasn't supposed to go to Cleveland, I was supposed to go back to Third Street—so I watched as the others boarded the campaign jet, and I stood there as it took off and disappeared over the clouds.

Could it be that simple? Could getting out of town—going where the bigger stories were—be a matter of just deciding, one fine day, to do it? Was the secret to joining the national reporters—the ones whose horizons weren't limited to the confines of Franklin County—not some intricate code to be deciphered, not something instigated by an engraved beckoning, but merely a matter of saying to yourself: I'm going to go?

Not that I was thinking in those terms that afternoon; mainly I was feeling a wistfulness that surprised me, a longing for the day not to end. I wonder now if Charlotte Curtis ever had a day like that—a day in Columbus when she looked toward somewhere far away, and silently made a vow. The plane became a speck. I went back downtown, to Sam, to the mezzanine.

17

Because our main lens on the world outside Columbus was provided by the United Press International wire-service report, the office was littered with UPI-related advisories and updates and correspondence. Whenever UPI would send the *Citizen-Journal* something through the U.S. mail—a brochure, a promotional pamphlet, a letter about terms of service—there would appear, somewhere on the paperwork, one or both of UPI's official slogans.

The first was "A UPI Man Is On the Scene." It was intended to instill confidence in the wire service: no matter where in the world news was breaking, the slogan assured client newspapers, a UPI man was there, covering it. The slogan was accompanied by an illustration of a UPI reporter wearing a dark suit and dark fedora, standing with his legs spread like a quarterback, peering down toward the notepad he held in his hands. The gender of the UPI reporter went unquestioned: if UPI was going to have someone out on the story, the newspapers that subscribed to the service could rest easy. The reporter was going to be a man.

The other UPI slogan was "Deadline Every Minute." It needed no translation. UPI, and its reporters, considered themselves always on deadline. Newspapers themselves may have had several deadlines throughout the day and night, but UPI never rested—that is what the slogan announced.

It was a heart-stirring notion, back then. Within forty years, with the sudden appearance and immense popularity of online news outlets— many of them offshoots of daily newspapers—the idea of a deadline every minute was assumed. It was part of the new game. If a reporter had a story, he or she had better get it up on the Web right now—*now*— because if he or she didn't, some other reporter, working for some other news organization or simply working alone with a computer and a mo- dem and the desire to tell people something, would get it up there first. The deadline-every-minute pride felt by the UPI reporters would soon enough become something not to boast about, because the concept would be met with a shrug. You have a deadline every minute? Who doesn't?

In the city room there was a clock—round, with a white face and black numbers—hanging from the ceiling next to a painted column near Sam's desk. Glancing at it became such a part of every C-J re- porter's and editor's daily routine that the constant glances were never even remarked upon. The clock might as well have been the Mona Lisa, or a nude calendar photo of Marilyn Monroe—that's how much of a magnet it was for every pair of eyes in the newsroom. You'd type and look, type and look, type and look—every person in the room fixed his or her gaze on that clock hundreds of times every work shift.

UPI may have had a deadline every minute, but we didn't. Our dead- lines, for the various editions, were at a handful of specific minutes, each day and each night. We knew them by heart. The people at home weren't checking their computer screens to see what we had for them— they knew they had to wait patiently for morning, when our work would land on their doorsteps.

In order for that to happen, we looked at that clock, and obeyed it. Sometimes everyone involved in a story would be looking at the clock next to the big square column at the same moment: the reporter as he or she wrote the story, Sam as he waited for it, the copy desk chief as he figured in his head when it might arrive in his wire basket, the layout man waiting to find a place for it on the front page. It was a comfort, that clock; it wasn't the enemy, it was an ally. It was with you every work shift. It brought you home.

"But seriously, folks, I wanna tell ya . . ."

Bob Hope was onstage at the Ohio State Fair, with Spiro Agnew at his side, and I was taking handwritten notes with such frenzied dedication that it must have appeared, to anyone observing, that the entire city was counting on me.

And I did believe, in a quiet and fundamental way, that the entire city was.

Because we were the *Columbus Citizen-Journal*—because Columbus was our first name—we accepted on faith, without really stopping to think about it too much, that we played a part in making it official, on a daily basis, that this place was, in fact, a community.

If our newspaper on all those doorsteps every morning contained the local news of interest to the people who lived behind those front doors—news so boundary-specific that it would be of little consequence to anyone who resided anywhere else—then by definition this amorphous collection of houses and apartments and factories and office buildings in the middle of Ohio must, indeed, be a community. The stories in our paper proved it. Why else would the *C-J* exist? Just by showing up each dawn, our paper assured our readers that the town was alive.

How we did it—how we provided that assurance—was pretty much up to us. Page One announced to the town each daybreak what had been the most momentous occurrences of the preceding twenty-four hours, but Page One, at dinnertime the night before, was still a blank easel down at 34 South Third. We were free to fill it in any way we wanted.

One of the most pleasing ways to fill it in, late in summertime, was with news of the Ohio State Fair. I loved it on the days when Sam would assign me to go there—I knew that I would be free to wander the fairgrounds all day and all evening, and that whatever I found during those unsupervised wanderings would make the front page the following morning.

Thus, I watched Bob Hope in front of a filled-past-capacity audience packed into the grandstand on a Monday night. Hope was flanked for part of his performance by Governor Rhodes and by Maryland Governor Spiro T. Agnew, who was running for vice president as part of Richard Nixon's ticket. Hope told a joke about how he had spent the afternoon playing golf with the other two:

"Just like politicians—not so good with woods, but you should see their eyes bulge when they get near the green."

The fairgoers roared, and I dutifully wrote down every word, which would appear halfway through my story in the morning under a banner headline—STATE FAIR CROWDS HIT ALL-TIME RECORD—and would be accompanied by a Hank Reichard photo of, on horseback, the fair's Queen of Queens, Marsha Jenks, "daughter of Mr. and Mrs. Merle Jenks of Jeffersonville."

The community seldom indicated that it regarded us as anything but fellow members, with fellow interests. In a dismal area of Franklin County known by the paradoxically peppy name of Wonderland, a series of eight fires had broken out—widely believed to have been set by "a gang of marauding youths," as, pleased and even proud to utilize such jargon, I referred to them in the *C-J*—and a photographer named Phil Long and I spent a day with the terrified residents. Not only did they speak with us—they allowed us to use their names, photos and home addresses.

"If someone doesn't do something to help us soon, we're going to have to start sleeping in the daytime and sitting up all night," a woman told us, and I identified her, with her permission, as Mrs. Grace Rudd of 4771 Rarden-av. "They drive around and then they burn, or they steal cars, or they slit tires," a man named Clifton Van Lear told us. "They got people so scared they won't tell the police. Holler at one of them, and your house burns the next day." Mr. Van Lear may have been scared to call the police, but it didn't occur to him to be scared of Phil, who snapped his photo, or of me, who put his address—4802

Diamond-av—on the front page the next morning. We were from the *Citizen-Journal*. They trusted us to be on their side.

We could be a little swashbuckling in our accounts. A woman, sensing that several of the arsonists were looking in on our interviews, said to Mr. Van Lear: "All this time you've been talking, they've been watching you. I've seen them. . . . You watch, your house is next." And when the people who had been observing us—the people suspected of being some of the arsonists—tailgated us as we drove through Wonderland, we printed that in the paper the next day, too: "A young man and woman in a blue Chevrolet followed Van Lear as he showed a *Citizen-Journal* reporter-photographer team the charred-out ruins of a house. When the C-J team tried to follow them they sped out of Wonderland and down Hamilton-rd."

"The C-J team"—a term as enchanting as Wonderland itself, something out of a comic book populated by rag-paper heroes.

Miss Allison—she had stayed on as secretary to the editor after Don Weaver's retirement—told me in whispered tones that Charles Egger would like to see me in his office.

Mr. Egger and I had not talked often during the summer; he was a quieter man than Mr. Weaver had been, he seemed almost shy, and I had no idea why he would want to meet with me. I didn't think I'd screwed any stories up, and even if I had, it would be Sam Perdue or Jack Keller who would tell me about something like that, not Mr. Egger.

But Miss Allison escorted me in there, and he wasn't halfway into his first sentence:

"The Scripps-Howard Washington bureau needs a copyboy to work for them for a week at the Democratic National Convention in Chicago. . . ."

"Yes," I said, cutting him off. "Yes."

"The press headquarters will be in the Stevens Hotel. . . ." Mr. Egger said.

It hadn't been called the Stevens for decades; it was the Conrad Hilton, long lauded as the largest hotel in the United States. Even I knew that. But I wasn't going to contradict him. This was going too well.

"Scripps-Howard Washington will pay your way there, and your hotel room and expenses," Mr. Egger said. "Your salary will be paid by us—your usual paycheck."

I floated back out into the city room. Sam had already heard.

"You're there to run errands for the Washington bureau," he said. "But if you want to, on your own time you can write stories about the convention for us."

As if I hadn't thought of that even as Mr. Egger had been talking in his office.

"Let me give you some names to look up when you're there," Sam said. I picked up a piece of copy paper and one of our thick pencils.

"There's A. W. 'Stoop' Mininni," Sam said. "He's a big man with the Franklin County Democratic party here. You tell him that I told you to find him. . . ."

At home I gave my parents the news, and within a day my father walked into my bedroom with a little yellow booklet.

"This is an expense book," he said. "You should write down every penny you spend. Itemize everything. You can't travel on business and just let the expenses pile up and assume you'll remember later. Ask for receipts everywhere you go."

It was the last thing I cared about, but I took the booklet from him. A few days later I flew to Chicago and took the bus from O'Hare to the Palmer House, where I was supposed to be staying. Mr. Egger had told me that there was no reservation in my name, but that one of Scripps-Howard's star correspondents, Jim G. Lucas, was ill, and that I should stay in his room. He said to just tell the desk clerk that I was Jim G. Lucas.

Improbably, it worked. This was before the days when hotels required credit cards at check-in; Mr. Egger had given me a receipt, mailed to him by the Washington bureau, that verified a pre-paid room for Jim G. Lucas, and I presented that receipt and got a key in return.

I threw my bags in the room and hurried to the Sherman House hotel—that was where Sam had told me the Ohio delegation was

staying—and one of the first things I saw in the lobby was Columbus
Mayor Maynard E. Sensenbrenner trying to check in. Apparently there
was some confusion.

"Sensenbrenner," he said with annoyance. "Maynard Sensenbrenner! Mayor of Columbus!"

The clerk had no such name.

"Mayor of Columbus!" Mayor Sensenbrenner said. The clerk was
not visibly impressed.

At dinnertime I sat alone in a booth at a drugstore lunch counter
in the Loop, and carefully filled in the first day's page of the yellow expense book my dad had given me:

"Hot dog. 50 cents. Coke. 15 cents."

I felt like a person who was suddenly on his own.

I almost didn't make it to the convention press headquarters at the
Conrad Hilton because I somehow locked myself in my hotel room
bathroom, and couldn't get out.

The Palmer House was an old and famous hotel with beyond-solid
vintage construction, and the doors were made of the heaviest oak. I
had locked the bathroom door when I got in the shower—don't ask
me why—and when I emerged from the shower the bathroom was full
of steam from the hot water, and the door was jammed.

After a few minutes of trying to unlock it I went into a panic. No
one knew I was here; I was registered as Jim G. Lucas. I had put a DO
NOT DISTURB sign outside my room's main door. With the town as full
as it was, no one was likely to try to enter the room with that sign out
there. If I couldn't get out of the bathroom, and remained in there with
no food or communication to the outside world for the next week, even
if my parents were to call the Palmer House and ask for me they would
be told that there was no guest with my name. I had a vision of maintenance workers, in a few weeks, breaking down the door and encountering my skeletal remains in the bathroom. Followed by a news bulletin
flashed around the globe: BONES OF JIM G. LUCAS FOUND IN CHICAGO
HOTEL.

But I finally, by wrestling with the lock and throwing myself against the bathroom door, unjammed it, and hurried to the Conrad Hilton. The entire and gargantuan basement level had been turned into a cavernous pressroom for the nation's reporters, each news organization having its own curtained-off area. I walked past the newsrooms of *Time* magazine and the *New York Times* and *Newsweek* and the Hearst Newspapers and the *Los Angeles Times,* and found the Scripps-Howard workroom. It was presided over by Jack Steele, a no-nonsense-looking man who was the chief of the Washington bureau. I tried to tell him about my bathroom, but he wasn't interested.

"Go upstairs to my hotel room," he said, handing me his key. "I left some folders up there. Bring them back here to me."

I rode the elevator to his floor, let myself into his room, and the phone rang. I picked it up—it was Mr. Steele giving me some more instructions. On the cradle of his phone—the part where the receiver rested—I noticed staring up at me the same custom-made item that I had found on my hotel phone at the Palmer House:

A clear yellow plastic doodad that was snapped onto the base of the phone, and, inserted into the plastic, a black-and-white photo of Chicago Mayor Richard J. Daley, smiling toward the ceiling. There was some wording indicating that Mayor Daley welcomed the guest in the hotel room to his city. I was to find out later that the Daley-says-hello photos had been attached to every telephone in every hotel room in Chicago that week. Mayor Sensenbrenner of Columbus may have been a fish out of water here, but there was one mayor who was the biggest fish in the ocean—in fact, he was the proprietor of the ocean, and had taken pains not to let anyone forget it, each time they picked up the phone to make a call.

When I returned to the pressroom—which was cooled in the hot August city to near-Arctic temperatures by the hotel's air-conditioning system—I saw a woman named Wauhillau La Hay, Scripps-Howard's marquee Washington feature-and-society writer, loudly informing Jack Steele that she had just walked over to Marshall Field's and bought herself a new heavy overcoat, courtesy of the company. "If it's going to feel like winter down here, then you're going to pay for my winter clothes," she said in a tone that can only, and admiringly, be described as reporter-in-old-time-movies brassy. She handed him the department-store receipt, and, in those days of endless newspaper revenues, he didn't put up an objection.

The week, for me, was something loftier than the galaxies. I was sent all over town to pick up press releases and run errands—at one press conference to which I was sent I saw the great columnist Russell Baker of the *New York Times* approach the politician running it, ex-tend his hand, and say casually: "Russ Baker." Which, of course, he must have said a hundred times a day every day, but which struck me as so cool—"Russ Baker," said deadpan—that for the rest of the week I found myself, when no one was looking, shaking hands with thin air and muttering the words nonchalantly to myself: "Russ Baker." "Russ Baker." "Russ Baker."

I rode the press buses to the International Amphitheater for the convention sessions every night, and the sensory wash of that place—the size, the color, the commotion, the thousands of milling and chatter-ing attendees, the lights—left me dazzled and all but dumbstruck. The Scripps-Howard Washington bureau reporters would send me onto the convention floor to conduct quick interviews with specific members of state delegations, so I could bring the quotes back to them; I looked up, high above the convention floor, to see, in their booth to the left, Chet Huntley and David Brinkley, and in his booth to the right, Wal-ter Cronkite. In the impossibly congested aisles I squeezed past some of the floor correspondents from the networks, wearing their bulky power packs: Frank McGee and Sander Vanocur of NBC, Mike Wal-lace and the young Dan Rather of CBS. Several times I made an ex-cuse to walk past the seat near the front of the floor where Mayor Daley himself sat, his eyes—who would have guessed it?—as soft blue and seemingly gentle as a sapphire ocean. One evening, at the nailed-together wooden press tables that flanked the podium, I saw, banging away at his portable typewriter, Jimmy Breslin on deadline. When he stepped away to get a cup of coffee I sidled past his machine just so I could sneak a peek at his lead, still rolled into the carriage. Our mezza-nine back on Third Street had seemed like the center of the universe to me, but now I realized what I probably had known all along: It wasn't.

I could see Cronkite up there, his back to the convention floor, speaking into a camera lens, and I knew that my parents were at home watching him in their bedroom.

I was more than aware, of course, that this 1968 convention was unlike any national political gathering in memory—hand-to-hand combat between Chicago police officers and anti-war demonstrators, National Guard troops and U.S. Army jeeps in the middle of Michigan Avenue, the smell of tear gas wafting up toward hotel rooms—but the fact was, I had no first-person memory of any convention other than this one. So the wild backdrop, while mesmerizing, became all but routine within a day or two.

I got up very early and I stayed up very late and, in the hours that Jack Steele gave me off from working for the Scripps-Howard Washington bureau, I wrote stories for the *Citizen-Journal*. I decided right away that I wasn't going to be following around Mayor Sensenbrenner or A. W. "Stoop" Mininni or any of the other Franklin County politicians whose names Sam Perdue had given me. It would have been a little absurd, I thought: the idea of writing standard local-delegation sidebars when, in the streets of Chicago, urban warfare was breaking out. So I wrote about what I was seeing: the mayhem and bloodshed in the midst of a fabled American city, the anger and finger-pointing inside the convention hall (even as a tuxedoed orchestra on a rear balcony played "Happy Days Are Here Again"), the fear that was everywhere.

And for me, after writing my stories, to see one of the Scripps-Howard teletype operators in the basement of the Hilton sending them across the wire to Columbus—to see a man who was being paid by Scripps carefully type my words into his machine, the same way he was typing the words of Dan Thomasson and Bill Steif and Ted Knap and the real Scripps-Howard Washington-based correspondents . . .

I watched the teletype operator as he did it, I saw his fingers hit the keys, and I knew that within seconds my story would be clacking its way onto a roll of paper in the *C-J* city room, inside one of those iron-bodied wire machines on the mezzanine, by the windows overlooking the alley. And I knew that the guys at the *C-J* would be seeing my words after they were stripped from the wire machine, would be reading my reporting from the convention.

"You having fun?" Jack Steele asked me, and he knew I was—there must have been a time when all of this was new for him, too.

He read a carbon of the story that I had just handed to the teletype operator. He knew I had not missed a minute of the copyboy duties I was committed to performing for him—he knew I was doing all the reporting and writing on my own time.

"When do you sleep?" he said.

"Next week," I said.

Which came way too soon. I wanted the convention never to end. When it did I flew back to Port Columbus and my father picked me up. He had a copy of that morning's *C-J* on the front seat of the car, opened to my last story from the convention, so I would see it.

At a stoplight on our way home a car pulled up next to us; it was driven by a kid named Steve Pariser who had gone to high school with me, and who was a year or two older.

"How was the convention?" he called into my dad's car window.

He knew. He had been reading the *C-J*.

When the light changed and we pulled away, my dad said, "So you must have quite a readership here."

I was secretly pleased to hear him say it, and I said, joking: "I'm a household word."

"So's 'toilet,'" my father said.

We reached our house and later that night, when everyone was sleeping, I went to a little alcove in the upstairs hallway that ran between the bedrooms. It was where we kept one of our telephones.

I picked up the heavy black receiver and clicked something onto the cradle. I had brought it back to Ohio with me from Chicago. From that night on, any time someone in our family lifted the receiver of that hallway phone, he or she was greeted with the smiling face of Mayor Richard J. Daley. The photo was in black-and-white; you would never have known just how blue his eyes were.

The Columbus city buses, after the convention experience, did not feel quite as exotic or charged with excitement as those press buses to and from the International Amphitheatre. Back to work at the *Citizen-Journal*, reporting on Columbus Board of Education debates or shootings in neighborhoods on the edges of downtown, I would ride the city bus to work each afternoon and sometimes I would see fellow passengers reading the *C-J*.

This never ceased to be a kick. Glancing a few rows ahead of me on the bus, seeing that someone was reading the story I had written the night before, I had to resist the urge to get up and tap the person on the shoulder and say: "That's mine." It wasn't so much pride of authorship that made me feel so good—it was that I was a part of the newspaper. Included in the enterprise.

That stenciled lettering with our paper's name—the stenciled painting on the glass doors that led from the elevators on the mezzanine to our city room . . . the *Citizen-Journal* lettering might as well have been a trumpet sounding a rousing herald. The lettering silently announced, as I walked in that door every day: Something important is going to happen in here before midnight. And none of us knows yet just what it will be.

Taking the back stairs to the mezzanine, though—skipping the elevator ride and hurrying up the stairway that the public didn't know about—for some reason made the whole thing even better. Arriving in the city room that way, to be greeted by all the reassuring noise, continued to feel, as it had started to feel that first copyboy summer, a little like letting myself in the back door of my parents' house. Just by using the *C-J* staircase and that rear door—wooden, unlabeled—allowed me to think: You really are at home here.

It was all I could do not to instinctively reach into my pocket and try to hang my keys on the rack on the wall—even though there was no rack on the wall here. There was at home—at home, when we came in the back door and into our family's kitchen, we'd automatically hang our keys on this funny-looking vertical rack with little rods sticking out of it. I felt just that at ease coming through the back door of the city room.

I think everyone who worked within those walls must have felt pretty much the same way. We sensed, every day and every night, that the stories we covered—the robbery, the fire, the murder—might be the most important events in the lives of the people at the center of them. For those people, the most important events ever, on the most important days ever.

But for us it would be gone by morning. We knew—or we learned quickly—that if we were to write a second-day story about the event we had covered for Page One yesterday, that second-day story wouldn't get front-page play. Whatever the new developments were, they were unlikely to be as stirring as what had landed the story on Page One when it was brand-new. That's why it was better—or so we thought— to be in the newspaper business than to be in any other business.

In the newspaper business, we could go blithely about our duties, day after day, in the midst of the world's bad things but at the same time immune to those bad things. As long as we had a new paper to put out the next morning, yesterday's bad things would be left behind, stuck in time, while we would be free to go on and on.

We had no idea where the advertisements came from.

We never saw an ad salesman.

If the *Citizen-Journal* was fat one morning because it was full of ads, or scrawny on another morning because the ads weren't so plentiful, those were not things to which we paid heed.

To worry about the number of ads would be like worrying if the paper was going to come out the next day—it was, we knew that, so the advertising revenues, or lack of them, were not a concern to us. We knew, because we'd been told, that the *Dispatch*, as part of the joint operating agreement, was responsible for all *Citizen-Journal* advertising sales and all

Citizen-Journal circulation efforts. So we just figured all of that was the *Dispatch's* business—literally—and we had no reason to think about it, and certainly no reason to fret about it.

"We're a little tight on the inside pages tonight," Sam might say to us, which translated to: Write short. But writing short was just one more instruction to follow, not a cause for furrowed brows or toss-in-bed concern. Every day we would arrive on the mezzanine and the latest edition of our newspaper would be sitting there on desks and tables throughout the office, and that was the proof of our robust health: Look what we did yesterday—it's right there. That newspaper didn't exist twenty-four hours ago, and here it is. We did it. And we're going to do it again today, and by tomorrow at this time something that doesn't exist in any way will be sitting right here on these tables and desks.

So even as the presses on Third Street rolled late each night—even as we could feel that tingle in our shoes—there was a sensation inside us of, if not exactly emptiness, then emptiness's first cousin. The sensation was not so much of a job completed, but of "Now what?"

Our newspaper was rolling, being born somewhere below us in the building, and the answer to "Now what?" was that in a few hours we would get to wake up with the rising of the sun and come here and, together, make all of this happen again. The solution, the antidote, to the emptiness was that we were going to be allowed to do this once more the next morning, and the morning after, and the morning after.

I felt so much a part of it all that sometimes I half-forgot that I was still in school, that I was due back in classes in September, that this was not my life.

There were moments of unmitigated joy. A week or two after I returned from the convention I was standing back at the *C-J* staff mailboxes, and the usual rolls of unopened newspapers from other Scripps-Howard cities were piled haphazardly on the ledge: papers from El Paso, papers from Cincinnati, papers from Evansville, papers from Pittsburgh.

I absentmindedly tore the wrappers off a few of the papers on top of the pile, and started leafing through them. I was reading an edition of the *Memphis Press-Scimitar* that had been mailed to us, and as I was going through it I stopped at a wire-service photo of the Chicago police fighting with demonstrators on Michigan Avenue, and beneath the photo was a story about the disorders. By me.

Scripps-Howard News Service, it said under my name, and I knew in an instant what had happened: Jack Steele, in that chilly basement pressroom at the Conrad Hilton, had read the carbons of one of the stories I was sending back to Columbus, had liked it, and had instructed the teletype operator to distribute it not just to the *Citizen-Journal,* but to the whole Scripps-Howard chain. He hadn't said a word to me—he had just done it. I felt like dancing, right there by the metal mailboxes.

I felt so much a part of it all. . . .

There were seldom double bylines in the C-J—seldom stories that were written by more than one person. It wasn't that the editors were philosophically against it; it simply never occurred to them, because we didn't have enough reporters on the staff to pair any of us up for double-byline stories. If two reporters were to work on one story, that would mean that there would be one less story in the paper in the morning, and who would want that to happen?

We didn't work on multi-part undertakings that would entail more than a few hours to report and write and would be scheduled to run months in the future. There were no "projects teams," as I was to encounter at newspapers years later—no elite subcategories of reporters who were split off from the rest of the staff to work on allegedly important and protracted long-term endeavors. There were no layers of departments—what you saw in that room on the mezzanine was what there was, and the newspaper the next morning was what you got. There was no journalistic theorizing or professional navel-gazing— what happened in that room was that one guy at a time was sent out to a story and told to write it quickly, because there would be more stories for him to write when that one was finished.

There didn't seem to be a management track. Management was the people we saw in the room, at the editors' desks—management was us, or at least some of us, and not an outside or upstairs or distant force about which to be apprehensive. When there was a change, management, as often as not, was just the same men moving to different desks.

Maybe the essence of what was going on in that room—in the city desk part of the room, in the sports desk part of the room—was this:

If we could immerse ourselves every hour, every day, in thinking about what was going on that specific hour, that specific day, and get it as close to right as we could in the paper the next morning, then we didn't have to give any thought at all to what was going to go on in the long run. The long run didn't matter, didn't really exist—we could push the long run aside.

Sometimes I looked at the people around me and I thought to myself that if this particular way of work wasn't out there, I didn't know what these men and women would do. If this job had not been invented— newspapering—I didn't know where these men and women would have gone, what they would have done with their lives. That was the great thing: this, this way of life, was made for them.

And there would be times, late at night, when the last deadline had passed and the room had thinned out, when I would look around that room and know for a fact that it had been waiting for me all my life.

On the last night of my summer I went to the little glassed-in area with the bamboo rods and I spread all of the *Citizen-Journals* from the past three months on the table.

This early-September ritual felt somehow comforting by now. I started with my first day of work and looked at every page—the stories, the headlines, the photos, the display advertisements—right up until today's edition. There would be one more paper that I would feel a part of—tomorrow's—and I would have a story in it, and then the morning editions of the C-J would continue to be born and I would be somewhere else, not knowing about them.

It was a warm night outside the building, and I knew that my friends were out drinking beer or showing off for girls or just letting the hours before and after midnight lead them to wherever those hours might lead. I had my back to the city room as I read the months of newspapers, and the door of the glassed-in area with the bamboo rods was open, and from behind me I could hear the shabby symphony, the sound of all those typewriters, each with its own voice and pitch. I didn't want to go home but after a while I did.

18

Maybe I knew on some level, as I left that night, that I would never work at the *Citizen-Journal* again; maybe I sensed, somewhere beneath the surface, that my life would be taking me elsewhere.

But even if I knew that—and I'm not at all sure I did—the one thing that never occurred to me, even for a second, was that the *Citizen-Journal* was already in trouble. The men who were running it then may have had no idea themselves, but the *Citizen-Journal*'s years were numbered, although if someone had said that to me as I departed the mezzanine that night I would have dismissed it as a not-very-good joke.

And newspapers themselves—the papers that rolled off the presses in every city and small town in the nation? The concept that, within forty years, they, as an industry, would find themselves in the most serious and disheartening kind of trouble?

Not conceivable.

Newspapers a fading and frightened industry? That would have been like saying that America's highways were endangered, or that its electrical wires and water pipes were in peril of going out of business. Some things were permanent; some things were impervious to being lost. They were public utilities.

Many years later, a country song would become a hit, its theme that of a man who fears that the woman he loves is getting ready to leave him. She hasn't said anything to him about it; on the façade of the relationship, all is well.

But he knows.

The key line in the song is:

I can't see a single storm cloud in the sky, but I sure can smell the rain . . .

I would like to be able to say that, on the night I walked out of the *Citizen-Journal* newsroom, I was intuitive enough to already be smelling the rain. That I understood, in my heart, that the way of life I had learned to adore was, somewhere off in the distance, getting ready to face the hardest of hard times.

But I didn't. Everything in the newspaper world felt wonderful. No clouds anywhere—not even the ones you couldn't see.

I went to work for the *Chicago Sun-Times* the month I graduated. There were four daily papers in Chicago—the *Sun-Times*, the *Tribune*, the *Daily News*, and *Chicago Today*, formerly *Chicago's American*. Things in the Columbus newspaper world, with the joint operating agreement in effect, had always been vaguely gentlemanly—the C-J and the *Dispatch* were competitors, yes, but there wasn't any bloodthirstiness. The two papers pleasantly coexisted because, it was understood, neither of them was at risk of dying (the JOA guaranteed that), and also, it was understood, because the *Dispatch* was assured of supremacy.

In Chicago it was different. The papers gleefully went after each other on their front pages and on the newsstands—behind every story and every headline was the implicit desire to show the other guys up. It felt like a fight, every day. The four papers were owned by two entities—Marshall Field and his family owned the *Sun-Times* and the *Daily News*, the Tribune Company owned the *Tribune* and *Chicago Today*—but there might as well have been four separate proprietors. The staffs took pleasure in publicly making their rivals stumble.

The game was distinct from, bigger than, what I had seen at 34 South Third Street. Ben Hayes and Tom Keys and Wink Hess, although celebrated bylines around Columbus, never seemed larger than life. That was part of their charm. In the *Sun-Times* building at 401 North Wabash, Irv Kupcinet and Ann Landers and Bill Mauldin would stroll through the city room—*their* city room—and it was all I could do not to stare. On the other side of the fourth floor—separated only by a narrow space with the wire-service machines inside it—was the *Daily News* city room, where, in a messy cubicle on the southeast corner, sat Mike Royko, then still in his thirties. I couldn't wait to get to work every day.

Reporters were supposed to call to the copyboys and copygirls when their stories were ready—most reporters shouted "Copy!", as the reporters at the *C-J* had, but a few of the older ones at the *Sun-Times* shouted "Boy!" I knew I could never do that—at twenty-two I was the youngest full-time reporter on the staff (tied with Doug Woodlock, who went on to become a federal judge in Boston)—and there was no way I was going to call one of the copyclerks "Boy." Some of them were older than I was.

So once I had introduced myself to them I would quietly call them over by name and hand them my copy. I didn't aspire to being grizzled, and there was no danger of that anyway.

I noticed right away that *Sun-Times* reporters, particularly those who covered crime, often used some variation of the phrase: "the *Sun-Times* has learned." When a story was especially splashy—when it dominated the tabloid-sized front page—the phrase was amended to: "the *Sun-Times* has learned exclusively."

It seemed to be part of the bigness of the newspaper business in Chicago—part of the swagger. The reporters were always learning things, and passing the secrets they had learned on to readers, who were expected to accept the veracity of those told secrets on faith.

At the *C-J* I don't recall anyone ever doing that—ever telling the readers, in a story, that "the *Citizen-Journal* has learned" something. The *C-J* wasn't the kind of paper that would learn anything on the sly, in dim back alleys. We just went out and talked to people and quoted them. On the mezzanine, we didn't see ourselves as very grand. But then, Ann Landers never walked among us.

My first big story was the Chicago Seven conspiracy trial—the federal trial in which the defendants, including Abbie Hoffman and Jerry Rubin, were accused of having conspired to disrupt the 1968 Democratic National Convention.

If the defendants had indeed done that, I was sort of happy that they had—the convention, only a year before, had been a lot more interesting to cover because of it. But now I wasn't a Scripps-Howard copyboy carrying my dad's yellow expense-ledger book—now I was in Judge Julius J. Hoffman's courtroom every day, listening to testimony.

It was a major running national story—the three television networks, in those pre-cable days, had courtroom artists and big-name correspondents in attendance, the *New York Times* and *Time* and *Newsweek* covered on a daily basis, and the country was paying attention. One day some of the defendants, to taunt Judge Hoffman, arrived in court wearing black judicial robes, which did not amuse him; it did, however, raise the national profile of the trial even higher.

The trial lasted for months, and like all trials that go on for a long time, even the most spectacular ones, there were slow days when not much fireworks were being generated. On one of those days my father happened to be in Chicago on business. I had gotten to know the bailiffs and court security personnel, and on that day I asked them if they would mind if I brought my dad to the press section of the courtroom with me. They said that should be fine.

The way the courtroom was set up, the jury sat on one side of the room, in two rows against a wall. Directly in front of them were the prosecution tables. A few feet away were the defense tables, and, next to them, two long rows of chairs—like a mirror of the jury box—for the press, against the other wall.

My dad met me in the lobby of the federal building at lunchtime, after the morning court session had ended. I took him to the elevators and we rode to Judge Hoffman's floor; we entered the courtroom through the press entrance (which was a cloakroom door), and we sat next to each other among the other reporters.

He seemed nervous. The defendants came in from lunch—they were very famous men by now—and my dad appeared almost startled to be sitting within a foot or two of them, and mesmerized as they bantered lightly with the reporters, as they usually did during down moments in the proceedings. Judge Hoffman entered from his private door, all rose, and the testimony and arguments resumed.

My dad pulled a little appointment book from his suit coat and took some notes. I don't know if he did it just to record his thoughts, or to have something to show his friends back at the Neil House at lunch when he got home, or if perhaps taking notes was what he thought he should be doing to prevent some court official from spotting him as an interloper and tossing him out. It wasn't much of an afternoon for banner-headline testimony, as I recall, and when court ended for the day I rode the elevator to the lobby with him.

I was going back to the *Sun-Times* building to write my story; he was going back to his hotel.

"What did you think?" I said.

"Well, it's a lot more fun than what I do all day at the Bron-Shoe Company," he said.

I knew he meant it and it was one of the few completely serious things he ever said to me. And he was right. It was nonstop fun, being a young newspaper reporter then.

"Give it to me in takes."

On deadline at night, that would be the request from the assistant city editor. The meaning of his words was:

Write one page at a time. Have a copyboy bring it to me as you're writing the next page. On an especially tight deadline, the city desk would edit that page of copy, pass it to the copy desk for further refining, and have it sent down to the Linotype operators by the time you were reaching the bottom of your second page. There was no opportunity to revise anything at the top of the story by the time you'd written the bottom of the story; even if you had wanted to make changes, the top would already be set in metal, ready to go to press.

There was no instinct or opening to be flowery on stories like those; if the morning edition was going to be printed on schedule and driven by truck to all the houses around the Chicago area, then one take at a time, in the dead of night, was how it had to be.

And—talk about fun; talk about what if felt like to be a young man working for a newspaper. . . .

Often after our shifts ended we would gather at bars in the Old Town area, around North Avenue and Wells Street. Some of them had licenses to remain open until four A.M.

And there were many nights, as the bars were closing, when, on North Avenue, we would see the clunky red *Sun-Times* trucks, beginning to deliver the morning edition to newsstands and vending boxes.

We knew the drivers; they knew us. We all worked out of that building on Wabash. There were no satellite printing plants; we wrote the stories in that building, the presses rolled in that building, the red trucks were loaded with bundles of newspapers at that building, and then the drivers sped away from that building.

So as we would come out of the bars in the hours before dawn, we would see the *Sun-Times* drivers and they would see us, and they would hit the brakes and offer to give us a lift home.

And we would climb into the truck—the truck filled with newspapers we had helped to write—and they would take us to wherever we asked to be dropped off. I remember one night in particular when Roger Ebert, who had not yet stopped drinking, got into the truck with me and with Paul Galloway, another *Sun-Times* reporter, and Ebert pulled a copy of the paper from the top of a bundle and read the movie review he had just turned in a few hours earlier. It was magic, nights like that.

And it was magic that would never go away, or so we assumed, because the need for this would never go away: the latest news delivered in the darkness by men who were paid to drive trucks, trucks jammed with piles of newsprint covered in messy black ink.

At some point in the 1970s—this was right around the time that the Pong video games were popular in taverns—the first Atex machines appeared in the rear of the *Sun-Times* city room.

Like the Pong games, they were rudimentary—in Pong, a computerized dot bounced back and forth across a screen, propelled by two opposing and not-very-convincing-looking Ping-Pong paddles; on the Atex machines, bright and fuzzy green letters of the alphabet appeared the moment a person touched his fingers to the typewriter-keyboardlike device below. One day there weren't any Atex machines in the city room and the next day there were. Just a handful of them at first—if they worked out, we were told, we would someday all be using them.

In the future, we were informed, you could write your stories on them and the stories would end up in the newspaper in the morning, without having to be set in type by hand. That was the goal, although we didn't really believe it was achievable. They might as well have been candy-bar vending machines, sitting back on the outskirts of the features department; they were mostly an exotic curiosity.

We were allowed to play around on them—they weren't setting type yet—and they were hooked up to a printer in the newsroom that allowed a person to print out, on a long continuous roll of paper like the rolls of paper in the wire-service machines, what he or she had just written. It took me only part of one day to realize that writing on these machines was better than writing on typewriters; you could back up and delete, you could insert, you could scroll between the top and bottom of a long story . . . it made the mechanics of writing much more pleasurable and efficient in just about every way.

I liked it so much that I started going back to the Atex machines to write my stories, even though at that point the machines were just a toy. I would write the story, then print it out on the long roll, then use a scissors to cut the sheet into typewriter-page-sized increments. I would send the pieces of paper to the copy desk.

My vision of the business side of newspapers was still the less-than-worldly one I'd had at the *C-J*: I thought that the men who ran the business did whatever it was they did on another floor, completely oblivious to what we did on the news floor. Thus, when the number of Atex machines began to increase at the *Sun-Times*—and, later, when I had accepted a job at the *Tribune*, and computer terminals began to appear there—I assumed that these were decisions driven by the desires of the editors, and not the business-side people.

Once, at the *Tribune*, when the computer terminals were just being introduced, some of the top men in the company came downstairs from their offices high in the Tribune Tower to take a look. They wore dark suits and shiny shoes and subdued-patterned neckties, and I thought they must be perusing the computers with mild disapproval. These men were, if anything, traditionalists.

I said to one of them: "These things will never beat typewriters, will they?"

He showed me a thin smile and said nothing.

They may have been conservative by nature, those business-side executives at newspaper companies all over America, but they were willing to step into the future if the reason was right. And what they saw when they looked at the computer terminals was enough to make them giddy inside. They were seeing a way to get rid of human beings—a way to be able to stop paying the Linotype operators. They were seeing a way to slash their payrolls. No wonder they looked so pleased.

So gradually the typewriters in the newsrooms were thrown out, and the computer terminals became ubiquitous. We were, in effect, setting our own type now; what our fingers tapped onto the keyboards became, by morning, words in print on the pages of the newspaper itself.

What we didn't see coming was that the computers would soon enough take over in ways we could not imagine. That the computer screens would become the newspapers—that the paper part of newspapers would become optional.

And that you wouldn't have to work for a newspaper at all to have your words read around town, or around the world.

My favorite syndicated columnist in the *Citizen-Journal* had been Jim Bishop. Unlike most of the other national columnists whose work ran on that *C-J* section front, he didn't deal in opinion—at least he didn't deal in pontificating. Instead, he told stories. He emphasized this in the title of the column itself. Most columnists just had their name, with their photo, run on top of their work. He called his column: Jim Bishop, Reporter.

He occasionally used one device that I particularly liked: if he was telling a story in which he didn't want to make the ending too obvious—if he didn't want to hit the reader over the head with his wrap-up—he would simply let the final sentence end in dots. By doing that, he let the column trail off, and allowed the reader to think for a moment, to ponder. Deadpan and, when executed correctly, devastating: *He walked down the hill.* . . .

After I started writing a column in Chicago I would sometimes use the dots—a direct lift, stylistically, from Bishop. We had never met— my introduction to his work had been when, as a copyboy at the *C-J*, I would carry proofs of the column page from the composing room to Don E. Weaver or Jack Keller, Bishop's column headshot showing a gray-haired man in a dark suit jacket, a white shirt and a narrow tie, looking resolutely off the page—but at some point in Chicago I wrote a column in which I mentioned him in a laudatory way. I don't even remember the context of the column.

A week or two later I received a letter with a Florida postmark. It was from Jim Bishop.

He was very ill, it turned out. He had either given up the column by then, or was thinking about it. In his letter he said that he had been in the hospital—maybe he was still in the hospital when he wrote to me, I'm not certain—and he had seen my piece.

He said it made him feel so good about the work to which he had devoted his life that he had asked someone at the hospital to tape it to the wall of his room, so he could look at it from his bed.

Of course the column he had taped to the wall was from the newspaper itself—either from the Chicago paper, or from another that had picked it up and run it. In one way or another, that clipped-out piece of newsprint had made its way to him; this was well before the days when you could read a newspaper story online, just as it was well before the days when Bishop could have sent me an e-mail.

Somehow, it seemed better, or at any rate more fitting, that way: an old newspaper columnist seeing a new column saying nice things about him. Alone in a hospital room near the end of his life, looking at something on the wall written by a reader far away. . . .

Jim Bishop was one of those relatively rare newspapermen, in that era, who also were well-known authors; his 1955 book *The Day Lincoln Was Shot* was a main selection of the Book-of-the-Month Club, during the period of American social history when the Book-of-the-Month Club was a huge force. Like many American families, ours—my father and mother—belonged to the Book-of-the-Month Club, and Bishop's book about Lincoln's last day was prominently displayed on a shelf in our den.

During my years at the *Citizen-Journal*, whenever Bill Moore would send me to buy him a pack of Larks at Gray's Drugstore or in the newsstand/gift shop of the Sheraton-Columbus, I would always see the circular metal carousel that held paperback books. You'd spin the carousel around to look at all the titles—many of them novels with semi-lurid covers of half-dressed women, but also a fair number of serious works of nonfiction. I would always gaze upon those paperback racks—there was one in the front of Rogers' Drugstore near my house, too, and there was never a time when I didn't check it out—and it would represent something amazing, something unreachable: those writers had composed entire books, and someone had published them, and the books had made it all the way to Columbus.

It seemed like such an unimaginable achievement. I suppose I assumed that each book sold millions upon millions of copies, that the authors of the books on the drugstore carousels reached audiences far more vast than those that we at the C-J could ever dream of.

I didn't yet realize that most authors would kill for the more than hundred thousand readers we at the C-J had every day—I didn't yet realize, as I would later, that except for the top echelon of bestselling authors, we reached more people on a single morning than almost any author did in the entire life of a book.

Of course, in that city room we were each just writing relatively brief news stories, and writing them quickly; for us, writing a book would have been exhausting just to think about. Yet you can make the argument that what we did every day was far more amazing than the amalgam of art and commerce that brought those paperbacks to our local drugstores. Yes, we were purely local at the C-J; our words were not read anywhere outside our circulation area. But to start from nothing every morning, and by the next morning to have produced an entire new edition and have it, right on schedule, in the hands of those hundred thousand . . .

I had looked at those paperback racks in central Ohio and had wondered about the marvelous lives of the men and women whose names were on the front covers of the books. Champagne and mink coats and first-class jets to Europe—that's how they had to be living. I'd stare, and then carry Bill Moore's cigarettes back to him.

In Chicago, in the middle of the 1970s, two young men came through town and it seemed that they represented everything powerful and everything possible in the newspaper business. If there was a moment when newspapering seemed consequential and authoritative and immune to erosion, this was it. The two young men made newspapering seem bulletproof—and they were just, at the time, two scrambling reporters who had done a very good job covering a story, and who were being rewarded for it.

Bob Woodward was thirty-one. Carl Bernstein was thirty. They were both still general-assignment reporters on the local-news staff of the *Washington Post*. Richard Nixon remained in office; he would not resign until later in the summer. Woodward and Bernstein's first book, *All the President's Men*, was just coming out, but the movie based upon the book was still in the planning stages. I knew them both from time I'd put in in Washington for the *Sun-Times* covering the Nixon-McGovern presidential campaign, and then the Watergate hearings. We spent the day together in Chicago.

"I need from both of you a sense of urgency," Phil Donahue said to them.

Woodward was having television makeup swabbed onto his face in a room adjacent to Donahue's studio. Bernstein was reading a copy of the *National Lampoon* 1964 high school yearbook parody.

"We can't be introspective, or sit around sucking on our pipes," Donahue said to them. "Make 'em mad, sad, or glad."

Woodward shot a quick look at Bernstein. Bernstein shrugged. They were becoming accustomed to this sort of thing.

After the broadcast, in the back seat of a limousine that their publisher had hired to drive them around town, they talked about what was inevitably going to happen next in their lives. Robert Redford had been signed to play Woodward in the movie version of the book; the Bernstein part, which would end up going to Dustin Hoffman, had not yet been cast. Woodward said that Redford had lately been following him around to observe how he talked, how he moved, how he lived.

"That's the first time I got a little embarrassed," Bernstein said to me. "The first time Redford came into the newsroom at the *Post*. When Redford came in, it was like we were suddenly on deadline. You know what I mean? The noise level built up. There was a lot of traffic in the room. A sense of tension. But it was only eleven o'clock in the morning. I wouldn't look up from my typewriter. I could hear the whispers, and I knew what it was, and I didn't want to see it."

"I don't know," Woodward said. "I don't look at it that way. I guess I separate my emotions from it, just like it's another part of the job. I suppose that's an emotionally personal problem with me. I won't go to my feelings. I thought about Redford just like I'd think about one of

Nixon's men. What is he here for? What does he want to do? What's the mixture?"

"Yeah, but still," Bernstein said. "When Redford walked into that newsroom, I started to think about everything that's happened. I started hoping that this whole thing wasn't turning into something that it's not. I'll just be glad when this is all . . ."

He paused to search for the word.

". . . settled," he said.

As they went from television studio to television studio, I noticed that they had worked out a set of hand signals that they flashed at each other, to remind themselves to keep their answers short and not tax the attention spans of their viewing audience.

The paperback rights to their book had just been sold for a reported one million dollars. During a break between TV appearances, Bernstein said:

"My first day at work at a newspaper, I was sixteen years old. It was the *Washington Star.* I got a job as a copyboy. Summer job. I knew I wanted to be a reporter literally the first time that I saw the city room.

"So it's my first day, and I'm wearing this brand-new cream-colored suit, because I figure that this is the way that you impress people and get a job as a reporter. And I'm loving the job, loving being around the reporters. At two-thirty in the afternoon, one of the older copyboys comes around, and he says, 'It's two-thirty, and the newest copyboy always has to wash the carbon paper.' I look at him, and he says it again.

"He starts to raise his voice, and he says, 'Unless you wash the carbon paper at two-thirty, it's no good for the rest of the day, and we won't be able to get the late editions out.' So I go around the newsroom, and I pick up every piece of carbon paper off of every desk, and I take it into the men's room. And I pile the carbon paper into one of the sinks, and I turn the water on full blast and I start scrubbing the carbon paper with my hands.

"The water is spraying all over me, and my beautiful new suit is getting all wet and grimy, and I keep scrubbing away. While this is going on, the managing editor walks in. He sees me, and he says, 'What in the name of Christ are you doing?' And I say, 'Washing the carbon paper, Mr. Noyes, it's two-thirty.' And he starts yelling, and saying that if the copyboys ever pull a prank like that again, they'll be fired, and he tells me to get the hell out of the men's room.'"

It all changed so fast. Late in the afternoon, the three of us were having a drink outdoors at a place on lower Rush Street called Riccardo's. The Wrigley Building loomed somewhere above us; across the way we could see, in the shadows of the setting sun, the loading dock of the *Sun-Times* building.

"The movie," Bernstein said. "Who should I get to play me? How about Desi Arnaz, Jr. And Mel Brooks as Deep Throat."

Newspaper life seemed so stuffed with possibilities, preposterous and funny and unlimited in its horizons.

"We'd better get going," Woodward said. "We're supposed to be at CBS in fifteen minutes."

Bernstein said: "By the time we get to the Catskills, we'll have this thing down pat."

I had gotten implausibly lucky. The *Sun-Times* had given me my own column when I was twenty-three, and I was still in my twenties when it was put into national syndication, which grew in numbers when I crossed Michigan Avenue and accepted an invitation to join the *Tribune*. The magazine I had most admired when I was growing up, *Esquire*, hired me to write its lead column, which we called "American Beat"; the television news broadcast I most admired, *Nightline*, hired me to be its first contributing correspondent, and I traveled the United States reporting show-opening pieces that served as lead-ins to Ted Koppel's live interviews.

Newspapering, and all the potentials and promises that came with it, seemed to be at the center of the world, and in the middle of all that it was sort of hard to smell the rain.

The one request that I had made when the column went into syndication was that the salesmen approach the *Citizen-Journal* in Columbus;

they did, and the *C-J* became one of the first papers to sign up as a client. Whenever I would go home I would make a point of going down to 34 South Third Street, where life on the mezzanine appeared to have changed not at all, except in surface ways. Some faces had disappeared, to be replaced by others; the copyboys and copygirls, I was told, were no longer required to make those food runs for the staff, because such duties seemed a little too servant-like in an ostensibly more no-one's-better-than-anyone-else era. The pastepots were gone, because computer terminals had replaced the typewriters, and revisions of stories on deadline no longer necessitated snipping apart pages of copy paper and pasting them back together.

But the room looked the same, and the face of the paper—its front page, its type style, its layouts, its headline fonts—was a face I loved. It felt like the face of a friend, the face of that newspaper; you couldn't read it anywhere else—I don't know how I would have felt about the *C-J* if I had been able to summon it up on the Internet with a click every day in Chicago, but that wasn't possible, there was no Internet and the only way to read the *Citizen-Journal* was to buy a copy of the *Citizen-Journal*. One of the facts of life in syndication was that client papers would often trim and harshly edit columns to fit the space they had available on a given day; I never liked to pick up a newspaper in some city and see that a story I had worked on diligently had been whittled down in a way that made it read clumsily or incompletely, but I winced especially when I was visiting Columbus and saw that a column had been crunched, because the readers of the *Citizen-Journal* were the ones for whom I especially wanted to do my best.

The life I had found beyond the mezzanine offered so many improbable moments that made me want to pinch myself that, had I literally done it, I would have been covered in bruises. I would be in an ABC News editing studio in London at three-thirty in the morning England time, finishing a piece on deadline and then putting it up on a satellite to New York where, within minutes, the *Nightline* theme music would sound and the story would lead the broadcast. When *Esquire* planned a special six-hundred-page-plus issue to commemorate its fiftieth anniversary, its editors assigned fifty writers to profile fifty men and women, living and dead, who had had the most significant influence on the world during the past fifty years. I was asked to write about Muhammad Ali, and as he and I traveled around the country and shared meals I silently thought about that day I had seen him at the CORE convention in Columbus, when I had been sent over to the Sheraton because Wink Hess had been insulted.

Smell the rain? There didn't appear to be a cloud within a thousand miles. When that issue of *Esquire* was published, the fifty writers, and all of the subjects who could make it, were flown to New York for a public celebration. We were summoned to Gracie Mansion for a breakfast at which the mayor was the host; in the evening there was a dinner at the Four Seasons for the writers and the subjects. Tom Wolfe and Norman Mailer and Kurt Vonnegut Jr. were present; so were Ali, and Dr. Benjamin Spock, and Philip Johnson. After dessert chartered buses carried us all to Lincoln Center, where, in honor of the issue, a black-tie party for two thousand guests was under way. In the men's room, I stood in my rented tuxedo at a urinal and looked to my right and, standing at the next one in his tuxedo (I have a feeling it wasn't rented), was William Paley, the founder of CBS. We were escorted, writers and subjects, to a balcony, where we were introduced to the crowd in the main room below.

We were, I remember thinking, on the mezzanine.

And with all that, the one thing that was a constant for me was this:

Wherever I was, whatever publication or broadcast for which I was writing, there always came a moment, just as I was about to turn the story in, when I instinctively hoped for the approval of Bill Moore or Sam Perdue. The newspaper would be holding space for whatever I might write; *Esquire* or *Nightline* would have reserved a hole in the magazine or the broadcast for my work. It was going to run; there was no question about that.

Yet there was always that moment, and it never went away, when I hoped against hope that Bill or Sam would read what I had just written, and that, across the room, I would see them nod—a sign that they thought it was good enough—and I would watch as they did what I knew they were doing next: take a copy pencil and write my byline on top of the first paragraph.

It was their approval, in that city room on Third Street, that I was always yearning for, no matter how many years had passed, and no matter where my travels had taken me. And one day in 1985 my parents called me and told me that there was some news in Columbus that they thought I would want to know about. The *Citizen-Journal* was going to die. It had just been announced. The last paper would be printed on the last day of the last month of that year.

19

It was nothing personal.

The *C-J*'s readers had not turned against it. The journalism in its pages had not declined in quality.

But the joint operating agreement with the *Dispatch*, which had been in effect since 1959, was due to expire, and the *Dispatch* had made a decision that, as a business strategy, was difficult to find fault with.

The *Dispatch* had traditionally been an afternoon paper—actually, in the term used by American newspapers for most of the twentieth century, an evening paper: the *Columbus Evening Dispatch*. That's where the money was, in the generations before network television news—in evening papers, to be read at leisure at the end of the workday.

But the changes in the nation's life brought on by the TV revolution had begun to diminish the impact of evening papers—my parents were not the only people spending less time with their evening paper, and more time with Walter Cronkite. It was going on in homes across the land.

The *Dispatch*, with reasoning that could not be objectively rebuked, had determined that it wanted to switch to morning publication. And, as the dominant paper in the partnership, it held all the cards.

The JOA would not be renewed.

Scripps-Howard, if it so chose, was free to buy its own printing presses and hire its own advertising and circulation staffs and build its own newsroom somewhere in town. It was free, if it so chose, to start over from scratch; if it wanted to strike out on its own in Columbus, there was nothing stopping it from continuing to publish the *Citizen-Journal* either as an afternoon paper, or as a morning competitor to the *Dispatch*.

But that would have been a prodigiously expensive, and chancy, proposition. Scripps-Howard decided to get out of Columbus while the getting was good.

And so it announced that the *Citizen-Journal* was folding.

Nothing personal.

Half a block south of the *Dispatch* building, on the site of the demolished old Hartman Theater, where touring Broadway shows had been presented for much of the century, a high-rise Hyatt hotel had been erected.

In the dwindling days of 1985 I checked in. There was a newspaper vending box on the corner; I put a coin into the slot and took out a copy of the next-to-last edition of the *C-J* that would ever be published.

In my room I read it—it was like having a one-way conversation with a best buddy who was on his deathbed and in his final hours—and then I tossed it onto the night table and walked in the frigid air over to the paper.

Same front doors on Third Street, same elevator (*"Durante always said goodnight to that Mrs. Calabash, but he never said who she was"*), same little landing on the mezzanine as the first day I had ever walked into the building.

Same painted lettering on the glass:

CITIZEN-JOURNAL

EDITORIAL DEPARTMENT

I walked in. They were putting out a newspaper.

————————

I sat on the edge of an unused desk and looked around me.

It was still early enough in the day that the staff was able to try to pretend it was like any other day. Phones were ringing; fingers were flying over keyboards; hands were absentmindedly grabbing for paper cups of coffee.

Except for the computer terminals on top of them, the desks appeared to be the same ones that had been there on the day I had first walked in twenty-two years before, bearing in my hands that story about the death of President Kennedy. Small things brought on a jolt of memories: the pattern of the tiles on the floor. The deadline clock hanging from the ceiling.

This room had taken me from my parents and had made my life something other—something better—than it had been before. I had always been a kid in their house, a constant presence, and then I was here at night instead. Starting that first C-J copyboy summer, our family's life changed. There was one less person at the family dining table each evening, because I was here and not there; I would spend my waking hours in this city room and I would quietly let myself into our house around midnight, when my mother and father and sister and brother were asleep. As I looked around the room it occurred to me: my mother and father had never been in here. This is the place that had taken their son away, and I had never showed it to them.

Over in a corner I saw the two top editors talking, looking together at a layout sheet. Dick Campbell was the editor-in-chief now, having succeeded Mr. Egger; Seymour Raiz was the managing editor. They were both Scripps-Howard lifers, having come down to Columbus from Cleveland. I had met them several times over the years when I would stop in at the C-J, but today I had not called in advance to say I was coming.

I approached them and we shook hands and I asked if they would mind if I wrote a column for the final paper. They already had my syndicated column for the next day, on some national topic or other, on hand, but I said I'd like to write a new one here, about this room. They said that would be fine and told me to pick out an unoccupied desk. I did, and hung my winter coat over the back of a chair.

Most of the reporters and copyeditors were people I didn't know; they'd come along in the years after I had left town.

One of them, Julie Hauserman, was sitting at the desk next to mine. She was working on a story—glancing at her notes, typing a paragraph, glancing at her notes again. The piece she was building from her notepad did not yet exist, and early tomorrow morning the words she would write—the next sentence, the next paragraph, whatever words she would come up with in the minutes ahead—would be in all those central Ohio homes.

I introduced myself. We talked for a few moments, and then she said:

"This morning my alarm radio went off, and the first story on the news was about the *Citizen-Journal* dying.

"They said it . . . and then they went on to the next news item.

"And it occurred to me: There are other stories. The city goes on. We're not the only story in town.

"We're just another story."

She went back to writing her own.

There were hours to go before I had to turn my column in, and I knew where I wanted to spend part of them, and who I wanted to spend them with. I walked back to the photo lab, and they were there. Dick Garrett. Hank Reichard. The snappiest guys I had ever known. *Shee-it, Henry.*

I could see the years in their faces. Dick had begun taking news pictures for the old *Columbus Citizen* in 1946, the year before I was born. Hank had come to the paper in 1951. Neither man had ever worked anywhere else.

Today Hank was developing by hand a photo he had just shot. The subject was a man named Ronald O'Brien, taking the oath of office as city attorney. It was scheduled to run in the final edition.

On the back of the photo, where for his entire career Hank had written "Photo by Hank Reichard," he now took a pencil and wrote: "Last photo by Hank Reichard."

Dick Garrett said to me: "It's funny. I don't even own my cameras. They've always belonged to the company. After I turn them in today, I'm going to have to go out and buy a camera to take pictures of the grandkids."

At a desk in the city room the telephone rang, and the man sitting at the desk, a reporter named Tom Holden, picked it up.

The caller was a woman from a dental association. Holden listened to her for a few seconds. Then he said into the receiver:

"Do we want to do a story on periodontal disease? Ma'am, in the first place, we just did a story on teeth. And in the second place, our newspaper is going out of business today."

Wandering around the room, seemingly lost in thought, was Sam Perdue.

He had stopped being city editor years before; he had been reassigned to write a column about state government—specifically, about the issues faced by government workers. There were a lot of those workers in the state capital.

As I approached him to say hello, a young reporter, having seen him pacing, asked him what he was doing.

"Just watching it all, like sand into the sea," Sam said.

Like Hank Reichard, Sam had begun work at the *Columbus Citizen* in 1951. On this day he was sixty-four. We stood in front of the same window overlooking downtown where he had once told me: "Nothing to write? There are *people* out there!"

Now we looked out that window together. "You know, Bob, I never learned how to sell the sizzle on the steak," he said. "I just saw myself as a working stiff. I don't know what I'm going to do now. Maybe I'll try TV. If they want an old guy with white hair."

A young reporter had a tape player on his desk, evidently to provide him with background music while he worked. I tried to imagine what Bill Moore or Jack Keller might have said to a staff member with the imprudence to have music playing in the city room, but it did no good to imagine, because it never would have happened. No staff member would have tried.

The Rolling Stones' "Sympathy for the Devil" was the song that filled the air around the reporter's desk. "We need something else," one of his *C-J* colleagues called out. "How about Bob Seger's 'The Famous Final Scene'?"

I thought about those nights with Seger up at the old Sugar Shack, before anyone knew his name, before he had made his records.

Another voice called out: "How about the Doors' 'The End'?"

All of the songs, old now, had been dreamed up, recorded, and become well known in the time since I had first walked into this room. They hadn't been written, or heard by anyone, then; now they were memories.

One of the older reporters, to whom the song titles meant nothing, worked in the midst of the noise and said, mostly to himself, "Looks like I ought to finish this damn story while there's still a newspaper around to put it in."

I started to work some more on the column I was writing, when I saw a man bundled up against the weather come through the glass door by the elevator landing, lugging a big box.

He put it on top of a counter. It turned out he wasn't there looking for anyone in particular. He didn't have an appointment. The box was a case of champagne.

He was a reader of the *Citizen-Journal*. No one more important, or less important, than that.

"I just wanted to thank you all for putting out a good newspaper," he said, and was gone.

Sitting near me was Susan Prentice, one of the younger reporters. She had grown up in Columbus.

"You know," she said, "this is the only place I ever wanted to work in my life."

I knew the feeling.

Around two-thirty in the afternoon, television and radio reporters, and outside photographers, were allowed into the city room for a half hour of interviewing and picture-taking.

I had never seen a television camera in the *C-J* newsroom before. There had never been a reason for one to be there. For the allotted thirty minutes, the presence of the outside reporters, and of the television lights, brightened up the atmosphere a little. Staff members talked into the television lenses, and the champagne that the reader had brought was poured into paper cups, and the *C-J* reporters and editors took snapshots of each other and exchanged home addresses and phone numbers. Someone—I don't know where he got this, but he must have been thinking about it in advance—threw some confetti.

Then, precisely at three P.M., building security guards in uniform appeared. Their job was to escort the outside reporters from the newsroom, because the interview session was over. The outside reporters had gotten what they needed.

They left, and the champagne was still in the cups, and the confetti was on the floor, and it was deathly quiet.

Arlen Pennell, a *C-J* photographer, set one of his cameras up on a tripod, and aimed it at the city desk.

281

He asked everyone to gather in front of the desk for a final team photo.

They did, and Arlen arranged them so that all their faces would be seen. I stood with him by his camera as he looked through the viewfinder.

"Come get in the picture," someone called to me.

I didn't think I belonged there; I had left the mezzanine many years ago, this was their paper, their team, not mine. But they were very nice about it; they motioned for me to join them.

So I did, and Arlen took one last look through the lens, and then, carrying a remote-control switch, walked over and got into the picture himself. He pressed the switch and the shutter clicked.

On the streets outside the windows of the city room it got dark early.

One by one, the staff members of the *Citizen-Journal* were leaving. They carried boxes and bags.

I finished my column and turned it in to the copy desk. I went into the men's room—unchanged, unmodernized since I had washed out all those pastepots during that first copyboy summer. On the mirror above the sink someone had scrawled, with soap: "C-J Lives!"

Back out in the city room, there wasn't much for anyone to do. A skeleton crew would be there during the evening hours, getting the edition ready to go to press. But for most of the reporters and editors, it was over.

"I just don't want to walk out of here," Susan Prentice said.

Frank Gabrenya, the paper's entertainment writer, stood by the door in his overcoat, not moving. "Getting the coat on was easy," he said.

Jack Torry, a reporter, said, "I can't stand this. I can't stand this. I know there must be worse things in the world, but I can't stand it."

I walked down Third Street to the Hyatt. I didn't have anything planned for the evening. I had a drink in the hotel bar, then went up to my room and watched some television. I tried to read a book.

After a while I knew I had to go back to the city room. There would be nothing for me to do there, I realized. But it just seemed that as long as the room was still there, I should be there, too.

The sidewalks of downtown were empty by that time of the night. I rode the elevator once more, pushed open that glass door once more.

By now just about everyone was gone. There were four, maybe six people remaining.

I walked around the city room. Up on the wall was the long piece of cardboard with all the important phone numbers inked on it: Police, Fire Department, Sheriff's Department, Jail, Clerk of Courts, State Highway Patrol, all of the local hospitals, National Weather Service.

I just felt so lucky, once again, to have found this room once upon a time, to have been permitted to be a part of it. Newspapering, at its best, is unashamedly a kind of prolonged adolescence. When you're on deadline with a good story, you never feel completely grown-up. You're a kid again—the adrenaline is flowing and the energy is total, and no matter how old you are you're a kid doing the thing that you do best.

That feeling I had first experienced in this room, that feeling late every night, even as the first papers were coming off the presses: "We get to do this again tomorrow." And now, impossibly, that was no longer true. Tomorrow, we would no longer get to do this. Not here.

Around eleven-thirty, copies of the final edition were delivered up from the pressroom. The front page looked good—the top half was a photo of the nighttime skyline of the city, and the headline, superimposed in white, said: GOODBYE, COLUMBUS.

The remaining staff members started to depart. They told me that there was a wake for the newspaper going on up on High Street, at a bar called Mellman's. They said I was welcome to join them.

But I couldn't leave. I couldn't leave. I looked up at that old deadline clock; it said that the time was 11:47 P.M. Isn't this something, I thought. The paper's dead, and everyone's gone. And I can't leave.

20

For a long time, it seemed that what happened to the *Citizen-Journal* was an anomaly, or at least not part of a troubling national drift.

The *C-J* died because it was the junior partner in a business arrangement in which the senior partner—the *Dispatch*—wanted what it had. That's what I told myself. The *C-J* had the temporary good luck of being a morning paper in the American era during which morning papers began to hold all the cards—and the good luck turned into bad luck when the JOA expired, and the *Dispatch* decided that it would prefer to be the morning paper.

That's what it seemed like to me. Certainly it never occurred to me that the death of the *Citizen-Journal* was any kind of precursor to a broader death spiral in the newspaper business. In fact, even as the *C-J* stopped publication in the middle of the 1980s, newspapers around the country were doing booming business. Where else were people going to read the news? Where else were merchants and merchandisers going to place their display ads?

In Chicago the two big newspapers had their offices on the banks of the Chicago River, so that barges carrying the enormous rolls of newsprint could enjoy close access to the loading docks that led to the pressrooms. When there was breaking news between editions, those presses would be stopped so the latest developments could be placed, on cylindrical plates, at the right places on those giant machines. Then the presses would restart. The fleets of trucks would wait for the finished product.

What could be more efficient than that? Boats, newsprint, presses, trucks: newspapers were everlasting—they were the past, the present, and the future.

The Linotype operators, all over America, began to go away.

Their skill—their art—was no longer needed.

Those computer terminals that had begun to appear in newsrooms as experiments precipitously became something other than experiments. The computers were setting type, and the type was being pasted directly onto forms that would end up as the next morning's newspaper.

The graceful, recurrent feats the Linotype men would routinely perform—the gorgeous intricacy of how they were able to set hot metal type in all the varying sizes, and fonts, and wraps—became, seemingly overnight, something that was done by the new machines.

I recalled how, at the *C-J*, the Linotype operators would make the byline—"By Wink Hess"—in one size and boldness and style of type, and then make the next line—"*Citizen-Journal* Staff Writer"—in a smaller, lighter type. So elegant-looking—both the work they did, and the product of that work.

Then, one day—gone.

But the assumption was that this was merely a cold business decision, a sign of progress on its grand march. The Linotype men might have vanished, but the newspapers?

Eternal. That's what we assumed, although one of the first things a newspaperman is taught is not to assume anything.

When the words we wrote first began appearing on computer screens other than the screens in our own newsrooms, we probably should have figured out that now everything was about to change, and quickly.

We were getting the sense that, somewhere out there, readers who were members of exotic-sounding new online services were able to read our words without picking up a printed newspaper. It seemed like an inexpedient way for people to receive their news—that's what a lot of us automatically thought. What were those readers supposed to do—print out the whole morning edition on some sort of home-publishing machines? It sounded like a bizarre hobby, an idiosyncratic niche—it sounded like a new version of shortwave radio. Maybe those people, whoever they were, were having fun with it, looking at our words on their big home computers. But it didn't have anything to do with what we saw as our task, which was making sure we met our deadlines so all the subscribers waiting for that thump on their front stoops wouldn't be disappointed at dawn.

Some of us noticed that the companies that owned our newspapers were actively promoting the home-computer-screen versions of what we were doing. The newspaper companies were urging people to read us on their computers—they were even buying billboard space next to expressways, telling rush-hour commuters what the Internet addresses of our papers were.

And they were emphasizing that reading the paper via computer was free.

The executives who ran the newspaper companies must have had a logical business plan. That's what we told ourselves.

E-mail was introduced to city rooms, and suddenly reporters were hearing from readers right away.

At work, I started asking the people who ran the Internet edition of the newspaper to try something. The Sunday column I wrote had a deadline of late Friday afternoon. I asked the editors of the Internet edition, just so we could see what would happen, to post it on the site on Friday evenings, instead of waiting until Sunday.

Within minutes of the column going up, I would begin to receive e-mails reacting to it. The readers were responding to a story that had not yet appeared in the newspaper. If, on Friday nights, they had wanted to go out and pick up a printed edition that contained the column, they would not have been able to. Yet they were reading it.

This, to me, felt great. Although a nagging thought did begin to form:

Theoretically, it seemed unnecessary for a person to work for a newspaper in order for his or her words to be distributed this way. The corporations that owned the presses, and that owned the legendary newspaper imprints? They didn't have a monopoly on this new kind of delivery system for words. Anyone, with enough knowledge of a computer, could do it—could write words, and send his or her words out, and have those words reach an audience. It did not require overhead, or massive tons of printing equipment.

In fact, owning the newspaper buildings, and being required to pay the salaries of editors and reporters and copyeditors and drivers . . . that could potentially put a company—a company that was in the business of distributing words—at a financial disadvantage.

And those people at home who were reading the Sunday columns on Friday nights on their computer screens?

They weren't being asked to pay a cent to read the columns early. The people who waited until Sunday, when the newspaper came out, to read it the traditional way—they were the ones who were obliged to reach into their pockets for cash.

This did not seem like an especially good deal for them.

In the days immediately after the twentieth century ended and the twenty-first began, I decided to conduct another experiment.

During the middle of a week, on a Wednesday, I asked readers who were seeing the column on their computer screens to look just to the left side of the text.

There was a little highlighted line that, if you clicked onto it, would provide an e-mail form.

I asked readers to click, and then to send me a note saying where in the world—the city, the state, the country—they were reading the column.

There was no such form in the printed newspaper's version of the column, and no e-mail address printed in the paper. The only people who would be able to send a note were the people seeing the column online.

The reason I was doing this, I wrote, was this:

> On a recent three-week stay on a quiet key off the west coast of Florida, the first thing I would do every morning was read three or four different papers from around the country on my computer screen. That day's editions—free, right there. In past years, on this same Florida key, I would walk over to the little grocery store to pick up some newspapers to read. Not this time. The papers, from far away, were mine with a few taps.
>
> Which is where the confusion comes in. The bosses of the newspaper industry must know what they're doing by giving their product away for free on computer screens; I certainly can't figure out why they do it, but as a reader—and as a newspaper writer—I really like it. . . .
>
> We who write for papers are told about "hits" and "clicks" and "page views"—but we have very little idea how many people are actually reading these words on glass screens, and where they are. And it occurs to me that this is a way to give myself at least a rough idea.

About an hour after the column went up that morning, I gave up trying to count the responses.

The mailbox was filling up faster than I could open the notes. I'd read one, and by the time I finished it the screen would be filled with more.

I started keeping a log of where the electronic letters came from—just the ones I had time to open and look at.

They were from all fifty of the United States. And from Brazil, Canada, New Zealand, Germany, Saipan, Portugal, Belgium, Greece, China, Sweden, Norway, Australia, Japan, Guam, the Netherlands, Singapore, Cyprus, Israel, Scotland, Puerto Rico, Poland . . . twenty-nine countries, just in the first burst of notes.

Some of the people had written brief messages:

"I am reading your article in Tulsa, Oklahoma. . . ."

"I am sitting at my desk in my office high atop Third Avenue and 57th Street in New York City. . . ."

"I'm in Strayhorn, Mississippi (that's about thirty-five miles south of Memphis). . . ."

". . . in Hong Kong . . ."

"Reading your column at my desk in the Pentagon . . ."

". . . from my horse farm near Moscow, Idaho, a university town about ninety miles south of Spokane, Washington . . ."

"Read your column here in Fukuoka, Japan, every day. . . ."

"I am reading your column in my apartment in the Bronx. . . ."

None of the people were touching newsprint. The column had been delivered to them by a planetary paperboy—the most powerful paperboy in the history of the world, riding his bike around the globe at the speed of light, tossing the latest edition onto every front porch, and not asking for a penny for the effort.

"Greetings from Bishop, California," one reader began his note. "As I look out the window from my home office, I see 14,000-feet-plus mountain peaks. To my back are the Eastern Sierras."

He wrote that he was out there, reading a newspaper from Chicago that had been provided to him for free.

"I wonder for how long?" he wrote.

Some of the people wrote that they were getting rid of their newspaper subscriptions.

"I've been reading your column for about two years now online," one reader wrote. "I even canceled my subscription. Why should I pay for a paper every morning when I can read just what I want for free, without getting my fingers dirty, and there are no recycling concerns? Not that I am doing it for environmental issues, just for convenience."

Another:

"As the number of people who read the paper online grows and grows, it will soon surpass, even double or triple, the number of people who read the printed version. At some point, some bright young executive will figure out that newsprint is an unneeded expense for the company (along with trucks, delivery people, ink). All of our sentimentality about the feel of print will be washed away by the financial numbers."

And:

"I have no idea why newspapers are doing this—but I love it! I can read great papers around the country without leaving my house, and it costs me nothing."

I wrote:

> *The publishing executives of newspaper corporations have decided to make one version of their product free on computer screens, and have asked people to click on. The people, willingly and sometimes gratefully, do it. At least some of those people—or so it seems—have made the decision not to continue to buy the ink-on-paper editions. You would assume that the newspaper publishers must have foreseen this possibility.*
>
> *So what exactly is going on here? Those of us who love newspapers—the real ones, the ones you hold in your hands—are trusting that our corporate bosses know what they're doing, that they're laying the groundwork for the future of our business. But every time I read an "I've-canceled-my-subscription-because-I-can-read-the-paper-online-for-free" letter, I become extremely nervous. This is our lives here; for all of us—publishers, editors, reporters, photographers—this is what we have devoted our working lives to.*

It seemed to be some corporate game of chicken that had somehow gotten way out of hand. It seemed that perhaps the newspapers were putting out their free online editions mainly because their competitors were—even if they belatedly were to decide that they would prefer not to do it, not to have gotten into this exercise in the first place, they were stuck. It seemed they were figuring out that if they were to stop putting out the computer-site versions of their newspapers—or started charging money—their readers would simply switch to another paper whose computer site remained free.

So the newspaper publishers, because their competitors were doing it, continued to write checks for the prodigious costs associated with their business, while giving away the product.

There was a phrase, in the world of nuclear weaponry, that applied to this:

Mutual assured destruction.

The *Washington Post*, long renowned as one of the world's preeminent newspapers, was seeing its circulation decline, and sought to remedy this by conducting a thorough study of what readers in its distribution area thought about the *Post*—in other words, why those readers weren't purchasing it in the numbers they once did.

In some of the households surveyed, the homeowners were asked how—just in theory—they would respond if the *Post* were delivered to them for free.

Some said they would decline such an offer.

Why, those homeowners asked, would they want stacks of newspapers sitting around?

Don Campbell, a lecturer in journalism at Emory University in Atlanta, wrote, in an essay in *USA Today*:

"The students in my advanced reporting class are among the few students at Emory University who hold a newspaper (other than the campus semi-weekly) in their hands when they read it. The only reason they do it is because I require them to bring the *Atlanta Journal-Constitution* to class, rather than access it online, and I give them occasional pop quizzes to make sure they're reading it.

"They don't like that a bit.

"They are journalism co-majors, but most of them had never read a daily newspaper before they entered my journalism program, and I have no illusions that any of them will read one in print after they graduate."

At the *Orlando* Sentinel in Florida, an executive wrote a memo to members of the staff:

"On Monday, March 31, the *Orlando Sentinel* will launch a new digital edition of the newspaper via a new business partner, Pressmart. As a result, the paper will no longer be available in physical form at the *Orlando Sentinel* offices."

So, according to the memo, the reporters, photographers and copy-editors who were putting out the paper every day would not, in their own newsroom, be provided access to copies of that paper.

Because of the rising cost of newsprint, just about every newspaper in the United States began reconfiguring the presses so that the page sizes were smaller.

Many papers also began using a less expensive, flimsier grade of newsprint, and reducing the total number of pages in each daily edition.

Newspaper industry analyst John Morton told *Washington Post* reporter Frank Ahrens: "The era of cheap newsprint for the newspaper business is over."

Readers were expected to understand and accept that they were being asked to pay for a physically diminished product.

The newspapers that had once swaggered and flexed their muscles were saying to their subscribers:

We're sorry, but we can no longer afford the paper we're printed on.

Hope you don't think any less of us.

The rapid loss in self-confidence manifested itself in a number of ways.

Instead of trusting their own instincts, newspaper companies increasingly resorted to focus groups and market studies to tell them why their readers seemed to have been growing indifferent. It was like marriage counseling in which one spouse—the newspaper companies—sought desperately to find out what had gone wrong and how to repair the rift, while the other spouse—the readers—agreed to talk about it, but with less interest in whether the longtime union could be saved.

The results could border on the unintentionally comical, or the wistfully sad, or in some cases both. The *American Journalism Review* reported that, in upstate New York, the *Rochester Democrat and Chronicle* had assembled a "front-page impact team" to come up with ways to attract readers.

Among the impact team's findings: that "more papers are sold when they contain breaking news, exclusive stories, or some kind of 'human drama' on the front page." If all three of those elements were above the fold on Page One, "it would be a big seller."

It took a committee, evidently, to figure that out.

In their search for ways to connect with readers in the new world of information delivery, some newspapers came up with ideas and analyses that, as presented, were enough to make your head feel like it wanted to explode.

The *New York Times* reported that "the fear persists that news aggregators like Google News have the potential to steal more traffic than they bring. Industry executives fret that aggregators are eroding what little control news sites have over users. Instead of entering a preferred news site through its front page, users are being routed to a single article, perhaps deep inside the site, and when they are done reading it, they move on."

I thought of Bill Moore, hunched over a piece of copy, getting it ready to go into the *Citizen-Journal*, where he knew every reader would easily, and eagerly, find it and devour it.

In another story in the *Times*, this one with a hopeful tone about new software programs that newspapers could use to reach their readers, it was reported: "Publishers can upload local ads to their cellphone sites using Verve's software or have Verve place national ad campaigns on their sites. Verve can deliver a particular ad to, say, people age 21 to 30 who live downtown and have searched for articles about the bar scene. *Philadelphia Magazine*, for example, sent readers of its Verve-developed Web site a message offering $4 grapefruit cocktails and half-price appetizers at a local bar."

I tried to envision Don Weaver, smoking his pipe back in his office—an act that, in itself, would be prohibited in today's newspaper buildings—as he contemplated sending news about grapefruit-cocktail offers to the telephones of readers of the *C-J*.

Forget about his confusion concerning how in the world he would print his news onto someone's telephone.

His real perplexity would form as he tried to comprehend the concept:

Grapefruit cocktails?

The very definition of news became altered. With continuous updates from multiple sources to readers' computer screens all day and all night, how could any development be considered an urgent news bulletin, when everything, by designation, was a news bulletin? With multiple cable television channels devoted twenty-four hours a day to nothing but news, what qualified as being newsworthy? How could there be the notion of an "Extra" when, on Web sites, every tick of the clock brought the electronic equivalent of newsboys who needed no sleep and no rest, shouting "Extra! Extra! Read all about it!"

The old idea of newspapers that systematically assembled and packaged their information for home delivery once each day began to seem like something from a vanished century, which, of course, it was. As newspaper owners publicly struggled to come to terms with this, and attempted to explain the industry's troubles to their readers, they willfully defied that old and wise admonition:

Never let them see you sweat.

The newspaper companies had sweat pouring down their foreheads, soaking their collars. And—out of their admirable habit of presenting the latest developments to their readers—they did not conceal their out-of-control perspiration, they let their subscribers observe it, they wrote and spoke incessantly about their newfound fearfulness and bewilderment.

Predictions like this one, by a newspaper analyst named Vin Crosbie, became commonplace:

"More than half of the 1,439 daily newspapers in the United States won't exist in print, e-paper, or Web site formats by the end of the next decade. They will go out of business. The few national dailies— namely *USA Today*, the *New York Times*, and the *Wall Street Journal*— will have diminished but continuing existence via the Web and e-paper, but not in print."

The shocking thing was not Mr. Crosbie's prediction. The shocking thing was that it was not particularly controversial—the shocking thing was that no one was shocked.

With the economics of traditional newspapers in freefall—it was as if a gigantic boulder had slowly been shoved toward the edge of a plateau for a very long time, and now, having reached and then gone over the edge, was hurtling uncontrollably down a steep hill and picking up speed by the second—less expensive ways of gathering and transmitting the news were being considered.

One of them—news generated not by professional (meaning "paid") reporters, but by the readers themselves—was much discussed. This user-generated content could be disseminated by the profit-oriented news companies at little or no editorial cost.

I smiled a private smile every time I saw the phrase that was most often used to describe this fledgling concept of newsgathering:

Citizen journalism.

The *Citizen-Journal*, during the years of its life, went by a second name
in many of the homes where it was read. The people who used that al-
ternate term for it probably did not even realize they were saying the
words. They—each of them—referred to the C-J as:

"My paper."

You would hear it all the time, not just in Columbus, but in every
city in the nation:

"I was reading my paper at breakfast this morning. . . ."

"I'm going to go out to the backyard with my paper for a
while. . . ."

"Has anyone seen my paper? . . ."

The newspaper corporations might not have belonged to the readers, but those readers nevertheless felt a true sense of proprietorship.
Those bundles of newsprint that were delivered to their doors every
day were a part of their lives—something consequential, maybe even
precious.

My paper.

With computers making it so easy now for readers in even the
smallest towns to click every day, if they choose, onto their personally selected repertoire of five, ten, twenty different news sites from
around the world—as many news sites as they want to look at—the
dissemination of news and opinion is more widespread and more sophisticated today than it has been during any time in history. Readers have gained something immeasurable and wonderful: instant,
free access to fine reporting and thinking from every part of the
globe.

When every paper in the world is available, though—when just
about every paper (although not on paper) in existence can be called
onto a screen, with the specific names of the newspapers viewed in a
given household varying depending on where in the world the residents of the household want to explore on a given day—it does raise a
question:

Does the phrase "my paper" continue to mean anything?

So it was against the backdrop of all this that, during the final weeks of what would turn out to be Barack Obama's victorious presidential campaign, we rolled into Columbus shortly after sundown on the CNN Election Express.

Dale Fountain, behind the wheel, pulled into the parking lot of our hotel. I had already finished writing for the day. The other two members of our autumn-long traveling party—Josh Rubin, CNN's producer on the bus, and Jordan Placie, the field engineer—were tired from the long trip, and were going to get a little rest before deciding what to do for dinner.

There was a sports bar/hot wings/burgers place called Roosters not far from where we were staying. I walked there alone.

In a booth, having a beer and deciding what to order, I heard my cellphone hit the musical tone that signaled a new e-mail had arrived. I opened the message, to see that it was CNN's every-evening update listing the network's leading stories of the day just past.

One of them, I saw, was the column I had written on the bus a few hours before, as we had traveled toward Ohio. It was about two people we had interviewed earlier that day in Tennessee. I clicked on the link; immediately the story appeared on my phone's screen.

There was a color photograph, taken by Josh, of the people with whom we had spoken; I didn't know where they were right now, but I was at Roosters, as was the colorful electronic image of them. When they, and I, had begun this day, we had never met and had never known we would meet. Now here they were, with me at dinner.

Also on the phone were the words I had written on the bus, and had sent skyward. Keystroke for keystroke, the words had been delivered not just to this phone, but to every screen in the world whose owners wanted to take a look at the coverage.

The waitress asked if I had decided.

I closed the phone, glanced once more at the menu, and thought about this astonishing, still-forming universe of newsgathering and delivery. Nothing, it seemed, would ever be the same; there was no going back to the old ways.

But what I mostly thought about, by myself in the restaurant booth, was that building at 34 South Third Street.

There was no way I could be in town and not try to go back to the mezzanine.

The *Citizen-Journal*, of course, would not be there—it had been dead for all these many years.

But, in all the ways that counted, it was still, now and forever, my paper.

21

Late the next afternoon, I called the main number at the *Dispatch* building.

Maybe I shouldn't have been surprised that, more than forty years after the day I first walked in, I didn't have to look it up.

There was a columnist there who I knew a little bit—his name was Joe Blundo—and I asked to be connected with him.

He answered on the second ring. This was toward the end of a Thursday afternoon; I asked him if he would be willing to take me to the mezzanine.

He hesitated for a moment; he told me that he had to leave at five P.M., for a family obligation in the suburbs. How soon could I be there?

I told him I was on my way.

The cabdriver let me out on Third Street. I walked through those doors once again.

There was a security guard at a desk next to the elevators. I said I was there to see Mr. Blundo; the guard asked if I had an appointment.

He placed a call upstairs, then told me that I would be met right there in the lobby.

I looked around as I waited. I knew that the *Dispatch*, like virtually every other American daily newspaper, was feeling the pressures. It was still "Ohio's Greatest Home Newspaper"—the sign continued to blaze on the top of the building—but the size of the pages had shrunk, the editions were thinner, the staff had been made smaller.

But at least it was still a newspaper. That's more than the *Citizen-Journal* could say. It had been gone more than twenty years.

The elevator door opened and Joe emerged.

I didn't say a lot to him about why visiting the mezzanine one more time meant so much to me, and he didn't have to ask. I think he knew.

"There's really not much up there to see," he said as we got into the elevator car.

It was the same one in which that woman, in the summer of 1964, had turned to me and talked about Jimmy Durante. I told the story to Joe; he raised his eyebrows and shook his head.

On the mezzanine landing we turned right and there were the same glass doors. No *Citizen-Journal* reference painted on them, and no remnants of where the words once had been.

He opened one of the doors and we were in a carpeted workspace.

These were business offices, he said—utilized to carry out some of the non-newsroom functions of the *Dispatch* company.

The carpet itself—soft, muted in color—was the first thing I noticed. The *C-J* city room had not been covered in carpeting, and the hard and basic flooring had added to the noise level of the old place. Today, the room was nearly soundless. It was almost closing time, and some people had departed for home already.

The entire center of the room, from one end to the other, was filled with a succession of high-walled cubicles. Nothing out of the ordinary there; that's what business offices look like these days. But the effect was to completely erase the feeling of what the *Citizen-Journal*'s newsroom had been. With no interior walls in that city room, no barriers between desks or departments, it had felt like a playground—you could see everything that everyone was doing in that room, there was no sanctuary, nowhere to shut yourself off in quiet contemplation. You saw every smile, heard every shout, measured every mood.

Here, now, each person on the mezzanine was provided with his or her own retreat. The cubicle walls undoubtedly were designed with maximum efficiency in mind. In the sea of measured-off workspaces, I tried to find the place where the old city desk had been, but could not.

There were private offices where the UPI wire machines used to stand.

The offices had been constructed along the windows that overlooked the alley. That probably made sense; executives and managers with their own offices are usually the ones provided with the added benefit of having exterior views.

But the view I had always loved best—the view from behind the sports desks, the windows from which we could look over the *Dispatch* lobby and out onto the streets of downtown Columbus—was gone.

A new wall had been constructed inside that west end of the room— it didn't seem to have any real purpose except to close in the room and cut off the view. I walked over to it.

In combination with the private offices that abutted it on the north wall, it completely did away with the vista that had greeted Sam Perdue and me the day he had stood and pointed and said: "There are *people* out there!"

I wandered a little; I was keeping in mind that Joe had done me a favor by bringing me up here when he was due at home, and I didn't want to delay him. And I'm not certain exactly what it was I was looking for, anyway.

The feeling wasn't melancholy; I didn't regret coming here. The business office looked no different from a hundred thousand other cubicle-crammed spaces in a hundred thousand other office buildings. There was no reason to be startled by what was here now, and certainly no reason to be sad.

What I was feeling mostly was the deepest kind of gratitude: gratitude that I once was allowed to live all those days and nights in this room when it was filled with laughter and noise, that I was permitted to be a member of the cast of characters whose voices, in my memory, still sounded in here, that in this room I got to help put out a newspaper that few people now remember, and fewer mourn.

It was a paper, I know, that didn't change the world. And I wouldn't change a thing about it. I thanked Joe, and silently offered a word of thanks for the good luck that had once allowed this place and me to find each other, and then I left to go back to the bus with its satellite dish aimed toward the stars.

Acknowledgments

There are some people who have made working on this book a pleasure, and I'd like to thank them here.

Phil Revzin, my editor at St. Martin's Press, continues to be an author's dream; his deadline instincts, his never-ending interest, his on-the-money suggestions, and his unfailing good humor are beyond impressive. My thanks, too, to his associates Jenness Crawford and Kylah Goodfellow McNeill for their help every step of the way.

Eric Simonoff, as he has been for many years, is not only a source of impeccable advice and counsel, but a trusted and treasured friend. My gratitude, respect and affection for Mort Janklow have only grown stronger since the beginning of our association.

The research staff at the Columbus Metropolitan Library has been generous, resourceful and persistent in assisting me during the writing of *Late Edition*. My thanks, too, to the staff of the Grandview Heights, Ohio, Public Library and to the staff at the headquarters of the E. W. Scripps Company for their help in looking into the history of the *Citizen-Journal* and its predecessor, the *Columbus Citizen*.

I'm grateful to *Esquire* magazine, where an early version of my account of the last day and night of the *Citizen-Journal* appeared.

David Bohrman, the Washington bureau chief and senior vice president of CNN, has long been a source of warm encouragement for my work and unerring understanding of the most human aspects of news stories. Alex Wellen, Richard Galant, and John Helton at CNN.com have been perceptive and valued editors. Josh Rubin, the producer aboard the CNN Election Express, has a wonderful ear for words, a tireless appetite for hard work, and an enthusiasm for reporting a story that make him a joy to spend time with. Josh, Dale Fountain, and Jordan Placie are as fine a group of traveling companions as any reporter on the road could ever hope for.

I wish I knew the name of the professor who, at a statewide convention of fledgling journalism students in Ohio more than forty years ago, made the suggestion from the speakers' lectern that keeping a daily diary was a good way to train oneself to become an observant reporter. The accounts of the events recorded in the journal I kept at his recommendation have helped me, over the years, to write not only *Late Edition*, but also *Be True to Your School* and *And You Know You Should Be Glad* before it. Because he advised the listeners in his audience to pay close attention to what was going on around them, and to write it all down, I have a record of those long-ago days and nights that has proven useful beyond measure in reconstructing what took place. Many times I have wanted to thank him—he is a part of every page of this book.

For their kindness toward me and toward my work during the time I was working on the story in the preceding pages, my gratitude goes to David Shipley, Richard L. Harris, Cal Thomas, Jim Bohannon, Bob Sullivan, Keith Blackledge and Bob Costas. And there is one person whose incomparable voice was a component of the air above us for so many years that it became a part of the nation's very atmosphere; for gestures of grace and thoughtfulness toward me that are so numerous I can't even begin to count them, my thanks and everlasting friendship to Mr. Paul Harvey.

About the Author

Award-winning journalist Bob Greene is a CNN contributor and a *New York Times* bestselling author whose books include *When We Get to Surf City: A Journey Through America in Pursuit of Rock and Roll, Friendship, and Dreams; And You Know You Should Be Glad: A True Story of Lifelong Friendship; Once Upon a Town: The Miracle of the North Platte Canteen; Duty: A Father, His Son, and the Man Who Won the War; Hang Time: Days and Dreams with Michael Jordan; Be True to Your School*; and, with his sister, D. G. Fulford, *To Our Children's Children: Preserving Family Histories for Generations to Come*.

As a magazine writer he has been lead columnist for *Life* and *Esquire*; as a broadcast journalist he has served as contributing correspondent for *ABC News Nightline*. For thirty-one years he wrote a syndicated newspaper column based in Chicago, first for the *Sun-Times* and later for the *Tribune*. His essays and reporting have been featured on National Public Radio's *All Things Considered* and on the op-ed page of *The New York Times*.

Readers may write to him in care of bobgreenebooks@aol.com.

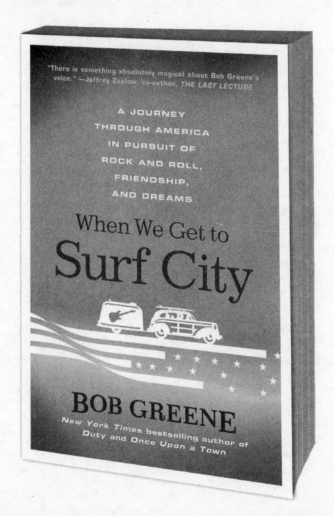